An Intelligent Framework for Smart Power Grid

Manali Chakraborty

CONTENTS

                                                          1

1.1 What is Smart Grid? 1
     1.1.1   AMI: Advanced Metering Infrastructure 3
1.2 Goal of Thesis 6
     1.2.1   Context 6
     1.2.2   Research Motivation 7
     1.2.3   Aim & Objective 7
1.3 Methodology 8
     1.3.1   Literature Review 9
     1.3.2   Protocol Design 9
     1.3.3   Analysis & Evaluation 9
1.4 Thesis Structure 9

Section I - Security in AMI   **13**

2 Existing Security Solutions Towards AMI   **15**
2.1 Characteristics of AMI Communication Network 15
     2.1.1   Why Cyber Security is Important for AMI? 16
2.2 Review on Routing Protocols and Security 17
     2.2.1   Multi-path Routing Protocols 17
     2.2.2   Opportunistic Routing (OR) Protocols 22
     2.2.3   Trust Models 23
     2.2.4   Research Gaps 23
2.3 Is Secure Routing Enough for Providing Complete Security in AMI Communication? 24
     2.3.1   Intrusion Detection Systems 25

		2.3.2	Energy Theft Attacks	26
		2.3.3	Review on Handling of Energy Theft Attacks in AMI	27
		2.3.4	Research Gaps	29

3 Secure Routing in AMI   31
    3.1   Pseudo Opportunistic, Multipath, Secure (POMSec) Routing Protocol 31
    3.2   Description of the Process 32
         3.2.1   Underlying Routing Protocol 32
         3.2.2   The Trust Model 33
         3.2.3   Proposed Methodology 36
    3.3   Experiments and Results 37
         3.3.1   Simulation Settings 37
         3.3.2   Simulation Results 38
    3.4   Conclusions 41

4 Energy Theft Attacks in AMI   43
    4.1   CORIDS: Cluster Oriented Reward based Intrusion Detection System 44
         4.1.1   The Proposed Cluster-Based Architecture for WMNs 44
         4.1.2   Description of CORIDS 46
         4.1.3   Handling Different Attacks using CORIDS 48
         4.1.4   Performance Analysis 51
    4.2   IDS for Detecting DIET Attack 60
         4.2.1   Smart Infrastructure for Communication 60
         4.2.2   Information Stored at Smart Meters 62
         4.2.3   Information Stored at Cluster Heads 63
         4.2.4   Proposed DIET Attack Model 63
         4.2.5   Description of the Proposed IDS 65
         4.2.6   Simulation Results 69
    4.3   IDS for Detecting CET Attack 77
         4.3.1   Proposed CET Attack 77
         4.3.2   Agent based Architecture 79
         4.3.3   Information Stored at Agent Nodes 79
         4.3.4   Information Stored at Smart Meters 81
         4.3.5   Proposed IDS 81
         4.3.6   Simulation Results 84
    4.4   Conclusions 86

Section II - Load Forecasting in AMI   89

5 State-of-the-Art Forecasting Models for Smart Grid   91
    5.1   Variations of Forecasting Models 92
    5.2   Mathematical Models for Forecasting 93
    5.3   Limitations of soft computing based approaches 94
    5.4   Regression based models 95
    5.5   Research Gaps 97

6 Mid-Term Load Forecasting Models for Smart Grid   99

	6.1	Motivation	100
	6.2	Challenges	103
	6.3	Contributions	104
	6.4	Proposed Methodology	106
		6.4.1 Selecting Predictor Parameters for Energy Forecasting	107
		6.4.2 Data Collection	108
		6.4.3 Relationship of Predictor Parameters with Predicted Value	108
		6.4.4 Comparative Analysis of Data Mining Techniques	109
		6.4.5 Verification of the Proposed Model	111
	6.5	Constructing Coefficient Database	112
	6.6	Results	115
		6.6.1 Applicability of The Model on Other Regions	119
	6.7	Some Interesting Facts	120
	6.8	Applicability of the Model on Industrial Sector	121
	6.9	Proposed Methodology	122
		6.9.1 Select Underlying Data Mining Algorithm	122
		6.9.2 Construct Multiplier Database :	126
	6.10	Conclusions	132

Section III - Design Issues in IoT based AMI   **133**

7 Existing Solutions towards Security in IoT based AMI   **135**
	7.1	Addressing Format of IPv6	136
		7.1.1 Existing Works	137
		7.1.2 Research Gaps	139
	7.2	ICMPv6 Abuses in IPv6	140
	7.3	Configuration and Compliance Issues in AMI	141
		7.3.1 Research Gaps	144

8 Implementing communication network using IPv6   **147**
	8.1	ICMPv6 Vulnerabilities	148
		8.1.1 Router Discovery	149
		8.1.2 Duplicate Address Detection	150
		8.1.3 Neighbor Discovery	151
		8.1.4 Proposed Intrusion Prevention System	152
		8.1.5 Results	152
	8.2	Address Configuration	154
		8.2.1 Proposed Addressing Format	156
		8.2.2 Performance analysis	157
	8.3	Conclusions	160

9 Configuration and Compliance Management Framework   **163**
	9.1	Working Principle of the Proposed Framework	163
		9.1.1 Component Management	164
		9.1.2 Configuration Management	166
		9.1.3 Compliance Management	170
		9.1.4 System Design	175

	9.1.5 Verification of the Configuration Management Layer	178
	9.1.6 Verification of the Compliance Management Layer	180
9.2	Conclusions	186

10 Conclusions & Future Works   **191**

References   **193**

LIST OF FIGURES

1.1	Smart Grid.	2
1.2	AMI and Smart Grid	4
1.3	Communication architecture of AMI in Smart Grid.	5
1.4	Motivations and Goals of our work.	8
3.1	Trust model of POMSec.	33
3.2	Network Maintenance part of POMSec.	36
3.3	Route Establishment part of POMSec.	37
3.4	Data communication between Source and Destination using ETSeM and POMSec.	38
3.5	Comparative data analysis for PDR and throughput of ETSeM, H-ETSeM and POMSec.	39
3.6	Comparative data analysis for End-to-end delay and Jitter of ETSeM, H-ETSeM and POMSec.	40
3.7	Comparative data analysis for Energy depletion rate of ETSeM, H-ETSeM and POMSec.	40
4.1	Blackhole Attack Analysis with Node Mobility	54
4.2	Blackhole Attack Analysis against Node Density	54
4.3	Blackhole Attack Analysis	55
4.4	DDos Attack Analysis for False Positives	56
4.5	DDos Attack Analysis for Detection Time	57
4.6	Variation of Detection Efficiency and False Positive with change in threshold	58
4.7	Comparison of CORIDS with MDA	60
4.8	Communication architecture of AMI in Smart Grid.	61
4.9	DIET attack model.	65
4.10	Flow diagram for data Processing phase of the proposed IDS.	67
4.11	Flow diagram for Detection phase of the proposed IDS.	68

4.12	Original Technical loss and registered Technical Loss for DIET attack with varying node density.	69
4.13	False negatives vs Node density for different attack scenarios.	72
4.14	Detection Efficiency vs Node density for different attack scenarios.	73
4.15	Electricity loss in proposed IDS.	74
4.16	Comparative results of false negatives and detection efficiency.	75
4.17	Comparative analysis for different attack scenarios.	76
4.18	Comparison of detection efficiency among different IDSs.	76
4.19	Comparison of false positives among different IDSs.	77
4.20	Peer-to-peer attack model.	78
4.21	Centralized attack model.	79
4.22	Agent based architecture of AMI.	80
4.23	Original Technical Loss and registered Technical Loss for CET attack with varying node density.	85
4.24	Various performance metrics of the IDS:(a) False Negative, (b) Detection Efficiency and (c) False Positive	86
5.1	General diagram of a forecasting model	94
6.1	Block diagram for construction of coefficient database.	105
6.2	Scatterplots for predicted power demand vs. (a) usage history, population density; (b) average maximum temperature, average minimum temperature, average percipitation; (c) GDP growth rate, number of holidays and residential and commercial load utilization respectively.	108
6.3	Actual usage vs. prediction values in (a) residential sector and (b) commercial sector, using four data analysis techniques for 2016	112
6.4	Actual usage vs. predicted value for residential sectors of Louisiana.	112
6.5	Actual usage vs. prediction data using proposed model for 2016 of [a] New Jersey-commercial, (b) North Carolina-residential, (c) Arizona-commercial.	117
6.6	Comparison of different forecasting models using MAPE.	117
6.7	Variation of predicted usage data using different coefficient sets for weather related control parameters for (a, c) commercial and (b, d) residential sectors of Kansas and Illinois respectively.	118
6.8	Variation of MAPE using different coefficient sets for weather related control parameters for commercial and residential sectors of Kansas and Illionois.	118
6.9	MAPE values for different states in both residential and commercial sector, using proposed forecasting model.	119

6.10	Actual usage vs predicted value in Himachal Pradesh - 2016.	119
6.11	Variations in MAPE for original and normalized dataset.	120
6.12	Block diagram for proposed forecasting model.	123
6.13	Energy demand prediction for North Carolina - 2015.	125
6.14	Comparison results using Random Forest for North Carolina.	126
6.15	Actual vs. Predicted energy usage for different U.S.A. States	128
6.16	Actual vs predicted energy demand of Florida (2014-15)	130
6.17	Variations of Upper and Lower limits of multiplier for Ohio	130
7.1	The structure of Global Unicast Address.	136
7.2	Version management problem in CBSD.	143
7.3	Dependency between components.	143
8.1	High level view of Intrusion Prevention in Router Discovery and Updation phase.	153
8.2	High level view of Intrusion Prevention in Duplicate Address Detection phase.	154
8.3	High level view of Intrusion Detection in Neighbor Discovery phase.	155
8.4	False Negative vs. Number of Malicious DCUs.	155
8.5	False Negative vs. Node density.	156
8.6	Proposed IPv6 addressing structure.	156
8.7	Flow chart for address configuration of a Smart Meter.	158
8.8	Flow chart for address configuration of a DCU.	158
8.9	Address space utilization for various addressing formats.	160
9.1	Workflow diagram of proposed framework.	168
9.2	Component relation structure.	169
9.3	Content of C_{Array} and P_{Array}.	169
9.4	Business Process diagram.	175
9.5	BPMN diagram of a smart meter.	180
9.6	BPMN diagram for the distributed generation in AMI.	181
9.7	List of Events	184
9.8	List of Events in Phase 3	187

LIST OF TABLES

2.1	Classification based on Route-Types and Data Transmission Mode	21
3.1	Parameter Settings for Simulation Environment	38
4.1	Simulator parameter settings	51
4.2	Parameter Settings for Simulation Environment	71
6.1	Definition of Comparison Metrices	110
6.2	Performance of Regression based Data Mining Techniques on New Jersey	110
6.3	Regression based techniques for residential and commercial sector of New Jersey	111
6.4	Mean Absolute Error and Mean Absolute Percentage Error	111
6.5	Predictor Variables on Weather Profile for Residential and Commercial sector	114
6.6	Values of Population Density for Residential and Commercial Sector	115
6.7	Values of Load Utilization Factor for Residential and Commercial Sectors	115
6.8	Remaining Predictor Variables for Residential and Commercial Sectors	115
6.9	US states according to climate, population density and electricity usage.	116
6.10	Coefficients of weather related predictor variables for Residential and Commercial sectors	118
6.11	Performance of Different Regression Methods	125
6.12	Division of region based on Average energy usage in previous 15 years	127
6.13	Upper and Lower Limit of Multiplier for different states	129
6.14	Minimum MAPE and corresponding Multiplier (Florida 2000-2014).	131
6.15	Multiplier prediction and Actual vs. Predicted energy usage (Florida)	131
7.1	Difference between TSD and CBSD	142
9.1	Coefficients of weather related predictor variables for Residential and Commercial sectors	178
9.2	Components of Smart Meter	182
9.3	List of patterns	184

9.4   List of Primitive Components and their functional and non-functional requirements   185
9.5   List of patterns for Phase 3 187

LIST OF ALGORITHMS

1	Working principle of POMSec.	34
2	CORIDS - Phase 1	48
3	CORIDS - Phase 2	48
4	CORIDS - Phase 3	49
5	Algorithm for detecting DIET attack	70
6	Configuration of the Coefficient Database	114
7	Find Multiplier	129
8	Algorithm for identifying dependent components	168
9	$Compliance\_Checking(C, P_1, P_2, \ldots, P_n, N)$	173
10	$Entailment\_Checking(C, P_1, P_2, \ldots, P_n, N)$	173
11	$Consistency\_Checking(Entailed\_Components)$	174
12	$Minimality\_Checking(Consistent\_Components)$	174

LIST OF ACRONYMS

A

AMI	Advanced Metering Infrastructure
AODV	Advanced Metering Infrastructure
ASR	Assignment Success Rate
ARMA	Auto Regressive Moving Average

B

BPMN	Business Process Modelling Notation

C

CBSD	Component Based Software Developement
CBR	Constant Bit-Rate
CC	Correlation Coefficient
CET	Collaborative Energy Theft
CH	Cluster Head
CORIDS	Cluster Oriented Reward based Intrusion Detection System

D

DA	Data Accumulator

DAD	Duplicate Address Detection	
DCU	Data Collection Unit	
DDoS	Distributed Denial of Service	
DIET	Distributed and Intelligent Energy Theft	
DoS	Denial of Service	

E

EIA	Energy Information Administration

F

FOL	First Order Logic

G

GDP	Gross Domestic Product

H

HAN	Home Area Network
HPC	High Performance Computing

I

ICMP	Internet Control Message Protocol
ICMPv6	Internet Control Message Protocol version 6
IDS	Intrusion Detection System
IEEE	Institute of Electrical and Electronics Engineers
IP	Internet Protocol
IPS	Intrusion Prevention System

IPv6	Internet Protocol version 6
IoT	Internet of Things
ISP	Internet Service Provider

L

LAN	Local Area Network
LLN	Low-power and Lossy Networks
LTLF	Long-Term Load Forecasting

M

MAE	Mean Absolute Error
MAC	Media Access Control
MANET	Mobile Adhoc NETwok
MAPE	Mean Absolute Percentage Error
MDMS	Meter Data Management System
MITM	Man In The Middle
MLR	Multiple Linear Regression
MPIPA	Multi Projection IP address Assignment
MTLF	Medium-Term Load Forecasting

N

NA	Neighborhood Advertisement
NAN	Neighborhood Area Network
NDP	Neighborhood Detection Protocol
NIST	National Institute of Standards and Technology
NS	Neighborhood Solicitation

P

PAN	Personal Area Network
PAR	Packet Arrival Rate
PDR	Packet Delivery Ratio
PR	Packets Received
PS	Packets Sent

Q

QoS	Quality of Service

R

RA	Router Advertisement
RAE	Relative Absolute Error
REPTree	Reduced Error Pruning Tree
RFID	Radio Frequency IDentification
RMSE	Root Mean Squared Error
RPL	Routing Protocol for Low-power and Lossy Networks
RR	Router Redirect
RRSE	Relative Root Squared Error
RS	Router Solicitation

S

SCADA	Supervisory Control And Data Acquisition
SG	Smart Grid
SLAAC	StateLess Address Auto Configuration
SM	Smart Meter
SMC	Smart Meter Connections
STLF	Short-Term Load Forecasting
SUN	Smart Energy Utility Network
SVM	Support Vector Machine

T

TSD   Traditional Software Development

U

UDP   User datagram Protocol

W

WAN   Wide Area Network
WEKA   Waikato Environment for Knowledge Analysis
WLAN   Wireless Local Area Network

CHAPTER 1

INTRODUCTION

It is esteemed that the growth in energy consumption will increase upto 28% globally [1], while, in Asia, it will grow by 51%. Besides, this report suggests that, due to population growth and enormous dependebility on technology to carry on the household chores, the electricity usage will increase mostly in residential sectors, followed by commercial and industrial sectors. In order to keep pace with this global trends, we must equip and modernize our existing electricity grid with hardware and software advancements, to ensure a smarter, faster and more efficient power grid. Far from being a futuristic thought, Smart Power Grid is emerging as one of the most promising technologies that will ease out many of these problems.

1.1 What is Smart Grid?

The conventional electrical power grid that has been used over decades has met our needs in the past. However, as the society advances technologically so does the expectations from various infrastructures surrounding us [2]. As depicted in figure 1.1, Smart Grid (SG) is an intelligent electricity network that integrates the actions of all users connected to it and makes use of advanced information, control, and communication technologies to save energy, reduce cost and increase reliability and transparency [3–5].

A typical Smart Grid should consist of six basic sub-systems: Power Generation System, Distribution System, Transmission Network, Data Management and Processing

1. Introduction

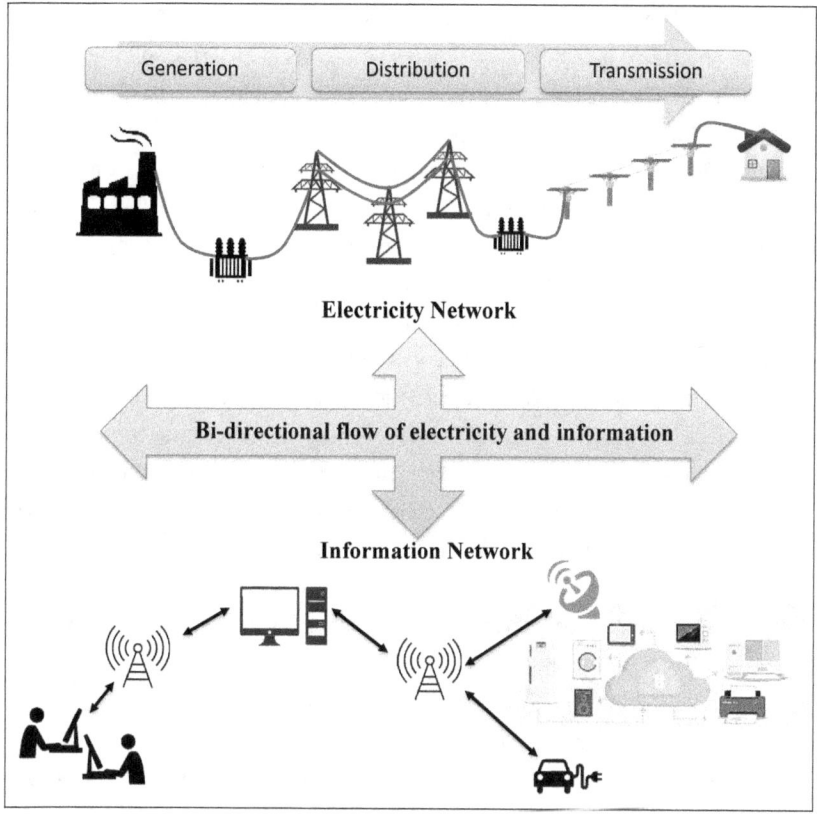

Figure 1.1: Smart Grid.

System, Smart Metering System and a Data Communication System connecting all the other systems to provide a two way communication. The first sub-system is the power generation that takes place in large power plants or renewables power plants; the second sub-system is the transmission that transports energy to the areas where it will be consumed; the third sub-system is the distribution that delivered energy to the end user; smart metering system monitors, measures and collects the end user data. In order to support the Smart Grid operation, Data Communication systems are needed for integrating all the other sub systems with Data Management and Processing system. The communication architecture of Smart Grid has three hierarchical layers: Home Area Network (HAN), Neighbourhood Area Network (NAN), and Wide Area Network

(WAN) [22]. HAN provides the communication between the Smart Meters in a home and other appliances in that home. NAN connects SMs to the Data Collection Units (DCUs), and WAN provides access between the DCUs and Meter Data Management System (MDMS).

Smart Grid is meant to modernize traditional power grids with the two-way data communication along with energy supply. In order to enhance the functionalities of the network, Smart Grid offers several applications to help both customers and utilities to optimize the energy usage and billing. Advanced Metering Infrastructure or AMI is one of the most important features of Smart Grid [15]. It establishes a direct communication between customers and utilities, including, meter readings at periodic intervals (sometimes on demand) to the Data Collection Units or DCUs, updated electricity tariffs at regular intervals to smart meters, electricity outage alert messages and sometimes it upgrades the meter firmware [16]. However, due to the unique characteristics of AMI, such as complex network structure, resource-constrained smart meter, and privacy-sensitive data, it is an especially challenging issue to make AMI secure.

The US Department of Energy [32, 33] specified the benefits of smart grids as follows:

- Smart Grids detect problems and automatically solve them (self-healing),
- Consumers can participate in the functions of the grid, changing their behaviour if it needs. Customers can easily access usage and other information (visibility),
- Smart Grids resist security attacks,
- Smart Grids accommodate all generation and storage options,
- Encourages innovation is highly efficient,
- A Smart Grid can optimize capital assets while minimizing operations and maintenance costs,
- Creating an electricity market as significant increases in bulk transmission capacity will require improvements in transmission grid management. Such improvements are aimed at creating an open marketplace where alternative energy sources from geographically distant locations can easily be sold to customers wherever they are located.

1.1.1 AMI: Advanced Metering Infrastructure

The figure in 9.4 depicts the relation of AMR, AMI and Smart Grid.

1. INTRODUCTION

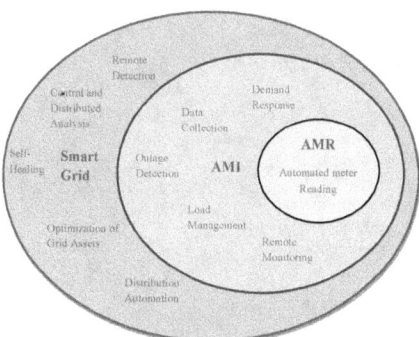

Figure 1.2: AMI and Smart Grid

Advanced Metering Infrastructure or AMI is one of the most important features of Smart Grid [15]. It establishes a direct communication between customers and utilities, including, meter readings at periodic intervals (sometimes on demand) to the Data Collection Units or DCUs, updated electricity tariffs at regular intervals to smart meters, electricity outage alert messages and sometimes it upgrades the meter firmware [16, 31]. However, due to the unique characteristics of AMI, such as complex network structure, resource-constrained smart meter, and privacy-sensitive data, it is an especially challenging issue to make AMI secure.

1.1.1.1 Communication Architecture in AMI

Figure 1.3 shows the communication architecture of AMI in Smart Grid. Smart Energy Utility Network (SUN) hierarchically consists of three components: Home Area Network (HAN), Neighborhood Area Network (NAN), and Wide Area Network (WAN) [18]. The HAN consists of the smart appliances and smart meters that are deployed at residential premises, commercial and industrial buildings, and electricity transformer and feeder points in a specific neighbourhood. These smart meters typically communicate by forming an IEEE 802.15.4 based mesh network that uses IPv6 for addressing individual devices. The RPL routing protocol is likely to be used to form the routing topology in the NAN tier. The WAN tier usually consists of the utility providers head end systems where metering data is collected. Unlike the NAN tier, systems in the WAN tier communicate using high-speed wireless or fixed-line access technologies. Field routers controlled by the utility providers, deployed on supply poles

1.1. What is Smart Grid?

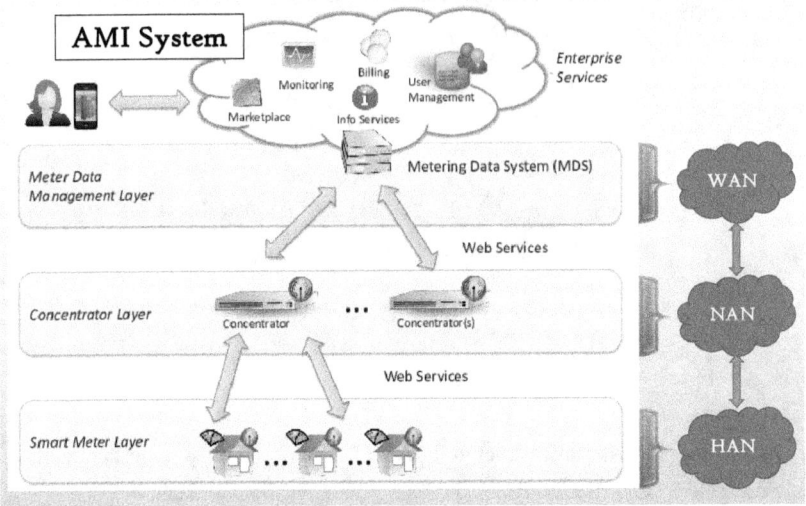

Figure 1.3: Communication architecture of AMI in Smart Grid.

in a neighbourhood, act as a bridge between the NAN and WAN tiers. These field routers have two interfaces, one that allows it to communicate with the low power lossy network (typically IEEE 802.15.4) on the NAN side and another one that provides access to the high-speed wireless or fixed-line networks on the WAN side. It is also possible for these field routers to participate in a NAN-to- NAN mesh, such that the final interconnection of smart meters with head end systems occurs only via the low-power lossy communication channel [19].

1.1.1.2 Roles of IPv6 in AMI

The backbone of the Smart Grid will be its communication network. This network is to connect the different components of the Smart Grid together, and provide two-way communication. IPv6 is a new technology which gained a massive attention, as a supporting layer in Smart Grid communication. The huge address space of IPv6 supports the network architecture of the Smart Grid communications. Besides, features like StateLess Address Auto Configuration (SLAAC) and IPSec support makes IPv6 more suitable for Smart Grid. IPv6 also supports prioritization of messages and different Quality of Service models, which complements several Smart Grid applications [20].

Therefore, the US National Institute of Standards and Technology (NIST) framework for Smart Grid interoperability [21] explicitly encourages the use of IPv6 for Smart Grid installations.

1.2 Goal of Thesis

1.2.1 Context

Compared to regular communication networks, Smart Grid communication systems have different goals, objectives and assumptions. Firstly, Smart Grid is a rapidly evolving topic. Few years back, smart meters are the lowest level of IP enabled devices in the communication network [22, 23]. However, in present days smart home appliances are also expected to be IP enabled, so that the smart meter can monitor and control the appliances actively. This leads to an extremely large network. Besides, the huge amount of data from Smart Grid is to be analyzed to monitor and maintain the whole network [22, 24].

Considering the vast scale of a Smart Grid, it is reasonable to expect that the cumulative vulnerability of the Smart Grid communication system might also be quite critical. Secondly, the traffic in a Smart Grid network will be traversing different types of networks, using a variety of media ranging from fibre optics/broadband (e.g. for meters to base control centre networking), to Zigbee/WLAN (e.g. for home networking). So interoperability is another key issue [25]. Also the traffic that will be generated by e-energy type applications in Smart Grid will be a mix of both real-time and non-real-time traffic being generated and distributed across different parts of a Smart Grid [26]. It is important to guarantee the real time performance and continuous operation features in a Smart Grid communication system.

In comparison with other commodities, the unique characteristic of electrical power is that it cannot be completely stored under the current condition of Smart Grid [27], i.e. the generation, transmission, and consumption of electrical power are all processed simultaneously [28]. The prediction of power demand and its potential fluctuation in a given period is highly important for the stability and economic efficiency of the power system [17]. Generation, transmission and distribution assets need to be built to meet peak demands, thus high peaks contribute to the biggest portion of electricity price. It can be seen that if the demand was controlled during peak time, there would be a huge decrease in the required asset and even more dramatic decrease in electricity generation cost [29].

1.2.2 Research Motivation

Smart Grid holds a great potential to realize a plethora of applications, such as, quick recovery after any sudden breakage/disturbance in lines and feeders, cost reduction, reduction of peak demand, integration of renewable energy sources etc. However, so far only a small fraction of these have been implemented and even fewer are made commercially available to end users. One of the major bottlenecks between the theoretical potential and its practical realization is the concern for security. The flexibility that the Smart Grid offers is like a double-edged knife that leaves an equal opportunity to the intruder as well the true user. Similarly, in order to fully explore the advantages of these applications, Internet of Things (IoT) becomes a necessity. However, providing security is the main concern here too.

1.2.3 Aim & Objective

The functionalities of a full-fledged Smart Grid demands developing a dynamic and fully autonomic infrastructure that would operate without manual intervention. Due to its autonomic nature, securing the Smart Grid is extremely important. An avid intruder can create a havoc by injecting spurious data in the communication network and this may lead to loss of human life and massive damages of grid equipments. The legacy security techniques can hardly fit well for the requirements of a Smart Grid communication system in the public networks such as internet. Thus, our primary research objective is to provide a secure Smart Grid.

On the other hand, like any new technology, IPv6 too comes with a bunch of issues on which more work needs to be done. One of these is addressing structure for proper utilization of 128 bits for Smart Grid components. Since, Smart Grid is built on an already existing and functioning system, it is necessary to verify the compliance issues before integrating IPv6 in the system.

Availability is another big concern for Smart Grids. To achieve uninterrupted power supply accurate forecasting is important. The ability to manage and to reduce peaks in the total load of the electricity supply chain is one of the most challenging problems in the implementation of the future Smart Grid where the electric infrastructure will work, more and more, by continuously adjusting the electricity generation to the total end-use load. Besides, the pattern of distribution and transmission of the grid will depend heavily on the supply demand information. Demand response application may introduce significant new cyber attack vectors such as a malware that initiates a massive coordinated and instantaneous drop in demand, potentially causing substantial damage to distribution, transmission, and even generation facilities [30].

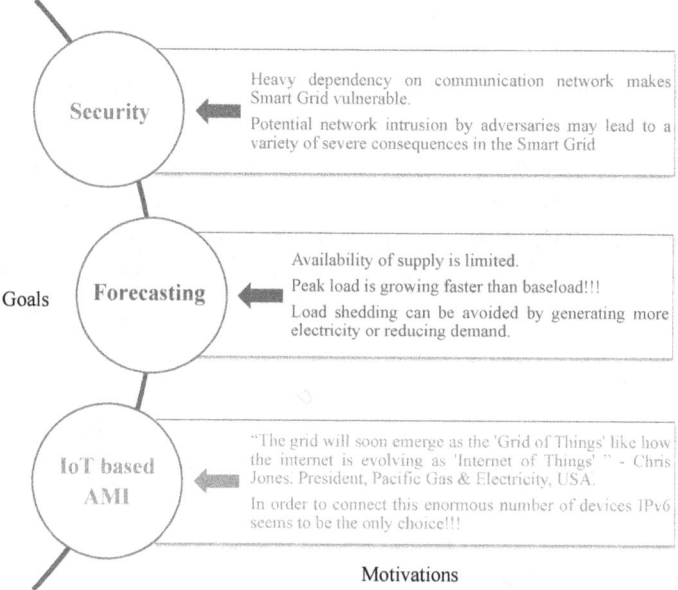

Figure 1.4: Motivations and Goals of our work.

Figure 1.4 describes the three primary goals of my thesis. Though Smart Grid offers a large number of research directions, we have only limited our thesis around these goals. This research aims to strike a trade off between efficiency and security, keeping in mind the diversity and interoperability of a huge system like Smart Grid.

1.3 Methodology

The research methodology exercised for this thesis consists of three key components: literature survey and critical analysis of the related work, protocol designs, and analysis and evaluation of the designed protocols.

1.3.1 Literature Review

The first task carried out in this research was to study the relevant literature on the two general areas of interest: Advanced Metering Infrastructure (AMI) of Smart Grid and its design issues and security concerns. The purpose was to become familiar with the SG concept (i.e., SG architecture, SG applications, etc.) and to identify security and privacy threats and attacks in the SG environment. However, so far only a small fraction of these have been implemented and even fewer are made commercially available to end users. One of the major bottlenecks between the theoretical potential and its practical realization is the concern for security. The flexibility that the wireless ad-hoc networks offer is like a double-edged knife that leaves an equal opportunity to the intruder as well the true user. Similarly, in order to fully explore the advantages of these applications, Internet of Things (IoT) becomes a necessity. However, providing security is the main concern here too. The literature was regularly reviewed throughout the duration of this research, with newly published work taken into consideration where necessary.

1.3.2 Protocol Design

Following the initial literature review and design requirements specification, protocols satisfying these requirements were proposed and designed. This stage of our work has led to some novel contributions.

1.3.3 Analysis & Evaluation

Smart Grid is an emerging technology with various improvements over the existing power industry. It is very difficult to build a Smart Grid test bed in a University set-up. Thus, to validate the results of our theoretical research, we simulate our algorithms for intrusion prevention using simulation software like Qualnet, contiki-cooja. We also use high level programming languages like C and Java to compare and analyze the performance. We have used Business Process Modeling Notation (BPMN) to validate one of our proposed algorithms. Besides, we have used data from U.S Energy Information Administration to implement our proposed theory in demand forecasting.

1.4 Thesis Structure

As we already mentioned in 1.4, this work is divided in three main parts.

1) **Part I** deals with the *security aspect of AMI*. It consistes of three chapters.
    - Chapter 2 provides a detailed review on the security solutions for communication architecture in AMI.
    - In chapter 3, we propose a secure routing protocol where trust evolution process is integrated with the route establishment process to provide security. Besides, a detailed comparison with other trust based approaches has been simulated and the results confirm that our proposed routing protocol proves to be an improvement over existing algorithms, as it provides security as well as better throughput, Packet Delivery Ratio (PDR), delay and energy efficiency.
    - Finally chapter 4 address the research problem of how to provide a second line of defense in AMI to prevent energy theft, DDoS and Blackhole attacks. We have provided three algorithms in this section and show that they can effectively handle these attacks as well as perform a passive monitoring on the network.
2) **Part II** addresses the problem of developing a *Generalised Forecasting model for Smart Grid*. This part consists of two chapters.
    - In chapter 5 we have reviewed existing forecasting models and identified the research gaps that we have identified with respect to Smart Grid.
    - An accurate energy forecasting model is proposed in chapter 6, that optimizes reliability and stability, while minimizing processing and computational load. In particular, we analyzed combinations of real life monthly user data and other predictor parameters to find some decision making information., which is used to find the coefficient for each parameter corresponding to different types of users to optimize the predicted demand. We further proposed an extension of our model based on Industrial sectors.
3) **Part III** focuses on two different design aspects while integrating IoT in Smart Grid: *Implementing communication network using IPv6* and *Configuration and Compliance issues*. It further consists of three chapters:
    - In chapter 7 we discuss the state of the art scenario of security and design issues while integrating IoT in Smart Grid. Especially in the above mentioned topics.
    - In chapter 8 we have identified the problems while incorporating IPv6 in AMI communication network, such as, security and addressing issues, and

proposed solutions to mitigate the ICMPv6 vulnerabilities in AMI, as well as a new addressing structure tailor-made for AMI hierarchy.

- Finally, chapter 9 mainly focuses on the design issues of IoT based AMI. In this part we consider two different problems: configuration and compliance, and provide solutions for each of them.

Chapter 10 concludes the thesis with a brief discussion on future research directions.

CHAPTER 2

EXISTING SECURITY SOLUTIONS TOWARDS AMI

Smart Grid is meant to modernize traditional power grids with the two-way data communication along with energy supply. In order to enhance the functionalities of the network, Smart Grid offers several applications to help both customers and utilities to optimize the energy usage and billing. Advanced Metering Infrastructure or AMI is one of the most important features of Smart Grid [34]. It establishes a direct communication between customers and utilities, including, meter readings at periodic intervals (sometimes on demand) to the Data Collection Units or DCUs, updated electricity tariffs at regular intervals to smart meters, electricity outage alert messages and sometimes it upgrades the meter firmware [35]. However, due to the unique characteristics of AMI, such as complex network structure, resource-constrained smart meter, and privacy-sensitive data, it is an especially challenging issue to make AMI secure.

2.1 Characteristics of AMI Communication Network

Now, due to specific demands of Smart Grid, the associated communication system should have these following characteristics [4], [64]:
- It should consider different type of traffic patterns in the network, e.g., unicast, multicast and broadcast.

- It need to be scalable and flexible to incorporate new renewable sources and distributed energy resources in the netwrok.
- Due to the large and evolving architecture of smart Grid, distributed or cluster based networks will be more suitable for it.
- The communication system should monitor the network devices and perform fault detection, isolation, and recovery.
- It should have the ability to uniquely identify and address every device in the network.
- It should support different QoS parameters for a variety of applications and functions which have different latency and loss requirements, different bandwidth, different security requirements, different real time and non reat time data constraints etc.

Besides, the communication system should be interoperable, dynamic, cost effective, open to active standards and public interfaces, backward compatible and most importantly secure to all the vulnerabilities from inside and outside of the network.

2.1.1 Why Cyber Security is Important for AMI?

Smart Grid are an emerging new technology which combines the traditional power grid and IT communication network to provide more efficient, resilient and reliable energy support [73]. On the other hand, with higher degree of autonomic control and decision making, it also becomes subject to several security concerns, especially cyber security. Smart Grid is different from traditional networks used in the other industries in various ways. It is generally considered as a heterogeneous, backward compatible, static, self adapting and self healing network, with a large number of devices, where two way communications is provided between Smart Meters and a Supervisory Control and Data Acquisition (SCADA) system. This requires special QoSs, like high restriction on delay, failure and voltage quality [74]. In Smart Grid, availability and integrity are typically considered more important than confidentiality [75]. Also the risk factor is quite high in Smart Grid as compared to traditional networks. Thus, the existing solutions for cyber security often fall short of the typical requirements for a Smart Grid.

2.2 Review on Routing Protocols and Security

A brief review of existing multi-path and opportunistic routing (OR) algorithms in different wireless networks is presented in this section, followed by a brief discussion on some trust models in section 2.3.

2.2.1 Multi-path Routing Protocols

Multipath routing protocols for wireless networks are mostly extensions of either DSR or AODV. In Split multi-path routing (SMR) [176], the intermediate nodes forward RREQs that are received along a different link and with a hop count not larger than the first received RREQ. The destination selects the route on which it received the first RREQ packet (which will be a shortest delay path), and then waits to receive more RREQs. The destination node then selects the path which is maximally disjoint from the shortest delay path. If more than one maximally disjoint path exists, the tie is broken by choosing the path with the shortest hop count.

The Ad hoc On-demand Multipath Distance Vector (AOMDV) routing protocol [177] is an extension of AODV to compute multiple loop-free link-disjoint routes. The RREQs that arrive via different neighbours of the source node define the maximum number of link disjoint paths that are possible.

A multi-path routing scheme that extends AOMDV by using a traffic-path allocation scheme has been proposed in [178] and it is based on cross-layer measurements of path statistics that reflects the queue size and congestion level of each path. The scheme utilizes the Fast Forward (FF) MAC forwarding mechanism [179] to reduce the effects of self-contention among frames at the MAC layer.

The route discovery process and selection of multiple routes is one of the fundamental issues in multi-path routing. A meshed multi-path routing M-MPR was proposed in [67] to provide mesh connectivity among the nodes. It also uses selective forwarding of packets among multiple paths. The selection is based on the condition of downstream forwarding nodes and an end to end forward error checking (FEC) is used to reduce the overhead of retransmitting the packets based on acknowledgement. Besides being energy efficient, higher throughput achievement has been claimed in [67] as compared to any other node disjoint multi-path routing protocol.

Another multi-path [55] routing for wireless networks combines the idea of clustering and multi-path routing together. Clustering is used to speed up the routing by structuring the network nodes hierarchically, and multi-path routing is used to provide better end to end performance and throughput. The solution in [55] is less prone to interference, than conventional multi-path routing. It is also quite simple as each path in the CBMPR just passes through the heads of clusters, resulting in a simple cluster level hop-by-hop routing. A reliable and hybrid multi-path routing, RHMR for MANET was proposed in [50]. It uses a proactive-like routing for route discovery and reactive routing for route recovery and maintenance.

LIEMRO [54] is another node-disjoint multi-path routing based on event based sensor network to improve QoS in the terms of data reception rate, lifetime, and latency. The primary path from source node to sink node is consist of the nodes with minimum packet transmission cost at each step. Similarly, the second path is established using the second best node at each step. Extra routes are only established if they dont decrease data reception rate at the sink node.

MHRP [68] is a Hybrid Multi-path Routing protocol that was designed to properly exploit the inherent hybrid architecture of WMNs. It uses Proactive Routing protocol in mesh routers and reactive routing in mesh clients. The client nodes in a wireless environment are often mobile and have fewer resources. MHRP reduces overhead from client nodes by efficient use of the resourceful router nodes towards route discovery and security mechanism.

Another multi-path routing for WMNs was proposed in MRATP [69]. It uses a traffic prediction model based on wavelet-neural network. The main idea of this paper is to set up one primary and some backup paths between a pair of nodes. The primary path is used to transmit the data, until any node on that path generates a congestion signal. Then the back-up paths are used to balance the load in the network. It is claimed that [69] reduces end to end delay and balances the load of the whole network efficiently.

In [53], a distributed, load balancing multipath routing algorithm has been proposed for wireless sensor networks. The algorithm has two different protocols: one for load-balancing and the other is a multipath routing protocol. The multipath routing protocol search multiple node disjoint paths, and then the load balancing algorithm allocates the traffic over each route optimally. Authors of this paper claimed to achieve higher node energy efficiency, lower average delay and control overhead than the other energy aware routing algorithms.

Another energy aware multipath routing algorithm for wireless Multimedia Sensor Network WMSNs) is proposed in [56]. In this proposed protocol each node first find its neighboring nodes and then built several partial disjoint paths from source to sink node. If any node in the primary path fails for less remaining energy, then the previous hop node of the failed node will find another partially disjoint path to transmit the data. The failed nodes are put into passive states, so that they can not further interfere in the route selection process. Initially, this protocol builds less number of paths from source to sink, and also has lower routing overhead. Thus performs better than Maximally Radio-Disjoint Multipath Routing [57] for WMSNs, in which one link failure leads to a alternative route rediscovery process, which increase the routing cost and waste the energy.

EQMH is another Energy Efficient and QoS based multipath protocol [58] for Wireless Sensor Networks. EQMH uses a queuing model to handle both real time and non real time data. This method considers remaining energy of a node, available buffer size of that node, Signal-to-Noise ratio and Distance of that node to the sink node to select the best node in a path. It also incorporates a Forward Error correction (FEC) method to recover from link failures. Thus, EQMH would avoid flooding and saves energy to increase the network lifetime.

A multi constrained QoS based Multipath Routing protocol (MCMP) [70], aims to increase the performance of a network, with certain QoS requirements, as delay and reliability and lesser energy consumption. A linear integer programming based algorithm is used to solve the end-to-end delay problem, formulated as an optimization problem.

In [71], a interference aware, load balancing an energy efficient multipath routing algorithm is proposed. Two paths are established between the source and sink node. The linking cost is minimized by selecting the nodes with more remaining energy and fewer number of hops to the sink node. After discovering the first path, the interfering nodes are marked out, so that they could not take part in the route selection for the second path. Thus the communication quality is improved by reducing the interference level of the nodes. A load balancing algorithm also balances the load between two paths to maximize network lifetime.

REER [59] is another energy efficient multipath routing protocol, that uses remaining energy of a node, Signal-to-Noise ratio and available buffer size of that node to predict the next best node in the route. This alogorithm has two methods of traffic allocation. Firstly, a set of node disjoint paths between source and sink node is selected and then the best route is chosen for data transmission. When this path cost falls bellow a certain threshold value, then the next best route is chosen to continue the data transmission. The second method breaks the transmitted message into several equal sized segments and then adds a XOR baed error correction code with them and transmits them through different paths. Thus guarantees the arrival of the packet to the destination without any delay.

RELAX [60] uses the relaxation effect of the battery to improve the network lifetime. The relaxation period of a battery helps it to regain a portion of its lost power. It also uses some metrics like remaining energy, Signal-to-Noise ratio, available buffer size to predict the best next hop node. RELAX splits the transmitted message into several equal sized segments, and then add XOR based FEC with them and transmit them through different paths. Thus, the protocol does not require flooding when there is a link failure and hence the lifetime of the network is increased.

SEDR [72], is a three phase routing scheme. They formulate the secret-sharing based disjoint multipath routing algorithm as an optimization problem, where, their objective is to maximize both the network security and lifetime. In order to ensure the security of the network, the proposed algorithm split up a data packet into several slices, using a secret sharing algorithm. And then forward those shares to the sensor nodes dispersively distributed all over the network with disjoint routes. Thus they provide security by increasing the diversity of the routing paths.

SEEMPr [61], tries to balance both the reliability and lifetime of a network, by providing the concept of criticality factor. The criticality factor determines the urgency of delivering a data packet. All packets dont have the same importance, so they forward the urgent packets via shortest path to the sink node, and transmit the rest of the packets via a different and longer path. Thus the energy consumption is distributed over the network.

The study above implies that two broad approaches are suggested for route discovery process. These are node-disjoint and link disjoint algorithms [58]. In node-disjointed approach, multiple routes are created with an assurance that no common node can exist between them. In the link-disjointed methodologies even if common nodes may exist between several routes, links between two nodes never overlap [50]. There is also another approach, called node-channel disjoint method, where a new route is selected only if it is both node disjoint and link disjoint with the previously selected paths [49]. The second column in Table 1 shows that the category in which each of the protocols cited above belongs to.

2.2. Review on Routing Protocols and Security

In a different perspective, Multi-path routing algorithms are of three types based on the mode of data transmission along multiple routes.

Type 1: In some cases, a back up path is used only when the primary path between a pair of nodes is down. This back up path is typically set up simultaneously with the primary path.

Type 2: In the second type, multiple paths are used simultaneously to balance the load of the primary path. Initially the primary path is used for data transmission. However, when there's heavy traffic on the primary path, the other paths also participate in packet transmission to reduce the burden from that primary path.

Type 3: In the third variant, every node disjoint path between a pair of nodes is used to increase the end to end performance by transmitting data among several paths [55].

The rightmost column in Table 1 shows that the category in which each of the protocols cited above belongs to depending on the mode of data transmission.

Table 2.1: Classification based on Route-Types and Data Transmission Mode

Paper	Route Types	Data Transmission Mode
[67]	Node Disjoint	Type 3
[55]	Node Disjoint	Type 2
[49]	Node-channel Disjoint	Type 1
[54]	Node Disjoint	Type 2
[68]	Node Disjoint	Type 1
[69]	Node Disjoint	Type 2
[53]	Node Disjoint	Type 3
[56]	Node Disjoint	Type 2
[58]	Node Disjoint	Type 3
[71]	Node Disjoint	Type 2
[59]	Node Disjoint	Type 2
[60]	Node Disjoint	Type 3
[72]	Node Disjoint	Type 3
[61]	Node Disjoint	Type 2
[176]	Link Disjoint	Type 2
[177]	Link Disjoint	Type 3
[178]	Link Disjoint	Type 3

The review above reflects that there already exist a large number of energy efficient, multipath routing protocols. However, the trust worthiness of participating nodes is often not considered by the above protocols. In [50], a secret-sharing algorithm has been used to secure the network. However, the degree of multiple path selection on a hop to hop basis depending on the trust-value of the next hop destination has not really been considered in the existing approaches.

2.2.2 Opportunistic Routing (OR) Protocols

Several works have been proposed in the field of OR. A survey on existing OR protocols in wireless network is presented in [63]. Although OR is attracting much attention owing to its improvement in network routing performance, there is not much work present in Smart Grid area.

PLC-OR [65] is a power line communication based opportunistic routing in Smart Grid. It uses static topological information of nodes to build a routing table. It always selects a single path to the destination to avoid duplicate packet reception problem at the final destination. Dijkstra's algorithm is used to find the shortest path between every relay node and destination. Authors claim to reduce the transmission cost by using a static PLC-AN.

Authors of [66] proposed another OR for Smart Grid. However, this algorithm differs from the previous one in terms of its ability to handle varying topology in a network. They also introduced a new parameter based on end to end transmission time for remaining path to calculate the best node among a set of forward nodes. The estimating method of TTRP is derived according to the outage probability of the PLC channel. Using simulation and theoritical methods they proved that selection and sorting the forwarding nodes according to TTRP can maximize the throughput.

Analysing the existing works on opportunistic routing protocol reflects that it performs better in a static network, otherwise the operational cost exceeds the performance gain of the network. Thus, the tradeoff between progressing gain and processing delay and cost will be one of the main important concern for OR. OR does not come with any inherent security model. Thus, providing a secure transmission will be another important aspect while implementing OR in Smart Grid. Furthermore, duplicate packet delivery is another problem for OR. It generally causes using isometric antennas and the broadcasting nature of the wireless channel. Authors of [65] claim to solve this problem by not allowing multipath routing, which restricted the selection of forwarding nodes within same transmission domain for a particular sender node. However, this inturn defeats the main purpose of OR, which exploits the broadcasting nature of wireless networks.

2.2.3 Trust Models

HIDS [47] is an honesty rate based collaborative intrusion detection algorithm for MANETs. Every node in the network has a unique identifier and an honesty rate or h_rate. The honesty rate of a node gets updated after a fixed time interval. h_rate of a node gets updated based on the packet forwarding information provided by one-hop neighbours.

TIDS [48] is a trust based intrusion detection algorithm for Wireless Ad-Hoc Networks. Each node in the network is initialized with a trust value as soon as it enters the network. As the node spends time within the network, its trust value gets updated. Trust value of nodes get updated based on direct references and indirect recommenmdations. Trust values of one - hop neighbours are evaluated as part of two different processes.

Li Xiong and Ling Liu proposed a new trust model in PeerTrust [54]. PeerTrust computes the trust of peers in a network as a function of 3 components. First, a peer node becomes trustworthy when other peers who have interacted with this peer are satisfied with its quality of service. It is the number of times the peer behaves normally while interacting with other peers. Second is the context of satisfaction. That is, it defines the total number of interactions that a peer has performed with its peers. Finally there is the Balance factor of trust which is used to reduce the effects of incorrect satisfaction information coming from malicious nodes.

After reviewing several routing protocols and trust models we can conclude that neither multipath routing nor OR is perfectly tailor made for Smart Grid. In order to maximize the performance of Smart Grid, a combination of both the paradigms is necessary. Besides, there rarely exist some works, where trust models have been used in route discovery. This inspires us to propose an intelligent, selective and secure routing protocol which can use the perks of both opportunistic and multipath routing protocols with additional security mechanisms.

2.2.4 Research Gaps

In traditional routing the route between a pair of nodes is always static and data packets are tramsmitted through intermediate nodes over that pre determined route. Whereas, multipath routing adds the desired level of redundancy to overcome link failures utilizing alternative routes [51]. Besides, in a multipath routing environment, link failures do not always result in the initiation of route discovery. This is because the network is k - fault tolerant, for small values of k and hence link failures do not bring network services to a halt [50]. Other than fault tolerance, multipath routing provides better load balancing and bandwidth aggregation etc. [52].

There exist several works, [55–61] which propose to utilize multiple paths for reliable data transmission between source and destination in wireless networks. However, in spite of all these benefits, multipath routing has three major disadvantages: 1) Sending a packet over multiple paths inevitably increases significant energy cost, which is one of the primary design concerns in WSNs; 2) Multiple route discovery and maintenance at every hop induces the operatinal cost of the network. and 3) Exploiting multiple paths also introduces more channel contentions and interference in te network, which in turn may increase the delivery delay as well as cause transmission failures [12].

Opportunistic routing (OR) [62], or anypath routing, is another routing protocol for wireless networks which exploits the broadcast nature. It does not use multiple routes, but selects best poosible relay nodes among a set of candidate nodes to improve reliability and overall system throughput. In OR, the sender node first broadcasts a data packet to its set of next hop relay candidate nodes. Then these candidate nodes select a best relay node among itself using some coordination algorithm and forward the data packet through that node. This process is continued until the data packet reaches its destination.

Now, multipath routing and OR, both have their advantages and disadvantages. Multipath routing provides better reliability and fault tolerance, whereas OR improves network performances and also supports different traffic patterns. However, multipath routing suffers from operational overhead of discovering and maintenance of routes in every hop, which inturn increase the contention in the network. OR also suffers from duplicate reception problem at the destination and single path breakdown problem. Thus, it will be more effective to develop a routing protocol integrating the positive sides of both these paradigms.

2.3 Is Secure Routing Enough for Providing Complete Security in AMI Communication?

Secure routing can be used as a first level of defense against a large number of attacks. However, it can not provide complete security to any system. There still exists a lot of

2.3. Is Secure Routing Enough for Providing Complete Security in AMI Communication?

attacks that needs special attention. Specifically, in Smart Grid, many traditional attacks can be performed to damage the network, as well as, some new attacks can be launched by exploiting the unique features of the grid. In order to detect these types of attacks, a second line of defense is always necessary. Intrusion Detection Systems (IDSs) can perfectly handle these attacks, if designed according to the specification. IDSs have not evolved with the purpose of proactively preventing attacks. Instead, their purpose is to alert about the attacks. An IDS attempts to differentiate the honest and malicious nodes in a network based on the behavior of the nodes [76]. Mitigation of the damage is an expected follow-up action after the IDS successfully detects the intrusion [77]. There exist several IDSs for various types of networks starting from wired to different wireless networks, such as, sensor network, Mobile Adhoc Netwok (MANET), wireless Mesh Network (WMN) etc. We have done a detailed survey on the evolution of all these IDSs in [78].

2.3.1 Intrusion Detection Systems

National Institute of Standards and Technology (NIST) identified wireless networks as one of the most important networking technology for Smart Grid [4]. Specifically, WMN gained a lot of appreciation from researchers as one of the most suitable communication technology for AMI. The redundancy and self-healing capabilities of WMNs provide for less downtime, with messages continuing to be delivered even when paths are blocked or broken. The selfconfiguring, self-tuning, self-healing, and self-monitoring capabilities of mesh can help to reduce the management burden for system administrators. Besides, the advanced mesh networking protocols coordinate the network so that nodes can go into sleep mode while inactive and then synchronize quickly for sending, receiving, and forwarding messages. This ability provides greatly extended battery life [78].

With the birth of Wireless Mesh Networks, newer challenges emerged. The hybrid architecture of WMNs is based on fixed infrastructure as well as it involves the client mobility of MANETs. Thus, researchers tried to adopt or extend the existing intrusion detection algorithms for MANETs. An interesting work on misbehavior based intrusion detection scheme for WMNs was proposed in [11]. The algorithm shows significant improvement by reducing false positives while selecting an appropriate value of threshold, but cannot eliminate it completely. The number of false positives increases with increase in the number of malicious clients within a fixed threshold value. RADAR [79] was proposed as a reputation based intrusion detection scheme. Routing loop attacks are detected with high false positives. RFIDS [80] uses one or more RF transmitters that emit Radio Frequency (RF) into the space along with a well planned network of RF receivers for detection. The proposed method gives better clarity, higher frequency and higher speed of processing. A lightweight PCA based intrusion detection system was proposed in [81] such that appropriate selection of threshold values can reduce the number of false alarms considerably. However, the authors do not mention anything about network traffic or false negatives. Another lightweight intrusion detection system was suggested in OpenLIDS [82]. The solution also avoids false positives. However, in the process, it fails to detect DoS flood attacks. Another two IDSs were proposed for defending Selective Forwarding Attack [83] in WMNs and detecting Selfish Nodes in WMNs [84]. They both claimed to have a high detection rate while having a low rate of false positives. But, there will be always some detection inaccuracy, due to some unrealistic assumptions. A community intrusion detection and pre-warning system based on wireless mesh network was presented in [85]. The system can establish network automatically by using the advantage of multi-hop communication of mesh network. Redundant node can be placed on important area to make sure reliability and resist destroy. Another community based IDS [86] presents a set of socio-technical challenges associated with developing an intrusion detection system for a community wireless mesh network. But this architecture does not explicitly address the challenges with system administrator. Another IDS was proposed based on Kohonen Networks [87]. Even if this solution is quite effective in terms of the number of false positives, it involves high computation overhead.

All of these works have designed to target some specific attacks, such as, blackhole, selective forwarding, DoS, clone attack etc. However, we have considered a Smart Grid specific attack, i.e., energy theft attack for our research. In the following section we'll discuss various types of energy theft attacks and IDSs that are designed to handle these attacks.

2.3.2 Energy Theft Attacks

Energy theft is one of the most important concerns related to the smart grid implementation. It is estimated that utility companies lose more than $25 billion every year due to energy theft around the world [34]. Energy theft may become an even more serious problem since the smart meters used in smart grids are vulnerable to more types of attacks compared to traditional mechanical meters. The unique challenges for energy theft in AMI call for the development of effective detection techniques.

2.3.3 Review on Handling of Energy Theft Attacks in AMI

Generally, energy theft can be accomplished using three ways [34], [36]. Firstly, by interrupting smart meters from recording correct electricity usages, secondly, by forging demand information in smart meters and lastly by injecting false/bad data in the communication line. Now, the first attack is the only one that existed for the traditional meters, the other two attacks are exclusively for smart meters. Besides, premise of energy theft in AMI can also be classified in three categories:

- Type-1: where the attacker modifies its own smart meter to maximize its individual gain.
- Type-2: where the attacker modifies numerous smart meters in his neighborhood to either maximize its personal gain or penalize the utilities.
- Type-3: the cooperative attack, where a bunch of attackers create a chain of attacks on a large scale to immobilize the system in a short time interval.

In the first scenario, it is quite easy to detect the attack by analyzing the electricity usage pattern. Classification based detection schemes are quite suitable for these types of attacks. In order to prevent the electricity theft attack in Smart Grid, providers try to physically secure the smart meter, so that no one can tamper it. GE has patented an energy meter that reads electricity consumption correctly, even if the in-going and out-coming meter terminals are reversed. This invention stopped illegal consumers from using their energy meter in the reverse direction to reduce their utility bill [175]. Besides, there exist several works to detect energy thefts which belong into the first two category. However, these types of attacks can be made more intelligent and difficult to detect, if implemented wisely. In this part, we have proposed an attack model for distributed and intelligent electricity theft and proposed a two tier trust based intrusion detection system. The third part: collaborative attack is much complicated to implement as well as detect.

2.3.3.1 IDSs for Energy Theft Attacks in AMI

There exist a good number of research works addressing solutions towards energy theft problem in Smart Grid. In order to mitigate energy theft attack, the AMI should ensure complete security throughout the life cycle of meter reading data, i.e., in data generation, acquisition, storage, processing, transmission and analysis [88]. The authors in [88] categorizes the existing IDSs as,

- Single data sources, where the IDS uses only smart metersdata to detect the attackers.
- Multiple data sources, where the IDS implements another set of agent or sensor nodes to monitor the network. The detection of attackers is based on the data coming from smart meters as well as the independent agent nodes.
- Privacy preserving data sources, where the IDSs use various computation methods without disclosing the actual usage data of any user to others.

In [37] authors proposed a Support Vector Machine (SVM) based detection model to construct users' load profile pattern and then detect deviations from the standard pattern in order to identify abnormal behavior Besides, to improve the performance of this model, authors incorporate fuzzy systems. The complete detection model identifies abnormal behaviors in the grid by comparing current load with recorded load profile and other additional information.

Authors in [38] proposed an Auto Regressive Moving Average (ARMA) based model to analyze the probability distributions of the normal and malicious consumption patterns of users. They have applied the generalized likelihood ratio (GLR) test to detect energy theft attacks. The proposed work is heavily dependent on the data capturing accuracy of the ARMA model. Besides, it is based on the assumption that the attacker would always choose to decreases the mean value of the real consumption.

Works presented in [39] and [40] also proposed a detection mechanism based on pattern matching and data classification. First, they proposed an classification method based on SVM and Rule based systems [39]. Then in [40], they introduce High Performance Computing (HPC) based algorithms to enhance the performance of their previous model. They have implemented some parallelized encoding algorithms to speed up the data classification, analyze and detection process. They have been able to differentiate the behavior of fraud customers from genuine users, using this model.

AMIDS [41] is another AMI Intrusion Detection model, where a data mining technique based Non Intrusive Load Monitoring (NILM) system can collect data from three different sensors. These sensors gather data to identify cyber attacks, physical attacks and power measurement based anomaly. Authors of this paper claim that the proposed intrusion detection system (IDS) can detect several attacks by using information fusion from different sensors and correlation of different alert triggers.

2.3. Is Secure Routing Enough for Providing Complete Security in AMI Communication?

A Radio Frequency IDentification (RFID) based theft detection technique is proposed in [42]. The proposed system is divided in two parts: ammeter inventory management and ammeter verification control. RFID tags are attached with meters and used to detect energy theft. In addition, the reader acquires the information transmitted from the tag and sends it to the company's ERP system through the network to determine whether it is the approved tag or a different one placed by electricity thieves. Although the RFID technology can be used to detect energy theft, the utility companies have to pay extra cost to install the system. In order to find out whether implementing RFID technology is beneficial for the utility company, cost-benefit theory is used to analyze different value changes caused by the proposed system.

Authors of paper [43] proposed a rather simple approach. they compare the meter readings of users with utilities reading. If the difference exceeds a threshold value, then that meter is marked as malicious and the connection will be terminated immediately.

2.3.4 Research Gaps

The detection methods for energy theft can be broadly categorize into three types [34], [44]: classification or statistical methods based detection techniques, monitoring based detection techniques and game theory based detection techniques. Classification based methods apply data mining methods and machine learning to energy usage patterns, collected from smart meters. They detect attacks by finding the deviation from the original data. These methods are cost effective and can be implemented easily. However, due to its lack of consideration for innovative and adaptive attack techniques, often some intelligent and minute attacks remain undetectable. Besides the false positive rates are on a higher side for these type of methods. Monitoring based techniques use sensor nodes, RFIDs and sometimes other smart meters to monitor the state of the network to detect the attack. This method has a better detection rate and lower false positive rate than the previous one. Continuous monitoring ensures the detection of very minute changes in the system. However, the implementation and maintenance cost of such system can become a disadvantage for implementation. Lastly, game theory based methods [45], [46] are new in this domain, very few works have been done to detect energy theft. Planning the strategies for each player and formulated their goals can be a bit tricky in smart Grid environment. The rules of the games should update simultaneously according to the change of situations in network and characteristics of players. Besides, these types of methods have greater false positive rates than monitoring based methods. It may be summarized that the monitoring based methods are best suitable to detect intelligent and minute attacks, providing the implementation and maintenance costs are minimized. Thus the main goal is to propose an effective monitoring system which ensures the trade-off between cost optimization and detection efficiency.

CHAPTER 3

SECURE ROUTING IN AMI

Traffic engineering governs the operational performance of a network and its optimization. Splitting the network traffic using multipath routing is one of the standard techniques of traffic engineering. Multipath routing maximizes network resource utilization and throughput by giving nodes a choice of next hops for the same destination along with minimizing the delay. On the other hand, Opportunistic routing minimizes operational cost and the burden of redundant route maintenance by using a constrained redundancy in route selection. POMSec: Pseudo Opportunistic, Multipath Secure routing is one such algorithm that combines the advantages of both the routing methods and additionally implements an underlying trust model to secure the communication in Smart Grid.

3.1 Pseudo Opportunistic, Multipath, Secure (POMSec) Routing Protocol

The proposed work is a secure and pseudo opportunistic, multipath routing scheme that offers efficient load balancing. Like traditional OR methods, our protocol dynamically selects a set of forwarding nodes for packet transmission. However, the number of routes for packet transmission is not static, and the number of routes varies with the status of each intermediate node, at every hop along the path. The degree of routes at each hop depends heavily on the trust worthiness of neighbouring nodes. As an example, it may act like single-path routing, if the nodes are trustworthy and the communication is reliable and meets network requirements. Otherwise, the number of paths increased. The selection process is run-time and dynamic.

The proposed protocol offers the flexibility that it may use multiple paths with high degree of multiplicity when the intermediate destinations are not that trusted. On the contrary, the protocol save resources, and checks congestion by choosing a single path or lesser number of alternate paths for the next hop according to the health value of its neighbour nodes. Because of these characteristics, our proposed algorithm has been referred as Pseudo Opportunistic, Multipath Secure (POMSec) routing protocol.

3.2 Description of the Process

This section briefly describes our proposed protocol for secure communication in Smart grid. Route selection in POMSec is dependent on energy depletion rate of the nodes, existing paths through the nodes and the trustworthiness of the nodes and their neighbours.

These following set of principles govern the proper execution of the proposed algorithm::
- Every node maintains two arrays – *Health* and *Trust*, of all its neighbour nodes.
- Every node has to store two variables – *Remaining Energy* and *Path*.
- Packet Receive (*PR*) and Packet Send (*PS*) counters are stored in nodes, along with the addresses of the nodes from which it receive the packets and to which it forward those packets. After a certain time frame (decided by the system operator), these counter values are sent to the node's one-hop neighbours.
- The health of each node N depends on trust-worthiness of the nodes, the remaining energy of it and on the number of paths through N.

3.2.1 Underlying Routing Protocol

The routing mechanism used for this protocol [89] is a restricted multi-path routing algorithm that dynamically selects the number of neighboring nodes through which packets would be transmitted. The word restrictive has been used to suggest that on a hop-by-hop basis, one or more paths may be selected to reach the final destination depending on the current status. The selection and degree of multi-path depends heavily on the trust value of the neighbours. As for example, just like single-path routing there could be only one selected node for the next hop, if the communication is reliable, trusted and meets other criteria. An intermediate may not forward the RREQ packet at all depending on the status of the factors mentioned. However, depending on the status, an intermediate may decide to broadcast to its entire neighborhood too. The selection is run-time and dynamic. The protocol is designed in such a way that the burden of routing is lesser on the weaker nodes and the nodes with more resources will have to perform more tasks. A node only increases the number of routes towards the sink node, when it finds that the next hop nodes are not capable enough to carry the total load. An outline of the algorithm is given in Figure 4.9. ETSeM offers a balanced approach of resource utilization for possible multi-path routing. Consequently, the data reception rate, defined as the ratio of the total number of packets received by the sink node and the total number of packets send by the source node, is much higher than any single path routing. Besides the end to end delay is decreased for ETSeM for the reason that the number of routes will increase with the decreasing health of nodes. Thus the load is balanced among the nodes and the multiple routes also increase the reliability.

Figure 3.4(a) illustrates the route selection proces following algorithm 1

3.2.2 The Trust Model

In order to secure our protocol we evaluated the trust of each node. The evaluation process is done by a node for its one hop neighbours and vice versa. The trust model has two main underlying concepts: *Direct Valuation* and *Indirect Reference* [48] as shown in 3.1.

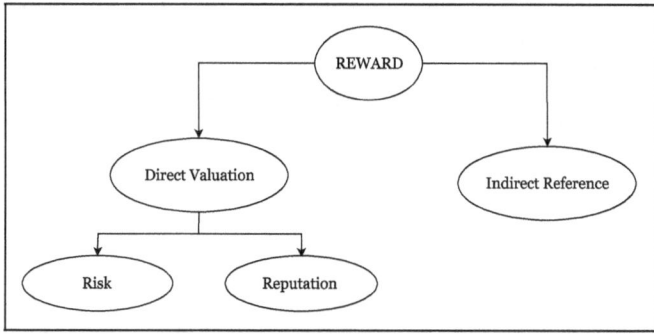

Figure 3.1: Trust model of POMSec.

3. Secure Routing in AMI

Algorithm 1: Working principle of POMSec.

1 initialization;
2 **for** *(EVERY node in the network)* **do**
3   Broadcasts a HELLO message;
4 **end**
5 **if** *a node (receives a HELLO message)* **then**
6   replies with a REPLY HELLO message containing four variables – PR, PS, REMAINING ENERGY and PATH;
7 **end**
8 **if** *a node (receives a REPLY HELLO message)* **then**
9   Extracts the value of the Variables – PR, PS, REMAINING ENERGY and PATH;
10   Calculate the HEALTH, for each of its Neighbour nodes;
11   Stores the address of each neighbour node with the value of their corresponding HEALTH, in an array;
12 **end**
13 **if** *a node is a (SOURCE node OR receives a ROUTE REQUEST message)* **then**
14   Checks its array for the HEALTHIEST node in its Neighbour;
15   **if** *(HEALTHIEST node > 90%)* **then**
16   Send a ROUTE REQUEST message to the HEALTHIEST node;
17   **else**
18   **if** *(HEALTHIEST node > 75%)* **then**
19   Send a ROUTE REQUEST message to the HEALTHIEST and second HEALTHIEST node;
20   **else**
21   **if** *(HEALTHIEST node > 60%)* **then**
22   Send a ROUTE REQUEST message to the HEALTHIEST, second HEALTHIEST and third HEALTHIEST node;
23   **else**
24   **if** *(HEALTHIEST node > 45%)* **then**
25   Send a ROUTE REQUEST message to the HEALTHIEST, second HEALTHIEST, third HEALTHIEST and fourth HEALTHIEST node;
26   **else**
27   Flood the ROUTE REQUEST message;
28   **end**
29   **end**
30   **end**
31   **end**
32 **end**
33 **if** *a node is a (DESTINATION node OR receives a ROUTE REPLY message)* **then**
34   it will initiate a ROUTE REPLY message to the nodes, from which it gets the ROUTE REQUEST message ;
35 **end**

3.2. Description of the Process

Direct Valuation refers to the trust value evaluated by a node. It is calculated using two different parameters: *Risk* and *Reputation*. *Risk* measures a node's behavior in recent past and *Reputation* assess a node's long term behavior. These two parameters helps to achieve an optimality by balancing the most recent behavior of a node in contrast to its long term behavior. On the other hand, *Indirect Reference* are considered from those entire one-hop neighbors that are common to both the evaluator node and the target node.

At time t, an evaluator node calculates the *Risk* and *Reputation* of its neighbour node i as,

$$Risk = \sum_{t} |PR_i - PS_i| \qquad (3.1)$$

$$Reputation = \sum_{t}^{t-n} |PR_i - PS_i| \qquad (3.2)$$

The *Indirect Reference* for m number of common neighbour Nodes (ND) between evaluator and target node, can be evaluated as,

$$Indirect\ Reference = \sum_{ND=1}^{m} \sum_{t}^{t-n} |PR_i - PS_i| \qquad (3.3)$$

The reward for a node for the last time slice, is calculated using these three metrics as follows [48]:

$$\text{"}Reward = (\alpha * Risk) + (\beta * Reputation) + (\gamma * Indirect\ Reference)\text{"} \qquad (3.4)$$

The above formula generates reward points for each nodes by assigning weights to α, β and γ. Also, these coefficients are normalized so that $\alpha + \beta + \gamma = 1$. Now, we can calculate the trust value as:

$$\text{"}Trust(t) = Trust(t-1) + Reward\text{"} \qquad (3.5)$$

If the value for the variable *Trust* of a node, crosses the threshold value, then it considered as an attacker. The trust value of a node may vary according to equation (3.5).

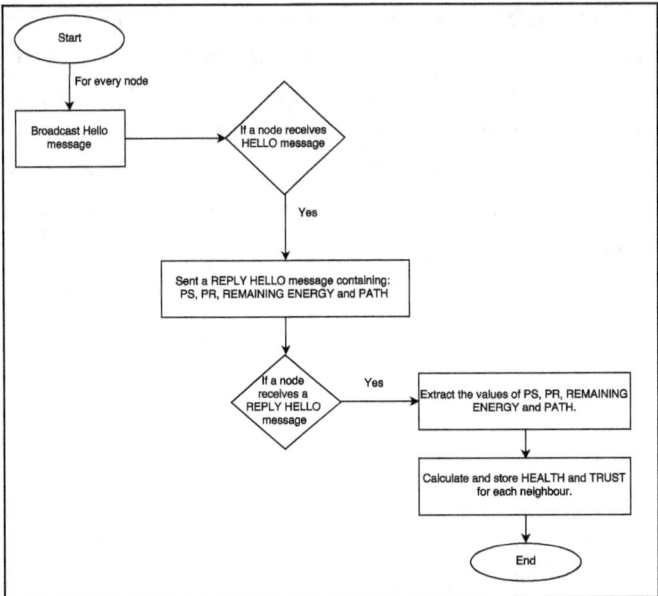

Figure 3.2: Network Maintenance part of POMSec.

3.2.3 Proposed Methodology

An outline of POMSec is described in figure 3.2 and 3.3. The value of the metric *PATH* is increased by one, whenever a node receives a *ROUTE_REPLY* packet. A source node can transmits data using the path that's derived this way. The load to the destination node is distributed proportionally through the routes according to the health of each node.

Figure 3.4(a) illustrates the route selection proces of the ETSeM algorithm given in [89]. The significance of the algorithm after incorporating the trust model along the route selection process is depicted in figure 3.4(b). Figures 3.4(a) and 3.4(b) has the same set of nodes. The black node in figure 3.4(b) is detected as malicious in spite of its health more than or equal to 90%. This is because the trust value of the node is less than the threshold. POMSec can avoid all such malicious nodes in the route selection process with the help of the underlying trust model.

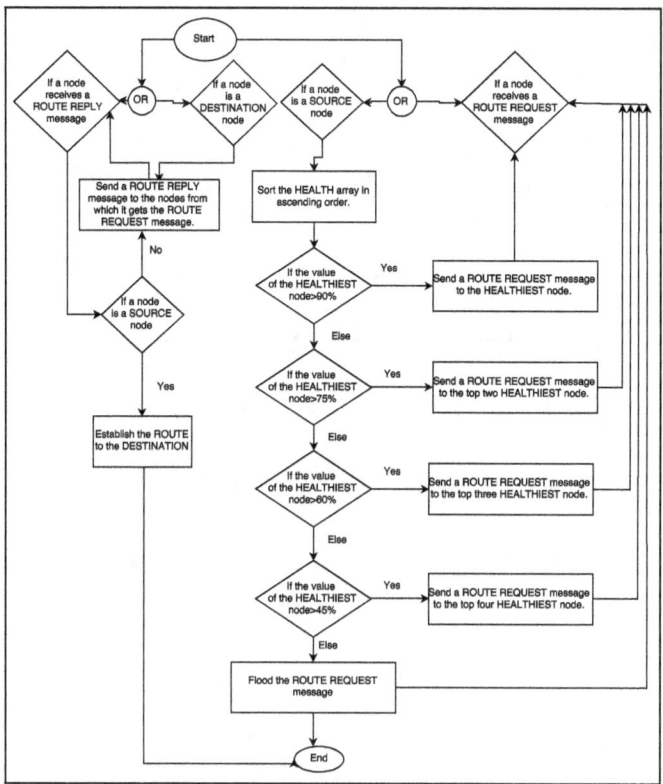

Figure 3.3: Route Establishment part of POMSec.

3.3 Experiments and Results

3.3.1 Simulation Settings

We have compared and analyzed the performance of POMSec with two different algorithms. First, another trust model, proposed in [47] is used with the ETSeM algorithm. Let's refer this change in the rest of this chapter as H-ETSeM. Thereafter, extensive simulations of POMSec, ETSeM [89] and H-ETSeM have been successfully performed in QualNet and the results have been plotted as graphs and discussed accordingly. The simulation scenario and settings are described in Table 4.2 below:

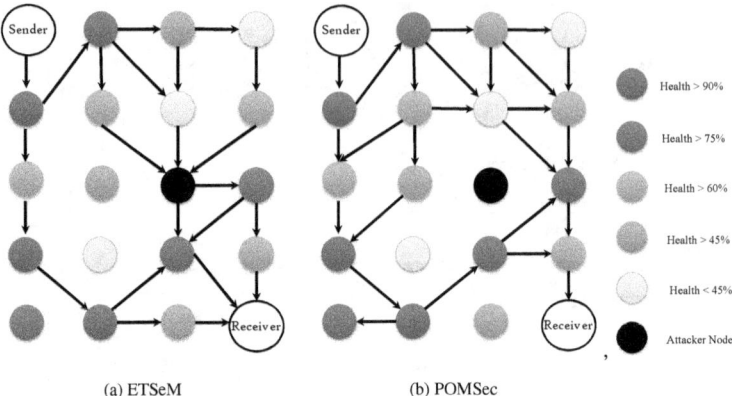

(a) ETSeM (b) POMSec

Figure 3.4: Data communication between Source and Destination using ETSeM and POMSec.

Table 3.1: Parameter Settings for Simulation Environment

Parameter	Value
Experimental area	$1500 * 1500 m^2$
Running time for each simulation	100 sec
Mac Layer protocol	DCF of IEEE 802.11b standard
Traffic Model	CBR
Number of CBR traffics	10% of the total number of nodes
Mobility	Random Waypoint
Initial Energy level for each node	5000

3.3.2 Simulation Results

A quantitative analysis of POMSec and detailed comparison with ETSeM and H-ETSeM are presented in this section. The node density for each experiment varies between 10 nodes to 50 nodes and the mobility is set at 30mps. We have used Constant Bit-Rate (CBR) traffic with 100 second runtime and 100 packets to transmit. A single CBR transmission is implemented for every 10 nodes, i.e., for fourty nodes there will be four different CBR traffics in the experiment. Data has been collected for every variation in node density and then averaged for final results. These results are then plotted on graphs.

3.3. Experiments and Results

3.3.2.1 Packet Delivery Ratio

The first simulation checks the Packet Delivery Ratio (PDR) of POMSec and also compares it with others. PDR is an important parameter in routing and quite standard too. PDR represents the ratio of successfully receiving packets at destination over the packets sent by the sender through CBR traffic. Figure 3.5(a) shows the PDR for original ETSeM, H-ETSeM and POMSec. POMSec demonstrates more stable and higher PDR than the other two algorithms, inspite of having a trust based evaluation method in route selection.

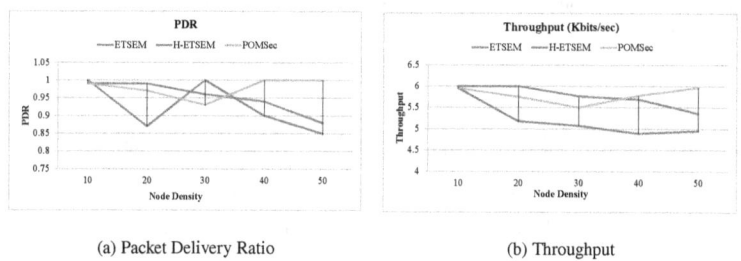

(a) Packet Delivery Ratio (b) Throughput

Figure 3.5: Comparative data analysis for PDR and throughput of ETSeM, H-ETSeM and POMSec.

3.3.2.2 Throughput

Throughput is a measurement of how much data passed through a network in unit amount of time. In this simulation we measured it in Kilobits/sec by observing CBR Server stats. The results in figure 3.5(b) shows that the throughput for POMSec is better comparing to the other two algorithms. POMSec obviously looks promising in terms of efficient path selection and decision-making and better throughput values.

3.3.2.3 End to End Delay

It represents the total time required by every CBR packet to reach its destination. Figure 3.6(a) depicts that POMSec offers much smaller delay than both the algorithms, which in turn proves the effectiveness of our trust model. H-ETSeM brings in more instability with increasing node density as compared to ETSeM. This actually confirms that the overhead for trust value updation increases with higher number of nodes.

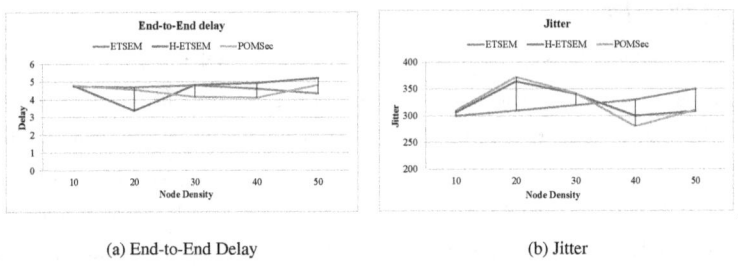

(a) End-to-End Delay (b) Jitter

Figure 3.6: Comparative data analysis for End-to-end delay and Jitter of ETSeM, H-ETSeM and POMSec.

3.3.2.4 Jitter

In networking, the word jitter represents the average of the deviation of a packet against the mean latency of the network [90]. Figure 3.6(b) shows that the Jitter of H-ETSeM and POMSec are quite identical, and as the degree of nodes increase in the network, it appears to decrease and become stable after sometime.

3.3.2.5 Energy Depletion Rate

Energy efficiency is one of the most critical QoS metric for various Wireless environments. The calculations for energy depletion of each node according to their expenses for packet transmission, neighbourhood discovery, trust evolution and route maintenance, along with the updation rule has been additionally coded in simulation environment. The results in figure 3.3.2.5 are very interesting and informative. Inspite of additional trust evaluation overhead POMSec has almost similar trend as ETSeM. This confirms that our trust model is much light weight and it does not add extra burdens in the routing.

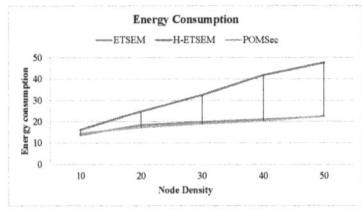

Figure 3.7: Comparative data analysis for Energy depletion rate of ETSeM, H-ETSeM and POMSec.

3.4 Conclusions

We have done a detailed study of the existing works in multipath routing and opportunistic routing in chapter 2. The survey reflects that many of them perform well in terms of throughput of the network and some of them are also energy efficient. However, none of these routing algorithms incorporate trust as a metric to determine the degree of multipath. Thats why we proposed an algorithm where trust evolution process is integrated with the route establishment process to provide security. Besides, a detailed comparison with other trust based approaches has been simulated in Qualnet and the results confirm that POMSec proves to be an improvement over existing algorithms, as it provides security as well as better throughput, PDR, delay and energy efficiency. POMSec has an unique feature that it distributed the traffic among nodes in such a way that the weaker nodes has lesser burden of routing than the nodes with more resources.

CHAPTER 4

ENERGY THEFT ATTACKS IN AMI

Power grid and energy theft has an eternal relationship. Though we moved towards Smart Grid, with an expectation for a more efficient, reliable and secure service, so does the attackers. Smart Grid and AMI systems incorporate a good number of security measures as we already discussed in 2, still it is open to various threats. Recent attacks on Smart Grids in U.S., Gulf State and Ukraine proved that the attacks on the grid have become more sophisticated. In this chapter we have introduced two new energy theft attacks: Distributed and Intelligent Energy Theft (DIET) attack and Collaborative Energy Theft (CET) attack. Besides, we have proposed three Intrusion Detection Solutions (IDSs):

1) The first one is a Cluster Oriented Reward based Intrusion Detection System (CORIDS), typically curated for Wireless Mesh Networks. This IDS can successfully detect various attacks, such as, Blackhole, DoS, Cybil and Clone attacks. However, this proposed IDS does not perform satisfactorily to detect our proposed DIET and CET attacks.

2) The above shortcoming of CORIDS leads us to an IDS that is tailor made for Smart Grid, rather AMI environment. The second IDS can successfully detect DIET attack, which is a Type-II energy theft attack. However, when it comes to collaborative attacks, the performance of the IDS degraded severely.

3) Finally we came up with an complete IDS, which can detect all type of energy theft attacks, i.e. Type-I, Type-II and Type-III.

4. Energy Theft Attacks in AMI

4.1 CORIDS: Cluster Oriented Reward based Intrusion Detection System

In this section we will explain in detail the Cluster-based architecture that we have proposed for our algorithm, how the mesh routers and mesh clients behave in this structure, what are the different types of attacks that we are addressing, and finally how the CORIDS algorithm works in detail.

4.1.1 The Proposed Cluster-Based Architecture for WMNs

We assume the hybrid architecture of WMNs. Mesh clients have mobility and resource constraints. Mesh routers are static and have unlimited resources. We organize the mesh clients in a hierarchical model. The entire network is divided into several disjoint or overlapping clusters. The clients are divided into clusters with each cluster having one mesh router as the Cluster Head (CH). Clusters are sufficiently spaced out so that no cluster in the network has more than one cluster head. A cluster is defined by the CH and all mesh clients which are within one hop distance (in the radio frequency range) from the The total number of clusters is bounded by the number of mesh routers in the WMN backbone. Client members of a cluster interact directly with the CH since they are in the direct radio range of the CH. Membership information about a cluster is maintained by the CH and is updated at regular intervals.

Cluster members send packets to other cluster members of the same or different cluster. These packets reach the CH of the cluster where the source resides. The CH checks its membership information with the receiver's address. If the receiver is in the same cluster, the CH sends it to the destination node. If the destination node belongs to some other cluster, then the CH checks its routing table information to decide where to route the packet. Inter – cluster communication is achieved when CHs share their information. Redundant multi-hop paths exist between CHs.

Only a CH can participate in the intrusion detection process. Each CH monitors the behavior of its cluster members. CHs store additional information about suspected nodes. Also, CHs store trust information of its cluster members. Since mesh clients have limited memory and power resources, hence, we do not involve the members in the intrusion detection system. Only CHs will run the CORIDS algorithm. CHs exchange trust information of their members among themselves at regular time intervals. Each CH updates the trust values of its members.

4.1. CORIDS: Cluster Oriented Reward based Intrusion Detection System

CHs can declare a node as malicious based on some parameters and their threshold values. A member can be declared as malicious by any CH through which the cluster member has transmitted or received packets. It must be kept in mind that mesh clients have mobility. As a result, a mesh client may send packets of some application through several CHs. Thus, behavior related information about a mesh client may get distributed over several CHs. If a node is malicious, it may misbehave intelligently enough such that none of the CHs cross the threshold value for some parameter. The malicious mesh client may remain undetected. However, combining information from all CHs the misbehaving node can be detected as malicious.

Since members of the mesh backbone are the CHs, they are static and have unlimited resources, great computational capability and no power constraints. These properties of mesh routers have been fully utilized to relieve the mesh clients from doing any kind of computations in the intrusion detection process. Very little resource utilization of mesh clients is performed as will be seen later. The various jobs that a CH is expected to do storage of information, routing, identification of cluster boundary and identifying malicious nodes from good ones.

CHs maintain two different parameters for each of its cluster members – the packet arrival rate (PAR), and the packet delivery rate (PDR). Since each packet originating from a source client is sent to the corresponding CH and each packet is delivered by a CH to the destination client, hence, PAR and PDR values for each client is maintained at the corresponding CH. Cluster members also keep track of the number of packets sent and received by it. This is done with the help of two other parameters – packets sent (PS) and packets received (PR). Both these counters are maintained in the mesh clients by kernel level protocols. It is assumed that an attacker cannot tamper with these values. Ordinary member nodes send their PR and PS information to their current CHs at regular time intervals. Whenever the PAR, PDR, PR or PS values of a mesh client are not within their respective thresholds, an intrusion is suspected. Trust values are updated based on these values and if the trust value for a mesh client falls below a threshold value, then it is declared as a malicious node.

During routing, when a CH receives a packet from one of its members, it updates the PAR parameter associated with that member. When the CHs deliver packets to their cluster members, they update the PDR parameter associated with the respective destination node. Original CHs may have to forward a packet to another CH based on its Routing table information. An intermediate CH, on receiving a packet from another

CH, checks its routing table information to decide whether to forward the packet or to deliver it to one of its members. The underlying routing protocol that is assumed for CORIDS is AODV.

4.1.2 Description of CORIDS

To relieve the mesh clients from wasting their resources on detecting intrusions, the CORIDS algorithm is executed only in the mesh routers. We would first like to define the parameters involved in the intrusion detection process.

- TR_{val}: Trust value of a cluster member as evaluated by its
- TH_{Tr}: Threshold Trust value; if the trust value of a mesh client falls below TH_{Tr} it is declared as malicious.
- PAR_X: Packet Arrival Rate for cluster member X as maintained by its CH.
- PDR_X: Packet Delivery Rate for cluster member X as maintained by its CH.
- TH_{PAR}: Threshold value of Packet Arrival Rate.
- N_X: Unique ID of node X.
- PS: Number of packets sent to the CH
- PR: Number of packets received from the CH

Before stating the working of the algorithm it is mandatory to mention the assumptions behind the proposed algorithm.

1) Every CH overhears the activity of its cluster members.
2) All mesh clients and mesh routers have a global unique ID.
3) CHs are relatively secured or they have enough resources to implement different layers of security.
4) The threshold values are pre – calculated and set for the entire network. These values are stored in the CHs. We would like to mention that depending on the priority of clusters, different CHs may have different values set as their threshold.
5) The PR and PS counters at the client side are maintained at the operating system level and these values cannot be tampered.

When a client enters the network, it must wait for itself to become a part of the network. As soon as it receives a ROL_CALL packet it immediately responds with an ECHO packet. It is only then that it becomes a part of the network. Whenever a CH identifies new members in its cluster boundary, it assigns them a globally unique ID and an initial value of TR_{val}. The trust value of each cluster member is stored in the Trust table of the CH. Monitoring of the network is performed every time a packet is received by the CH from a member or delivered by the CH to a member. All data and control packets are signed by the source of the packet. Whenever a data packet reaches a CH from a cluster member X, it only attaches the unique ID of the client with that packet. This packet is then propagated through the network.

The CORIDS algorithm provides a three step solution to the intrusion detection problem. In the first phase of the algorithm, CHs collect information about their cluster members which is stored in the CHs of other clusters. This phase is necessary as it may so happen that a cluster member, due to its mobility, sends data packets through several CHs. If the node is under the influence of a DoS attack, it may try to block network resources by generating excessive traffic. It is a basic assumption while defending any kind of attacks that the attacker is very intelligent. So the malicious node may start sending too many packets but evenly route them through different CHs. Thus, if a cluster member has multiple CHs, then its PAR information will most likely be distributed over these CHs. Aggregating this information before making any kind of decisions is mandatory.

Merging of information from different Cluster Heads becomes necessary when a Cluster Member receives or sends packets through different Cluster Heads. PAR / PDR information for a Cluster Member, as stored in a Cluster Head, reflects only the number of packets received or delivered to that Cluster Member via that Cluster Head. However, PR / PS information stored in a Cluster Member represents the history of packets received by and sent from the node. So in order to correctly assess the behavior of Cluster Members we need to merge the PAR / PDR information.

At the beginning of every epoch, Cluster Heads send IDS_Request packets to all its Cluster Members on one frequency and IDS_Update packets to all neighboring Cluster Heads on another frequency. Each Cluster Head stores PAR / PDR information in a table along with the particular Cluster Member's Node Address. IDS_Update packets contain a list of Node Addresses along with their PAR / PDR information as collected by that Cluster Head. So when a Cluster Head receives an IDS_Update packet from another Cluster Head, it scans through this list and checks if there is any node which is a member of both the clusters as represented by these two Cluster Heads. All distributed information about a particular Cluster Member (if that member belongs to more than one cluster), are merged in all the Cluster Heads which have information about that

Cluster Member.

In the second phase of the algorithm, a CH interacts and collects control information from its cluster members. After collecting information from its cluster members, the CHs execute the CORIDS algorithm in the third phase. They update the trust values associated with each of their cluster members. Once Trust values are updated, cluster members can be declared as malicious if required. cluster members, which are once declared as malicious, are informed to other CHs. Algorithms 9, 10 and 11 explain phase 1, phase 2, and phase 3 of CORIDS.

Algorithm 2: CORIDS - Phase 1
---
1 initialization;
2 CHs store PAR, PDR, PR and PS information of Cluster members with their corresponding ID;
3 After a fixed time slice, CHs broadcast their respective client information to all other CHs in the network;
4 When a CH receives such an update packet, it scans the packet and checks to see if information is available about some node that also belonged to its own cluster. This is done by checking the node ID N_x associated with each parameter set;
5 If any N_x matches with those of its cluster members, then it updates the information associated with that node ID N_x;
6 Steps 3 and 4 are performed by all CHs;
7 Proceed to Phase 2;

Algorithm 3: CORIDS - Phase 2
---
1 Mesh clients within every cluster send the values of their PS and PR parameters to their respective CHs;
2 Mesh clients send their PR and PS data along with their respective node ID, N_x;
3 The CH maintains a table of all cluster members within its own cluster;
4 Proceed to Phase 3;

The Algorithm is executed by the CHs in a distributed manner and at random but regular time intervals.

4.1.3 Handling Different Attacks using CORIDS

The basic motivation behind our algorithm is that we update trust values of nodes based on current information (reward – based). The trust values of compromised nodes should

4.1. CORIDS: Cluster Oriented Reward based Intrusion Detection System

Algorithm 4: CORIDS - Phase 3

1. CHs compare the PAR and PDR values of a cluster member with its corresponding PR and PS values and also their respective thresholds;
2. Attacks are classified based on these values;
3. Rewards are calculated for all nodes. Normally behaving nodes are positively rewarded whereas misbehaving nodes are negatively rewarded;
4. Trust values of cluster members are updated using the evaluated reward values;
5. The updated Trust values are compared with a predefined threshold trust value. If the trust value of any Cluster member falls below the threshold value, then it is identified as a malicious node;
6. Stop;

be decreased while that of normal nodes should be increased. When a node enters the network, it is assigned an initial trust value given by equation 4.1.

$$TR_{VAL} = (2^n - 1)/2 \qquad (4.1)$$

Here n is the number of bits assigned for storing trust values. A node whose trust value falls below the threshold value of trust (TH_{Tr}) is declared as malicious. We now look into some of the different situations and attacks that may occur, how the attacks are detected and how clients are rewarded. In our simulation, the Trust value is initialized to 16384 for all the client nodes. We have used an integer variable to represent trust. The values for two-byte integer range from -32768 to 32767. We assign the midway value in the positive scale, i.e., 16384. It is equivalent to 0.5 on a normalized scale of [0, 1].

The packet transfer rate is taken as 1 per second. Since our IDS algorithm repeats in every 20 sec., ideally a node should generate a maximum of 20 packets in between successive epochs. We allow a buffer of 5 more packets keeping in mind that traffic can be heavy at times. If the number of packets is more than 25, we decrease the trust-value of a node by 300 ∗ (number of extra packets generated). This value of 300 has been decided arbitrarily. When trust value falls below the threshold value of 10000, we declare a node as malicious. The threshold value is so decided such that we can detect an attacker as soon as possible. This is how Denial-of-Service attacks are detected. If a node behaves normally then its trust value increases by a fixed amount, as defined in equation 3. The Blackhole attacks are detected following a similar approach.

A node behaves normally. Good nodes are characterized by the property that their PAR, PDR, PS and PR values are consistent. Good nodes should be duly rewarded. A node X is assumed to behave normally if $PAR_X < TH_{PAR}$, $PAR_X = PS$ and $PDR_X = PR$. Such a node is rewarded as defined in equation 4.2.

$$Reward = R \times (PAR_X + PDR_X)/2 \qquad (4.2)$$

DoS Attack (generation of spurious packets): Denial of Service attack is primarily a resource utilization attack. It causes congestion in the available network resources. One such type of DoS attack is spurious packet generation and flooding them throughout the network. The DoS attack can be distributed in nature if several nodes start generating spurious packets from different points of the network. A node X is definitely under DoS attack if the Packet Arrival Rate for that node exceeds the threshold value, i.e., $PAR_X > TH_{PAR}$.

$$Reward = -R \times (PAR_X - TH_{PAR}) \qquad (4.3)$$

Blackhole Attack (routing misbehavior by dropping packets): The routing protocol has been so modified that packets are routed only through CHs. Since CHs are intrinsically secure, a blackhole attack can be launched only during route setup. The attacker can maliciously claim to be the final destination for an application and generate a route reply packet. Once a route is set up between the sender and the attacker, all packets would be sent to that attacker node.

However, CHs increment their PDR values only when the destination address matches with that of its cluster member. Thus, although the packet is delivered to the malicious node its PDR value is not incremented at the On the other head, whenever a cluster member sends or receives a packet, its PS or PR parameter gets incremented. Thus, there is a mismatch between the PR and PDR values of the malicious node at the A node X is surely in blackhole attack if Packet Delivery Rate for the node is less than the Packet Received parameter, i.e., $PAR_X < PR_X$.

$$Reward = -R \times (PR_X - PAR_X) \qquad (4.4)$$

Using the different parameter values, we are able to evaluate the rewards that every cluster member has acquired since the last execution of the algorithm. Once we have the rewards for all cluster members, we can evaluate and re-compute their trust values. Trust value of a cluster member is updated according to equation 4.5.

$$TR_{VAL\_x}(t) = TR_{VAL\_x}(t-1) + Reward_X \qquad (4.5)$$

Now we check if $TR_{VAL\_x}(t) < TH_{Tr}$. Based on this result, we either declare a node as malicious or safe.

4.1.4 Performance Analysis

Our findings are based on simulations of a WMN network model using Qualnet. The simulation scenario and settings are listed in table 4.1 below.

4.1.4.1 Evaluation Metrics:

A common criterion for evaluating an anomaly detection scheme is the trade-off between its capability of detecting anomalies and the ability of suppressing false alerts. In our experiment, we examine the detection efficiency and false positive percentage of our algorithm. 10 simulation epochs were executed for averaged results. We also show a trend of the average number of iterations required for each experiment. Also, we have compared our results with the MDA algorithm [11] in terms of false positive percentage and detection efficiency.

Table 4.1: Simulator parameter settings

Parameter	Value
Terrain area	1500X1500 m^2
Simulation time	200 sec
Mac Layer protocol	DCF of IEEE 802.11b standard
Network Layer protocol	AODV routing protocol
Traffic Model	CBR
Number of CBR applications	10 % of the number of mesh clients
Mesh router : mesh client	1:5
Types of attacks implemented	DDoS attack using Spurious Packet Generation and Routing Misbehavior attack using Blackhole
Mobility Model	Random Waypoint
Initial Trust Value of nodes	16384

4.1.4.2 Evaluation of Performance Parameters:

When we have simulated our experiment we have arbitrarily set some of the nodes as malicious. The % of malicious nodes varies from 10% to 50%. For detecting either blackhole or DoS attack, we have taken one set of readings by varying node density and another set of readings by varying mobility. Now, for example, when node density is 50, we take 5 sets of data by increasing the number of malicious nodes from 5 through 10, 15, 20, 25. During every simulation, we know the number of malicious nodes and we arbitrarily set that many nodes as malicious from our configuration. Since we know which nodes are supposed to behave maliciously, we check with the Intrusion data generated by CORIDS.

Since CORIDS is a reward – based IDS, we assign either positive or negative rewards to nodes. Depending on the rewards earned, the algorithm adjusts the trust values of the nodes. When trust values fall below a threshold, they are declared as malicious. This is what comprises the Intrusion data of our algorithm. So at the end of our experiment, we check to see which nodes have been detected as malicious by CORIDS.

Suppose we had set 'x' nodes as malicious before our simulation, and CORIDS detects 'y' nodes as malicious at the end of our experiment, out of which 'z' nodes belong to the list of malicious nodes set by us (z<=y, z<=x). Then the detection efficiency can be calculated as –

$$\text{Detection Efficiency} = z/x * 100 \qquad (4.6)$$

If $z = x$, then detection efficiency is 100%. Now, $(y - z)$ may be greater than equal to 0. If 'y' is greater than 'z', then it implies that CORIDS has detected some benign nodes as malicious. These are the false positives which can be expressed as a percentage as follows –

$$\text{False Positive} = (y - z)/x * 100 \qquad (4.7)$$

If $y = z$, then there are no false positives. This is how we calculate Detection Efficiency and False Positives.

False Negative is closely related to Detection Efficiency. Detection Efficiency is a measure of the number of malicious nodes correctly identified as intrusions and False Negative is a measure of the number of malicious nodes that could not be detected by

4.1. CORIDS: Cluster Oriented Reward based Intrusion Detection System

the IDS. Since Detection Efficiency is expressed as a percentage, False Negative can be easily calculated as –

$$\text{False Negative} = (100 - \text{Detection Efficiency}) \qquad (4.8)$$

In our simulation settings, CBR traffic is generated at the rate of 1 packet per second and our epoch duration is 10 seconds. So in every epoch, 10 packets are in transit – either sent, received or forwarded. So we consider a tolerance of 30% which is 3 packets. A node may drop up to 3 packets or generate 3 extra packets in one epoch. This is classified as normal behavior and the node has its trust increased. If a node drops or generates 4 or more packets more than normal, then it is classified as malicious behavior and its trust is decreased.

4.1.4.3 Results and Analysis

We simulate the CORIDS algorithm in several stages. First we implement blackhole attacks and test the performance of our algorithm. The performance metrics have already been mentioned above. In the next stage, we simulate our algorithm for detecting DDoS attacks. The same set of readings is taken. Finally we compare the performance of our algorithm with the existing MDA [11] algorithm.

Blackhole Attack First we test our algorithm by implementing the Blackhole attack. This attack has been implemented in our simulated environment as follows. When there exists a CBR application, the first step is for the sender to discover a path to the receiver. When the path is being setup, if a malicious node receives a RREQ packet then it immediately responds by returning a RREP packet, claiming to be the receiver. As a result, the path is set up from the sender to the blackhole.

A critical analysis has been done for all the graphs. First, we measure the performance of CORIDS for Blackhole attack detection with variation in mobility. The False Positive percentage remains in the range of 0-5% . The detection efficiency lies in the range of 85 – 100% . Using the above formula (3), the false negative percentage comes out to be in the range of 0 – 15% . Each of these parameters has been evaluated by varying mobility from 10mps to 90mps and varying the percentage of malicious nodes for each node mobility value. All these parameters have reasonably good values for CORIDS to qualify as a good intrusion detection algorithm.

4. Energy Theft Attacks in AMI

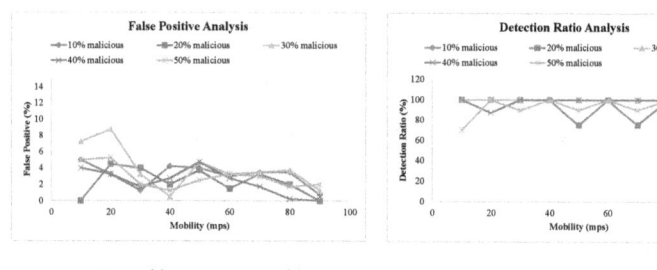

(a) False positive vs. Node Mobility

(b) Detection Time vs. Node Density

Figure 4.1: Blackhole Attack Analysis with Node Mobility

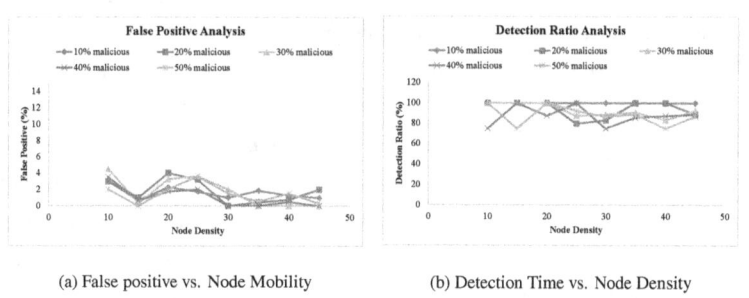

(a) False positive vs. Node Mobility

(b) Detection Time vs. Node Density

Figure 4.2: Blackhole Attack Analysis against Node Density

We then take a different set of data for detecting Blackhole attacks. This time we keep the mobility of the nodes constant at 30mps and vary the density of nodes from 10 to steps of 5. For each data set we take readings by changing the density of malicious nodes from 10% to 50%. This time we observe more consistent behavior. The False Positive percentage remains in the range of 0-4%. The detection efficiency is seen to lie in the range of 85–100%. Using the above formula (3), we see that the false negative percentage comes in the range of 0 – 15%. Each of these parameters has been evaluated by varying node density and varying the percentage of malicious nodes for each node density. All these parameters have reasonably good values for CORIDS to qualify as a good intrusion detection algorithm.

We see that the number of epochs of our algorithm required for malicious node identification is almost constant over varying mobility. When we analyze the performance

4.1. CORIDS: Cluster Oriented Reward based Intrusion Detection System

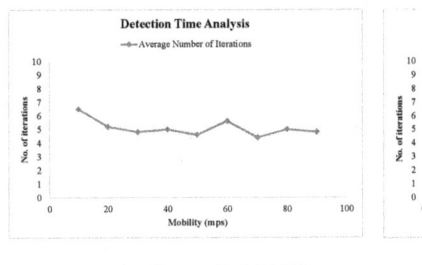
(a) Detection Time vs. Node Mobility

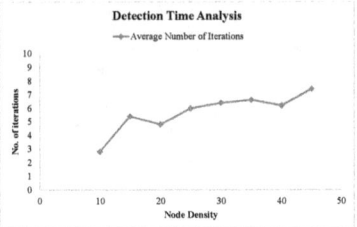
(b) Detection Time vs. Node Density

Figure 4.3: Blackhole Attack Analysis

of our algorithm in terms of the number of epochs required, we observe some kind of stability. While detecting blackhole attacks, varying mobility keeps the average number of epochs in the range of 4.5 to 6.5. Varying the node density keeps the average number of iterations in the range between 5 and 7. This is a significant advantage as mobility usually effects the performance of most intrusion detection algorithms. The number of epochs of our algorithm required as the node density increases is slightly increasing. However, the rise is not sharp. Thus, there is not much variation in the number of iterations required for detecting malicious nodes.

There are two scenarios in which a node behaves normally to increase its Trust value and then starts misbehaving. In the first case, the node increases its trust value as soon as it joins the network and then starts behaving maliciously consistently. In such a situation, the only way that this effects our algorithm is the Detection Time. It will take greater number of iterations / epochs to reduce the increased trust value of the node below the threshold.

A more serious situation is the Selective Forwarding attack or Greyhole attack where a node drops packets selectively. The node is positively rewarded for the majority of packets that it forwards towards the destination and negatively rewarded for the packets that it drops. As a result, the trust value of the node will never fall below the threshold if the attacker intelligently manages the ratio of forwarded packets to dropped packets. In such a situation, CORIDS fails to detect the attacker and it is counted as false negative.

Distributed Denial-of-Service Attacks DoS attacks can be implemented in several ways. In our simulation, we have implemented it as generation of spurious packets by a malicious node, thereby, leading to congestion. Network services can no longer be provided to mesh clients. Thus, spurious packet generation can lead to Denial-of-Service. The attack is implemented in a distributed manner in the sense that several nodes in the network can start generating spurious packets simultaneously.

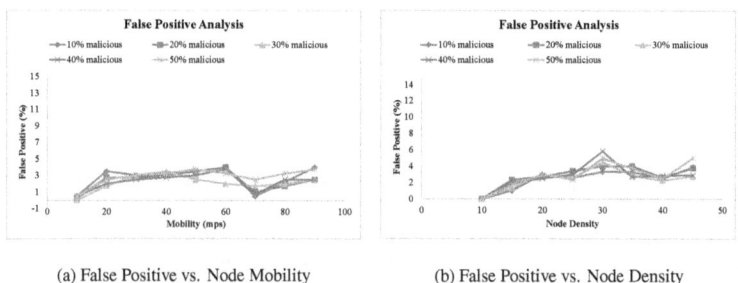

(a) False Positive vs. Node Mobility   (b) False Positive vs. Node Density

Figure 4.4: DDos Attack Analysis for False Positives

The false positive analysis for the CORIDS algorithm is very impressive in case of DDoS attack. Change in mobility does not affect the performance of our algorithm. This is depicted by the linear nature of the curves. Also the close proximity of the 5 different lines clearly brings out the consistent behavior of our algorithm in spite of varying the density of malicious nodes. When the algorithm was run by varying node density and keeping the mobility constant at 30 mps we encountered good results again. The false positive percentage was restricted in the very low and narrow range of 0 – 4 % . The behavior of the algorithm was very consistent in spite of increasing node density and percentage of malicious nodes.

Unlike Blackhole attacks, we did not plot the detection efficiency of our algorithm for DDoS attack as the detection efficiency was always 100% . This is a significant result which needs to be highlighted. The number of epochs required for identifying DDoS attackers was again somewhat a linear function when plotted against variation in mobility. While detecting DDoS attacks, varying mobility keeps the average number of epochs in the range of 3 to 5. Varying the node density keeps the average number of iterations in the range between 3.5 and 5.5.This reiterates the fact that an increase in node mobility does not degrade the performance of our algorithm significantly. A huge plus point. The number of epochs for detecting DDoS attacks in the presence of varying node density was also almost constant. This adds to the effectiveness of the

4.1. CORIDS: Cluster Oriented Reward based Intrusion Detection System

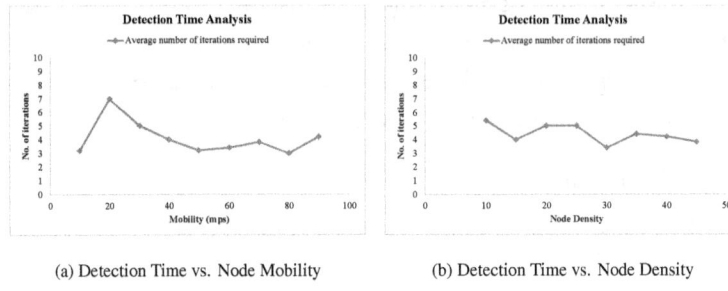

(a) Detection Time vs. Node Mobility

(b) Detection Time vs. Node Density

Figure 4.5: DDos Attack Analysis for Detection Time

CORIDS algorithm as most intrusion detection systems falter under heavy loads.

Performance Variation with Different Threshold Values The first graph shows the variation of Detection Efficiency with change in threshold values. We tested the performance of CORIDS with both higher and lower values of threshold. The higher the threshold value the more sensitive the system is to attacks. So detection efficiency is not affected by higher threshold values. This is clear from the graph as well. For threshold values of 0.3 and above, the detection efficiency of the system remains above 85%. But for lower threshold values, the detection efficiency starts decreasing as it requires a sufficient amount of misbehavior from the malicious nodes to decrease their trust values below the threshold. This is what we see in the graphs as well. Thus, we conclude that for threshold values below 0.3, the detection efficiency decreases or the false negative increases.

However, we also tested the performance of our algorithm against larger threshold values and observed that it affected the False Positive percentage. Small variations in PAR – PS statistics or PDR – PR statistics were sufficient to decrease the trust value of the nodes below the threshold and declare them as malicious. This is visible in the second graph that we obtained from simulation.

The graphs show that detection efficiency remains considerably low for threshold values of 0.7 and below. When the threshold is set above 0.7, the False Positive percentage increases and also increases with increase in node density. Thus, these simulation results show that the performance of CORIDS remains stable and efficient in the threshold range of 0.3 to 0.7. For values of threshold below this range, the detection

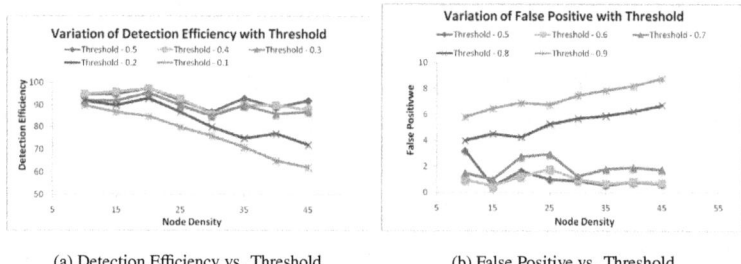

(a) Detection Efficiency vs. Threshold (b) False Positive vs. Threshold

Figure 4.6: Variation of Detection Efficiency and False Positive with change in threshold

efficiency decreases and for values of threshold above this range, the False Positive percentage increases.

4.1.4.4 Comparison with MDA Algorithm:

Finally, we took our data and compared it with the performance of the MDA [11] algorithm published in 2008. The MDA algorithm was chosen as it is one of the most significant work in trust based intrusion detection system for WMNs. The MDA algorithm declares a node as malicious whenever its trust value falls below a certain threshold, similar to the CORIDS algorithm. It also offers a better false positive value compared to other existing works. We compared the performance of the two algorithms under varying density of malicious nodes. The evaluation metrics were the same – false positive percentage and detection efficiency.

The working of CORIDS has been explained in details in section 4.1.2 of this chapter. Let us look into the working principle of MDA. MDA assumes that any two mesh clients 'x' and 'y' communicate through a common set of routers. This common set is defined by those set of routers that have previously communicated messages between 'x' and 'y' OR have separately communicated messages from 'x' and 'y'. In other words, this common set refers to those routers that have an existing trust history of the clients 'x' and 'y'. These are the routers that participate in the Misbehavior Detection Algorithm.

The past trust values T_x and T_y are calculated for the mesh clients 'x' and 'y'. MDA divides the common set of routers { M } and trust values T_x and T_y into g groups ($g \geq 1$) as { { T_{x1} },{ T_{x2} },..., { T_{xg} } } and { { T_{y1} },{ T_{y2} },...,{ T_{yg} } } . Here 'g' represents

4.1. CORIDS: Cluster Oriented Reward based Intrusion Detection System

the number of routers in the common set $\{M\}$. T_{xk} represents the Trust value of mesh client 'x' as evaluated by mesh router 'k'. The trust values are then arranged according to groups as $\{\{T_{x1},T_{y1}\},\{T_{x2},T_{y2}\},\ldots\{T_{xg},T_{yg}\}\}$ and the correlation is calculated using the following equation –

$$\rho(T_x, T_y) = \frac{cov(T_x T_y)}{\sigma T_x \sigma T_y} \qquad (4.9)$$

where σT_x and σT_y are the standard deviations of clients 'x' and 'y'. MDA then calculates the average correlation –

$$\rho_{avg} = \sum_{i=1}^{g} \frac{\rho}{g} \qquad (4.10)$$

Finally, the average correlation thus calculated is compared with a predefined threshold value. If $\rho_{avg} \leq threshold$, declare the mesh client 'y' as malicious.

A detailed analysis reveals why we choose to compare CORIDS with MDA. Firstly, both CORIDS and MDA are based on threshold based trust evaluation. That is, in either case, a node is declared as malicious if its trust value falls below a certain threshold. This implies that both the algorithms are vulnerable to the same kind of misbehavior. Secondly, both algorithms evaluate the trust of mesh clients based on their trust history as maintained by the mesh routers. The only major difference between the two algorithms is the Trust evaluation process. MDA uses correlation whereas CORIDS is a Reward – based intrusion detection algorithm. All these features make it interesting to observe the behavior of CORIDS as compared to MDA.

The grey line shows the performance of CORIDS as compared to that of MDA as shown by the black line. The false positive percentage is extremely low (about 2%) and consistent for our algorithm. For MDA, the number of false positives is a linearly increasing function. Also the false positive percentage is quite high starting from 10% . In terms of detection efficiency, CORIDS performs consistently better with an efficiency of 90% and above. For MDA, the detection efficiency is a linearly decreasing function of the density of malicious nodes. Also, the maximum detection efficiency achieved by MDA is 60% .

Thus we conclude that the CORIDS is a lightweight algorithm that uses very little control messages and executes from the backbone routers only. Control messages are restricted to each cluster. The percentage of false positives is relatively low for CORIDS and remains consistent with variation in node density and node mobility. There are no

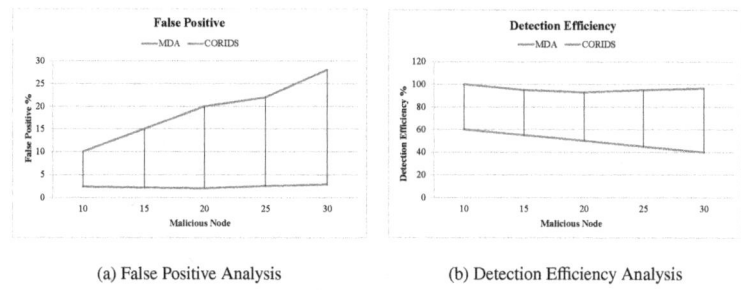

(a) False Positive Analysis (b) Detection Efficiency Analysis

Figure 4.7: Comparison of CORIDS with MDA

false negatives when CORIDS is used to detect DoS attacks. This is demonstrated by the fact that the detection efficiency of CORIDS remains consistently high for blackhole attacks and is 100% for DoS attacks.

4.2 IDS for Detecting DIET Attack

We have proposed a two-tier solution to detect the proposed DIET attack and perform a passive monitoring on the system, to provide an additional level of security. Besides, we have compared our IDS with a specification based IDS for AMI [8], which is one of the most cited paper in this domain.

4.2.1 Smart Infrastructure for Communication

Figure 4.8 shows the communication architecture of Smart Grid. Smart-energy Utility Network (SUN) hierarchically consists of three components: Home Area Network (HAN), Neighborhood Area Network (NAN), and Wide Area Network (WAN) [18]. The HAN provides the communication between the Smart Meters in a home and other appliances in that home. The NAN connects SMs to the Data Aggregators (DAs) and Data Collection Units (DCUs), and WAN provides access between the DCUs and Meter Data Management System (MDMS). DAs collect data from hundred of SMs registered under it and send them to DCUs. DCUs are responsible for communication with MDMS. Smart Grid has a quasi hierarchical structure, where the number of intermediate levels in the network varies with demographic and socio-economic condition of any particular region [95]. The smart meters act as hosts in a network, DCUs are the routers of

4.2. IDS for Detecting DIET Attack

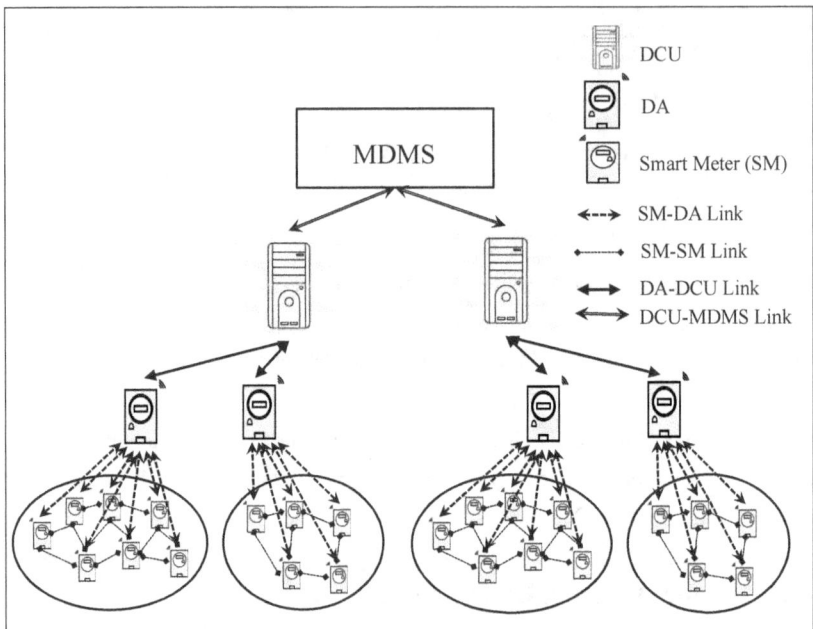

Figure 4.8: Communication architecture of AMI in Smart Grid.

the network and DAs are intermediate connectors. We assume that Smart Meters are managed by its immediate upper level DA or DCU, depending on the hierarchy. We assume that Smart Grid is a cluster based network, where each DA acts as a cluster head and can accommodate utmost 1000 of Smart meters. When a SM X is installed in a grid, it should find a DA to bind with. X will continue to communicate through DA in the network.

Firstly, we propose Near Term Digital Radio architecture [94] for the Clustering scheme used by our IDS. In this specific architecture, the cluster is divided into several physical subnets. Each subnet consists of the Cluster Head or DA and the Cluster Members or SMs which are at one – hop distance from the DAs. All SMs within a cluster can communicate with the DA using the same frequency and can communicate with other SMs within the same subnet using another frequency. These two channels are assumed to have different frequencies, so that there is no interference. DAs can also communicate with its upper level DCUs and DCUs with MDMS. The MDMS sends its messages to the DCUs, which then propagates the information through other DAs and finally it reaches to SM.

Communication between DAs, DCUs and MDMSs are supposed to be secure. However, SM to SM communication link may be compromised by attacker. In order to model our proposed, new Smart Grid specific energy theft (DIET) attack scenario, we have used several network attacks, such as, extracting meter credentials and Man in the Middle (MITM) attack.

4.2.2 Information Stored at Smart Meters

The basic job of a smart meter is to track the energy usage of its customer and communicate with a DA. Generally a SM send their electricity usage after every 15 minutes of interval to the cluster head (DA) and receives various instructions from the DA. Now, in order to implement our IDS, we assume that,

- Every SM has an unique MAC address within its cluster.
- A smart meter can acquire its neighbor SMs' address through Neighbor Discovery procedure and can communicate with them over a wireless medium.
- A SM send a Electricity Usage (EU) message to the DA after every 15 minutes and broadcasts the same message at the same interval so that all of its neighbors can keep a tab of its electricity usage.

$EU_{i,t}$ denotes the energy usage of SM i at time interval t-$(t$-$1)$, where i denotes it unique MAC address.

- Every SM maintains an array Neighbor's Electricity Usage (NEU) for storing the information about the energy usage of its neighbors $NEU_{i,t}[j]$, denotes the electricity usage of SM with unique MAC address j, at time t as stored at smart meter i.

Every time when a SM_i receives a broadcasted message from its neighbor SM_j at time t it adds the value of its electricity usage with the previously stored value for SM_j in the array, and updated its NEU as,

$$NEU_{i,t}[j] = NEU_{i,t-1}[j] + EU_{j,t}$$

Where, t-$(t$-$1)$ = 15 minutes.

Thus, a SM stores its neighbor SMs' electricity usage in a cumulative array.

4.2.3 Information Stored at Cluster Heads

Cluster heads acts as a bridge between customers and utility. The main function of cluster heads, or DAs, or DCUs (depending on the hierarchical structure of the Grid) is to receive the electricity usage information of its SMs and provide billing information, electricity pricing and various informations to the SMs, depending on the applications. Besides cluster heads are also responsible for analyzing the data and detect any anomalies or abnormal behaviors in its cluster and report to the MDMS. We assume that,

- Each cluster head maintains a Smart Meter Connection (SMC) graph to store the topological information about its cluster. The graph is represented by an array of linked lists, where the size of the array defines the total number of SMs in the cluster and the size of each individual list represents the number of neighbors of that SM.
- Besides, every DA, i.e., cluster head will maintain a 2-D array ES(N,T) of energy supplied to each smart meters in its cluster, Where N is the total number of smart meters, registered with the cluster head and T denotes time. ES[i][t] denotes the energy supplied to the smart meter with MAC address i at t time-stamp

Each cluster head communicates with the SMs within its cluster, and then transmits the aggregated data to its upper level DCU or MDMS.

Data structures, EU, NEU and ES are initialized after every 4 hours. And the Smart meter Connection (SMC) graph is updated after the joining of every new SM in the cluster.

4.2.4 Proposed DIET Attack Model

In [91], the authors have addressed the issue of energy theft in smart grids using AMI. However, the authors elaborate on Type-1 attacks only and how they can be achieved in the AMI. The implementation of such attacks requires the attacker to hack into his Smart Meter using a Man-in-the-Middle attack. Once the attacker has his Smart Meter credentials, he can drop packets, inject new packets, as well as modify the usage information stored within the Smart Meters.

However, the situation is quite different for Type-2 attacks. Here, the attacker tries to hack and modify the data packets of its neighboring smart meters and then forward those malicious packets to DCU. Now, the first level of security can be easily provided by the AMI by implementing a modified version of the Needham Schroeder protocol [92] (like the Kerberos protocol or the Needham-Schroeder-Lowe protocol) to prevent replay attacks and Man-in-the-middle attacks. This prevents any eavesdropper from spoofing its neighboring Smart Meters during mutual authentication. Once this is ensured our only concern remains in securing the network communication. Whenever a Smart Meter tries to send a periodic update to the DCU about it's usage, the attacker may intercept this packet, drop it from the network and inject a new packet (with the neighbors credentials) with modified usage statistics.

We have considered a special case of Type-2 energy theft attack. The Type-2 energy theft attack can be made quite difficult, if the attacker modifies the energy usage of a meter with a very negligible amount. 6% to 8% Technical Loss (TL) in transmission and distribution (T&D) is considered as normal in traditional power grid [93], but with Smart Grid the TL in T&D is reduced to 4% to 6% [32], i.e., if the allocated energy is 10 KW for a particular smart meter, then 9.4-9.6 KW of electricity is expected to be used by the smart meter. Now, suppose a smart meter registered 9.55 KW of electricity usage and sends it to the DCU. The attacker captures the packet and modifies the data to 9.45 KW. Apparently, the modified amount is so negligible to the customer that it would not bother him while billing. The DCU would also not be able to detect any anomaly. On the other hand, if the attacker modifies 100 smart meters like this, then it would create a 10KW Non-Technical Loss (NTL) in the system.

There can be two intentions behind this type of attack: the attacker can either maximize its personal gain by reducing its electricity usage by the same amount as stole from the neighboring meters, or just minimize utility's gain by introducing a generous amount of NTL in the system.

- Personal Gain: The attacker may reduce its usage statistics by X% and uniformly distribute this power consumption value among its neighboring Smart Meters. From the DCU's perspective, the total power consumed by the Smart Meters appears to be proportional to the Power allocated to that DCU. The energy theft goes undetected. Here, the utility company does not bear the brunt of the attack.
- Utility Loss: In this other type of attack, the attacker does not look for personal gains; but is rather motivated by a more malicious intent of inflicting financial losses to the utility. The attacker achieves this by considering the Technical Loss during Transmission and Distribution. It drops all packets from neighboring Smart Meters containing usage statistics and injects new packets having usage statistics slightly less than the original (within the TL threshold). The DCU interprets this

as TL during T&D although consumers have consumed this power but have not been billed for the same.

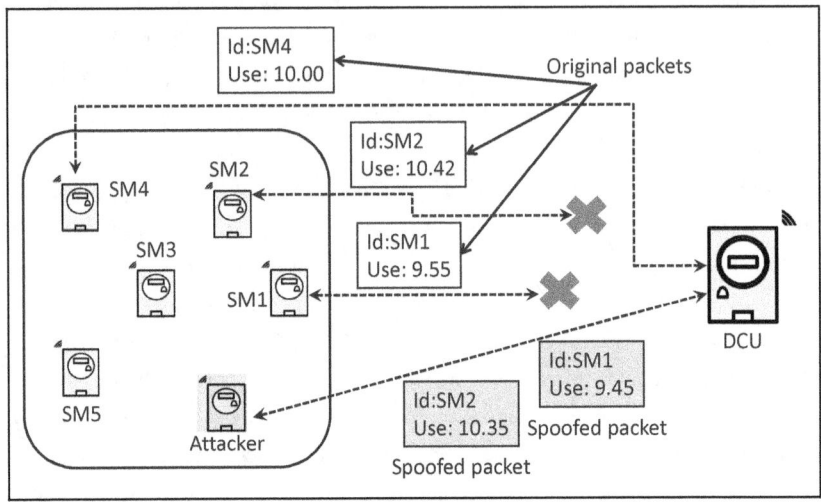

Figure 4.9: DIET attack model.

Figure 4.9 explains our DIET attack scenario. Here, the attacker captures the data packets from SM 1 and 2, and modifies them slightly, so that it lies within the TL threshold and send them to the DCU. The transmission between SM 4 and DCU remains secure.

This attack will proved to be more effective in densely populated areas, where the attacker can have a huge number of smart meters as its neighbors Implementation of this attack become easier in a urban locality with numerous multi storied buildings, where a huge number of smart meters are placed across a long vertical line, but in a small horizontal section. As the attacker can access numerous SMs within its neighbor proximity, the scale of attack can be made more devastating in such scenarios.

4.2.5 Description of the Proposed IDS

In order to detect the DIET attack, we have proposed an IDS model. The detection mechanism will be performed in the cluster heads after certain time intervals. The IDS can detect Type-1 and Type-2 energy theft attacks. We assume that the Intrusion Detection System (IDS) will be running periodically with a time interval of 4 hours.

4.2.5.1 Used Parameters in The IDS

We would first like to define the parameters used in the proposed IDS before explaining the working principle of our algorithm.

1) CH = Cluster Head.
2) SM = Smart Meter, SM_i, SM_j denotes smart meters with MAC address i and j respectively.
3) $EU_{i,t}$ denotes the electricity usage of SM_i at time t.
4) δ defines the allowed technical loss margin for each SM.
5) $EURec_t[i]$ defines the total electricity usage of SM_i at time t as recorded by the CH.
6) $NEU_{i,t}[j]$, denotes the electricity usage of SM with unique MAC address j, at time t as stored at smart meter i.
7) DEP_VL_i denotes the *Dependability Factor* of SM_i.
8) DEP_TH denotes the threshold value for the *Dependability Factor*.
9) *Attacked Nodes* defines a list to store the SMs which have been attacked by the attacker.
10) *Negative Neighbors* of SM_i is the list of neighbour nodes which causes an anomaly in the detection phase of the IDS.
11) *Possible attacker Node* holds the MAC address of those SMs which show abnormal behaviour in terms of stored information of its neighbor SMs.
12) *Attacker Nodes* contains the nodes which are detected as attacker.

4.2.5.2 Working Principle of Proposed IDS

The working principle of our algorithm can be divided into two phases: Data processing phase and Detection phase.

Data Processing Phase: In data processing phase, each SM in a cluster send its electricity usage data to the cluster head at 15 minutes interval. Besides, they also broadcast the same message over a separate channel, meant for only SMs in a cluster. Upon receiving this messages, each SM update itself regarding its neighbors' usage history. Cluster heads perform a preliminary detection at every 15 minutes, to detect type-1 attacks. Besides, CH also stores this periodic usage values in order to maintain a consistent usage log of each SM. The flow diagram of information for data processing phase of

4.2. IDS for Detecting DIET Attack

IDS, among various components in the AMI communication hierarchy is depicted in figure 4.10

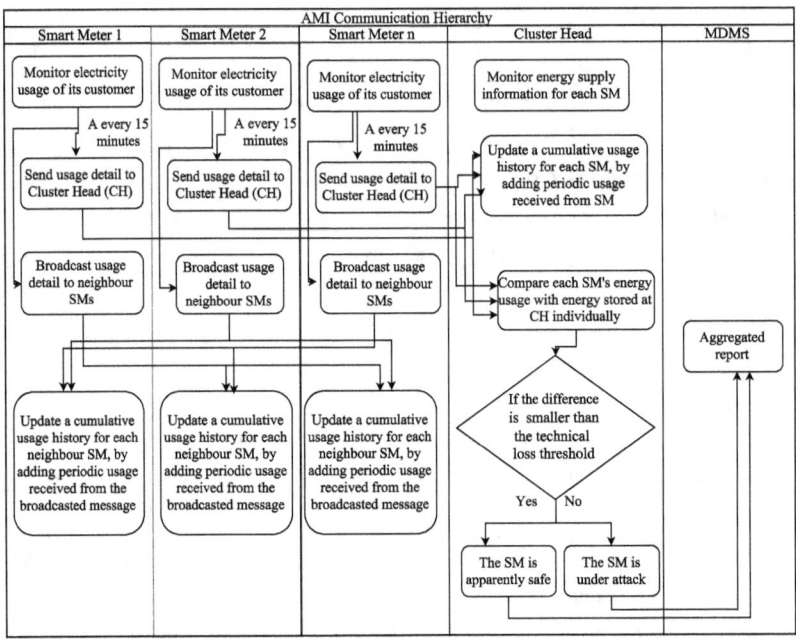

Figure 4.10: Flow diagram for data Processing phase of the proposed IDS.

Detection Phase: We assume that the detection phase will execute at every 4 hours instead of 15 minutes. The reason behind this is to reduce the packet transmission overhead and network congestion. At every 4th hour CH will request its SMs to send their $NEU_{i,t}[j]$ array. Upon receiving this packets from all the SMs, CH extracts the neighbor information for each SM_i, and compares those values with $EURec_t[i]$. If all the neighbors' information match with $EURec_t[i]$, then SM_i is marked as safe, otherwise, the CH marks SM_i as *Attacked Node*. The CH then identifies the neighbors whose information matched with the stored information for SM_i and marks those as *Matched Nodes*, and the other neighbors of SM_i as, *Mismatched Nodes*. Now, the main idea of DIET attack is that the attacker is working alone. So, in case of an attack, the attacker's information will match with the recorded usage of SM_i, while the other neighbors will have a different information, but same collectively. Thus, the CH then compares the total numbers of *Matched Nodes* and *Mismatched Nodes* of SM_i and marks the minority group as *Negative Neighbors*. The intersection of *Negative Neighbors* of all SMs in a cluster is detected as *Attacker Nodes*. Whereas, the other *Negative Neighbors* are marked as *Possible Attacker Nodes* and the CH decreases the *Dependability Value* of these nodes at each detection cycle. These nodes can unmark themselves by showcasing good behavior and gaining *Dependability Value* at next detection cycles, or can be marked as *Attacker Nodes* if the *Dependability Value* goes under the threshold level.

The detailed procedure for attack detection is described in 4.11.

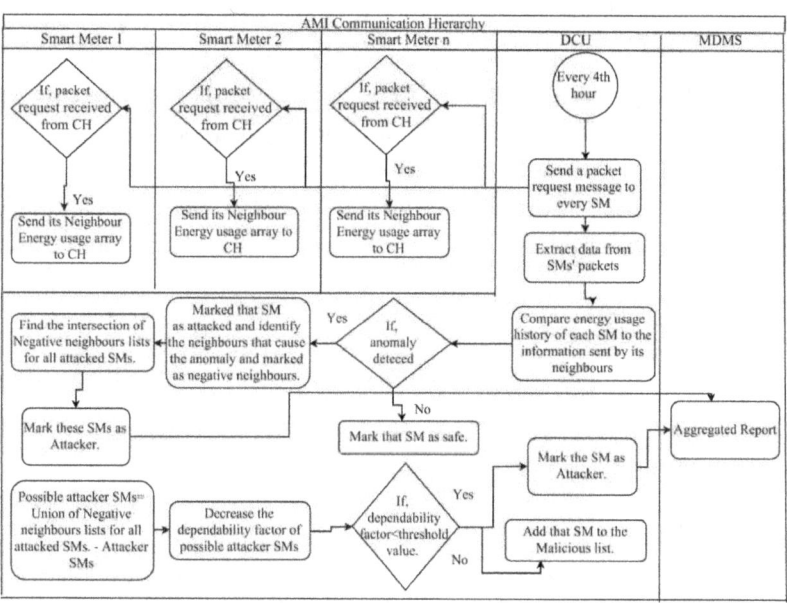

Figure 4.11: Flow diagram for Detection phase of the proposed IDS.

4.2.5.3 Algorithm for The Proposed IDS

The algorithm for both the phases of our proposed algorithm is described in algorithm 5. Step 2-8 of this algorithm defines the data processing phase and the rest of the part is used to detect DIET attack. Here n is the total number of SMs under a Cluster Head and m is the maximum number of neighbors for each individual SMs among n SMs in

4.2. IDS for Detecting DIET Attack

the cluster.

Once, the algorithm detects the attacker nodes and put them in *Attacker Nodes* list, the CH, then checks the *Attacked Nodes* list and replace their forged energy usage values by the original usage statistics with the help of its neighbors' information.

4.2.6 Simulation Results

We have implemented The DIET attack and the proposed IDS in Qualnet 5.2. The simulation settings and the used scenario are described in table 4.2.

4.2.6.1 DIET Attack Simulation

Firstly, the DIET attack is implemented and the results are analyzed. We have considered varying node density of 11 to 55 nodes for our experiment. Data has been collected for every variation and then the averaged values are plotted in the graph. In order to implement DIET attack, we assumed that each Cluster Head can have atmost 10 SMs under its surveillance, and the energy supplied to these SMs is remained fixed at 10kW. δ is defined as 5% of supplied energy, i.e., 0.5kW.

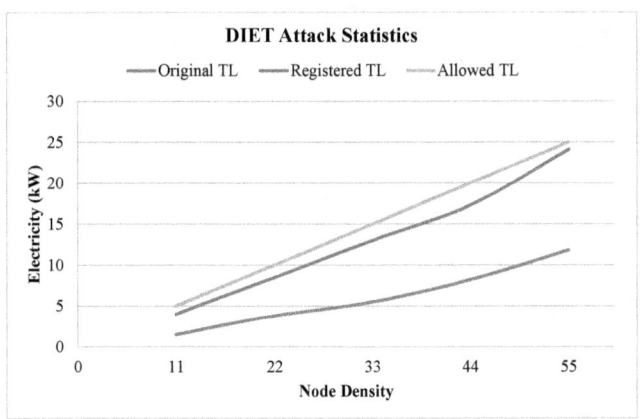

Figure 4.12: Original Technical loss and registered Technical Loss for DIET attack with varying node density.

Figure 4.12 depicts the allowed, original and registered TL for implemented DIET attack. Energy theft = (registered TL - original TL). Now, the registered TL is still under the threshold of allowed TL, thats why the theft can not be detected by the system.

Algorithm 5: Algorithm for detecting DIET attack

1 Start;
2 At every 15 min, CH receives a $EU_{i,t}$ message from SM_i;
3 **if** $(ES_{i,t-1} - \delta <= EU_{i,t} <= (ES_{i,t-1}))$ **then**
4   SM_i is safe;
5     $EURec_t[i] = EURec_{t-1}[i] + EU_{i,t}$;
6 **else**
7   SM_i is under attack;
8 **end**
9 After every 4 hours, CH will ask its SMs to send their NEU array;
    /* After receiving all the arrays, CH checks the following   */
10 **for** *(i=1 to n)* **do**
11   **for** *(j=1 to m)* **do**
12   **if** $(EURec_t[i] == NEU_{j,t}[i])$ **then**
13   match_count++;
14   Add SM_j to the list of *Matched Nodes*;
15   **else**
16   mismatch_count++;
17   Add SM_j to the list of *Mismatched Nodes*;
18   **end**
19   **end**
20 **end**
21 **if** *(match_count==m)* **then**
22   SM_i is safe;
23 **else**
24   Add SM_i to the list of *Attacked Nodes*;
25   **if** *(mismatch_count> match_count)* **then**
26   Mark *Matched Nodes* as *Negative Neighbors*;
27   **else**
28   Mark *Mismatched Nodes* as *Negative Neighbors*;
29   **end**
30 **end**
    /* Let, r be the total number of attacked nodes   */
31 *Attacker Nodes* = Intersection of *Negative Neighbors* for all the *r* SMs in the list *Attacked Nodes*;
32 *Possible Attacker Node* = Union of *Negative Neighbors* for all the *r* SMs in the list (*Attacked Nodes – Attacker Nodes*);
33 Decrease the DEP_VL of every SMs in *Possible Attacker Node* list;
34 **if** $(DEP\_VL_x < DEP\_TH)$ **then**
35   Mark SM_x as *Attacker Node*
36 **else**
37   Add SM_x to the list of *Malicious Nodes*
38 **end**
39 End;

4.2. IDS for Detecting DIET Attack

Table 4.2: Parameter Settings for Simulation Environment

Parameter	Value
Experimental area	$1500 * 1500 m^2$
Running time for each simulation	100 sec
Mac Layer protocol	DCF of IEEE 802.11b standard
Network Layer Protocol	AODV
Traffic Model	CBR
Number of CBR traffics	10% of the total number of nodes
Cluster Head : Smart Meter	1 : 10

4.2.6.2 IDS Implementation

In order to evaluate the performance of our proposed algorithm, we have considered three metrics: false positive, false negative and detection efficiency. False negative and false positive are both very important metric towards Smart Grid. Identify a legitimate SM as an attacker (false positive) can harm the customers', as well as utility's reputation and cause for temporarily disruption of service for that innocent customer. On the other hand, not being able to identify an attacker can lead to financial loss, malicious billing and can even cause havoc devastation.

We have considered four different attack scenarios to evaluate our algorithm.

- **Attack Scenario A** has 100% of DIET attacks, i.e., where an attacker modifies its neighbor SMs usage data, but within the TL threshold. We assume that typical Type-1 and Type-2 attacks are not present for this situation.
- **Attack Scenario B** has 50% of DIET attackers and another 50% of both Type-1 and Type-2 attackers.
- **Attack Scenario C** has 25% of DIET attackers and another 75% of both Type-1 and Type-2 attackers.
- **Attack Scenario D** has equal share of all the three attackers, i.e., 33.33% of DIET, Type-1 and Type-2 attackers.

False Positive: Our proposed algorithm does not identify any false positives for our entire simulation time with various node density and number of attackers It only detects genuine attackers and put them in *Attacker Nodes* list. However, it adds some genuine SMs in *Possible Attacker Nodes* list and decreases the DEP_VL for those nodes at some iterations.

4. Energy Theft Attacks in AMI

False Negative: False negatives are used to measure the accuracy of the system. If the total number of attackers present in the system is x, and the IDS detects y of them, then the false negative can be calculated as:

$$\text{False Negative} = ((x-y)/x)*100 \%$$

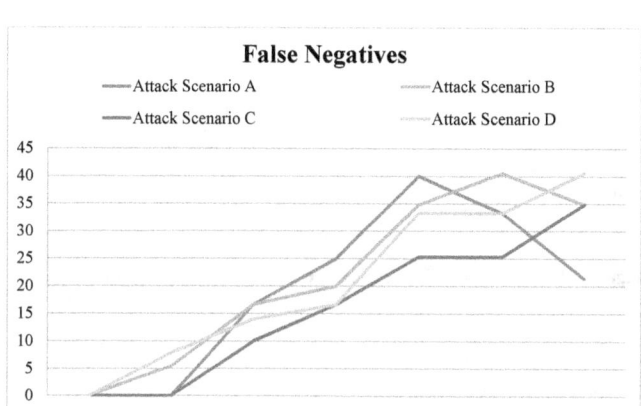

Figure 4.13: False negatives vs Node density for different attack scenarios.

Figure 4.13 depicts the total percentage of false negatives against varying node density for various attack scenarios. Number of attackers in the system are also increased proportionally with the number of nodes. Figure 4.13 shows that for attack scenario A and C, the false negative is null for the first two instances. However, it started increasing gradually thereafter, and reaches its peak when the node density is 55. After that the false negative tend to decrease in scenario A. Now, while analyzing the graph, we find that, for every instances, our proposed IDS either successfully marked every attacker node or add them to the list of *Possible attacker Nodes*. With 55 nodes in the scenario, the IDS is able to identify every attacker node as a possible attacker, however, due to the lack of enough neighbor support, it cannot mark the attackers immediately Though, the trust evaluation process will help them detect gradually. Thus, we can confirm that our proposed system can eventually detect all the attackers.

Detection Efficiency: Detection efficiency can simply be calculated as, (100 - false negative), provided there is no false positives in the system.

4.2. IDS for Detecting DIET Attack

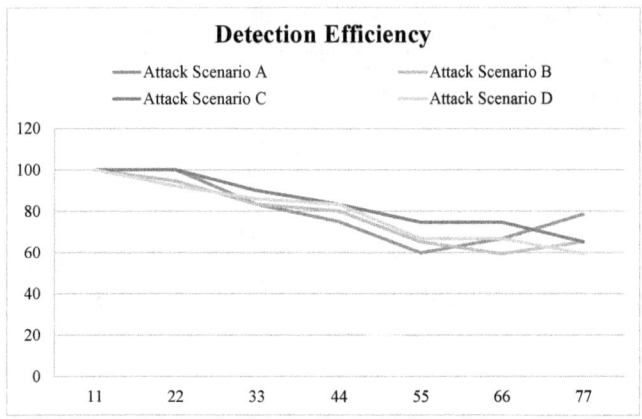

Figure 4.14: Detection Efficiency vs Node density for different attack scenarios.

Figure 4.14 shows the detection efficiency of our IDS. Since there is no false positives in our IDS, the graph for detection efficiency is simple reciprocal of false negative.

The detection efficiency for our proposed IDS remains 100% for smaller number of nodes (i.e., up to 22 nodes for our simulation scenario.). However, with increasing number of nodes and attackers, the detection efficiency tends to decrease gradually. The detection mechanism of our proposed IDS depends heavily on the anomalies in the data provided by SMs in a neighborhood. With fewer nodes in the scenario, it will be easier to analysis the data and hence the detection of an attacker. On the contrary, when the node density increases, it affects the complexity of data analysis and hence the detection efficiency. However, to address this situation and provide a stability in the system, our IDS marked all suspicious nodes as *Possible Attacker Nodes*, and decreases their dependability factor as well, so that the system can be aware of that nodes and do not let those nodes to further affect the decision making process. When the dependability factor goes beyond the threshold value, then only a node will be marked as attacker.

Energy Loss: Finally we measure the energy loss for our IDS, and figure 4.15 demonstrated that the proposed IDS is successfully able reduce the electricity loss due to DIET attack.

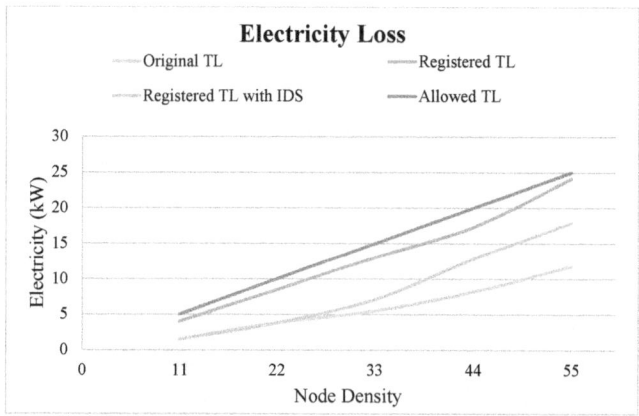

Figure 4.15: Electricity loss in proposed IDS.

4.2.6.3 Comparison with Existing Works

In this section, we have done a detailed comparative analysis of our proposed IDS with a specification based IDS proposed in [8]. In this paper, authors deployed sensors in NAN to monitor the communication network and detect malicious activities in the AMI based on formal verification of the specifications and monitoring operations. Authors claimed that the proposed IDS can detect both known and unknown attacks in network level, including MITM, black hole attack etc. Since, our proposed IDS handles DIET attack, which in turn associates with MITM and stealing of meter data credential attacks, we consider the IDS, proposed in [8] as an appropriate choice for comparison. We have implemented the IDS of [8] for different attack scenarios, as mentioned in section 4.2.6.2.

Figure 4.16 provides the comparative analysis of our proposed IDS and specification based IDS proposed in [8]. We have considered the performance of both the algorithms for four different attack scenarios and with seven different node densities over 11 nodes to 77 nodes, and then averaged the results. The IDS in [8] monitors the state of communication network and verifies with existing specification rules. It does not consider the content of packets transmitted over the network, rather it keeps tab of total packet received and sent, time stamps of different events, frequency of packet transmission etc. Thus, it cannot detect Type-I attack, as in this case, a SM modifies its own packets and transmits them. On the other hand, in DIET attack, a SM steals

4.2. IDS for Detecting DIET Attack

its neighbor SMs' credentials, manipulates their meter data within tolerance level and retransmits to the DA. Thus, at the end points, the packet received and sent metrics for a particular SM will remain unaltered. Hence the attack will remain undetected. However, when node density increases, so does the traffic and if the sensors detect an abnormally large number of packet transmission on a particular channel, then it can detect the attack sometimes. However, for typical Type-II attack, the attack can be detected by considering cumulative energy usage parameters.

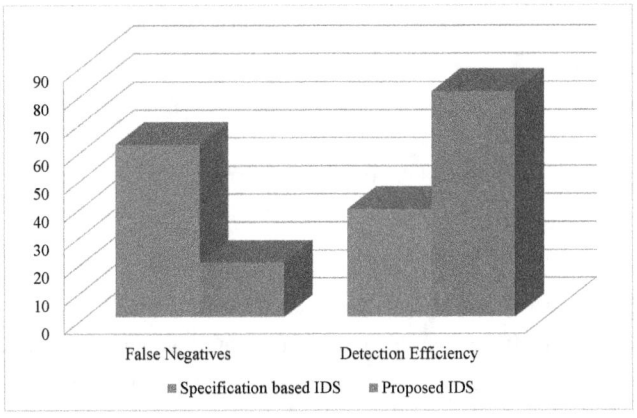

Figure 4.16: Comparative results of false negatives and detection efficiency.

Figure 4.17 gives the performance of two IDSs for attack scenario A and D. In attack scenario A, our proposed IDS performs much better than the other one. Specification based IDS [8] performs better with increased node density. Still it never performs like our proposed IDS. However, for attack scenario D, the IDS of [8] performs much better, but still the false negatives are much higher than our proposed IDS.

We have compared the performance our IDS with other existing IDSs. Figure 4.18 and 4.19 provide comparative analysis of our proposed IDS and two existing IDSs based on SVM [10] and ARMA-GLR [9] models respectively. Our proposed IDS offers better detection efficiency than [10]. Figure 4.18 shows that the IDS in [9] performs much better than our IDS. On the other hand figure 4.19 shows that our IDS is free from false positives, which is a disadvantage for both of the works presented in [10] and [9].

As we already mentioned, false positives and false negatives are two important metrics to evaluate the performance of any IDS. Now, energy theft is an attack scenario

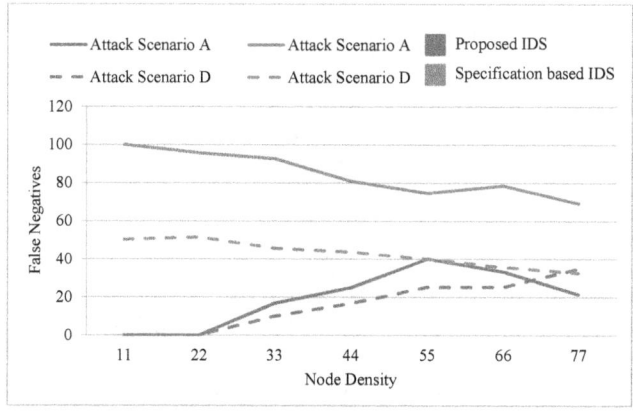

Figure 4.17: Comparative analysis for different attack scenarios.

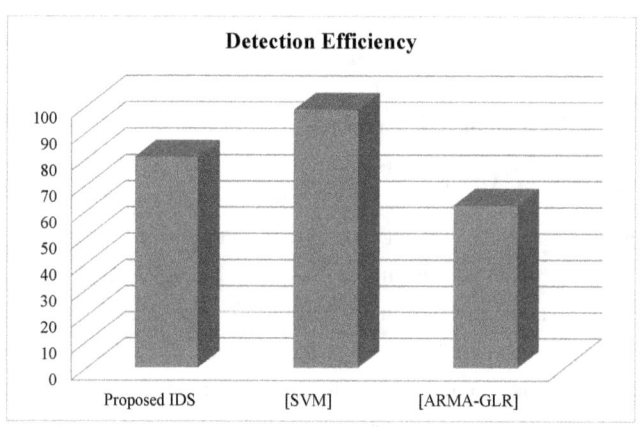

Figure 4.18: Comparison of detection efficiency among different IDSs.

which involves the customers directly. The attackers disguised themselves as customers. So we have to give extra care to detect attackers. False positives may harm the reputation of genuine customers, which incurs in bad reputation for the utilities. Thus, while dealing with energy theft attack, false positives are much more important than false negatives. Thus we designed our IDS in such a manner that it marks a node as attacker only after being 100% sure of that. Otherwise, it can mark suspicious nodes as possible attackers, and monitor their further behavior This in turn justifies the results of figure

4.3. IDS for Detecting CET Attack

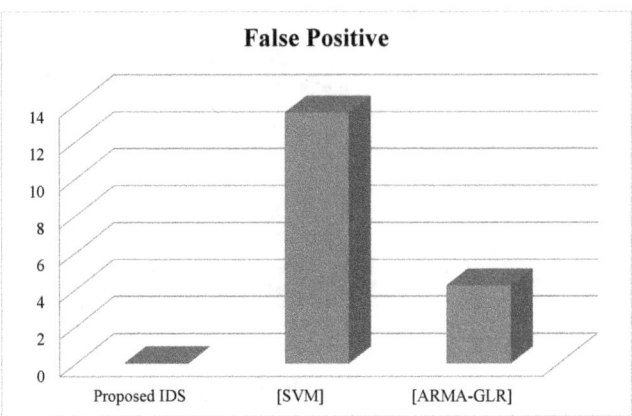

Figure 4.19: Comparison of false positives among different IDSs.

4.18 and 4.19.

4.3 IDS for Detecting CET Attack

4.3.1 Proposed CET Attack

A Collaborative Energy Theft (CET) launches the attack with numerous numbers of attackers, who can communicate within themselves. In this attack scenario, attackers form a communication network to share information regarding the attack. Generally we can detect energy theft attacks using trust based methods, as the attackers act in standalone fashion. The rest of the nodes in the network can vouch for an attack or some misbehaviour within the network. However, in CET, the attackers can cooperate. As a result, the neighbourhood of the attacker will have some other attacker nodes, and they can manipulate the decision of other trust worthy nodes, or can form a majority over false information and mask the attack.

This attack will proved to be more effective in densely populated areas, where the attackers can have a huge number of smart meters as its neighbors. Implementation of this attack become easier in a urban locality with numerous multi storied buildings, where a huge number of smart meters are placed across a long vertical line, but in a small horizontal section. As the attackers can access numerous SMs within its neighbor proximity, the scale of attack can be made more devastating in such scenarios.

4. Energy Theft Attacks in AMI

We assume that the attackers can collaborate among themselves using two different topological structures: P2P and Centralized.

P2P or Peer to Peer model: In this model, the attackers form a chain and communicate with each other by transferring information. The chain is formed such that atleast 50% of the neighbours of each node in the network is part of the malicious network. An attacker captures the data packet from one of its neighbour smart meter, changes the information in the packet and sends it to the DU. This information is shared with the other attackers. The total amount is adjusted by deducing a small value from data in some packet and adding the same value to data in some other packet. The attackers update the network table accordingly. The total usage of the network remains the same, so that the DCU can not detect the presence of an attack in the network.

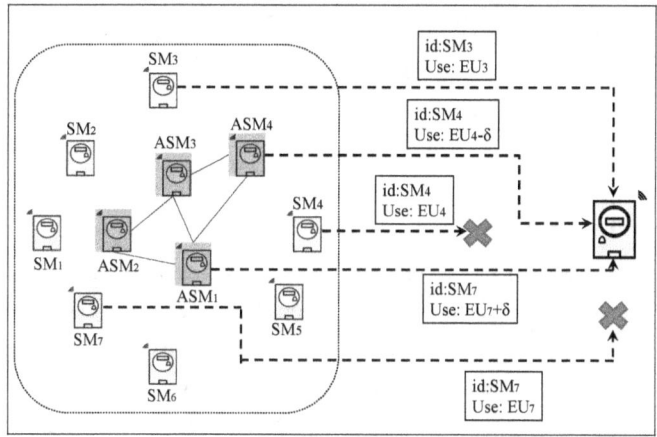

Figure 4.20: Peer-to-peer attack model.

Centralized Model In this model also the attackers forms a chain but there a central attacker node which is denoted as a head and all the other attackers communicate only with the head. When an attacker captures a data packet from its neighbours, it transmits the details to the head. The head updates its usage value by some amount which is adjusted with the data packets captured by the malicious network thus increasing it's personal gain. The values of all the data packets are sent to all malicious nodes in the network. As the total usage in the network remains unchanged, the DCU is unable to detect the occurrence of an attack.

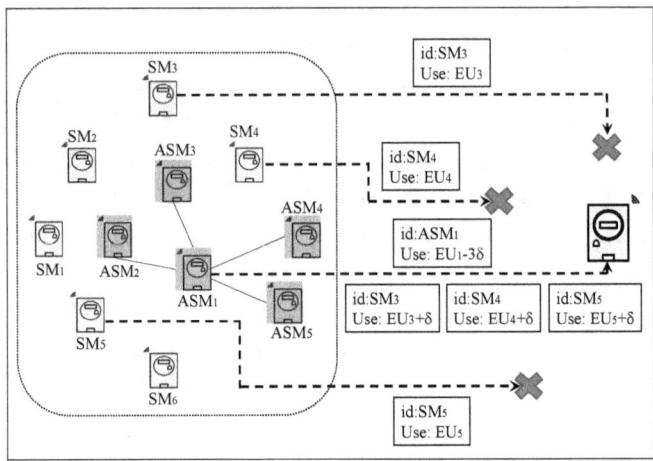

Figure 4.21: Centralized attack model.

4.3.2 Agent based Architecture

As we already mentioned in the previous section, a simple trust based model is not effective enough to detect a collaborative attack. Hence, we proposed a agent based IDS that can detect CET attack. Figure 4.22 depicts our proposed architecture, where an independent set of agent nodes are deployed in the AMI to collect data from smart meters individually and transmit them to DCU. These agent nodes do not interfare with the already existing communication channels between smart meters and DCU. Instead, they have another set of communication channel, which is comparatively more secure, and without any public interference.

4.3.3 Information Stored at Agent Nodes

The primary job of an agent node is to collect the energy usage data of smart meters, that lies in its one hop distance and communicate with a DA. An agent node can communicate with more that one DAs. Generally an agent node senda their collected data upon receiving instruction from DA or DCUs. However agent nodes cannot send

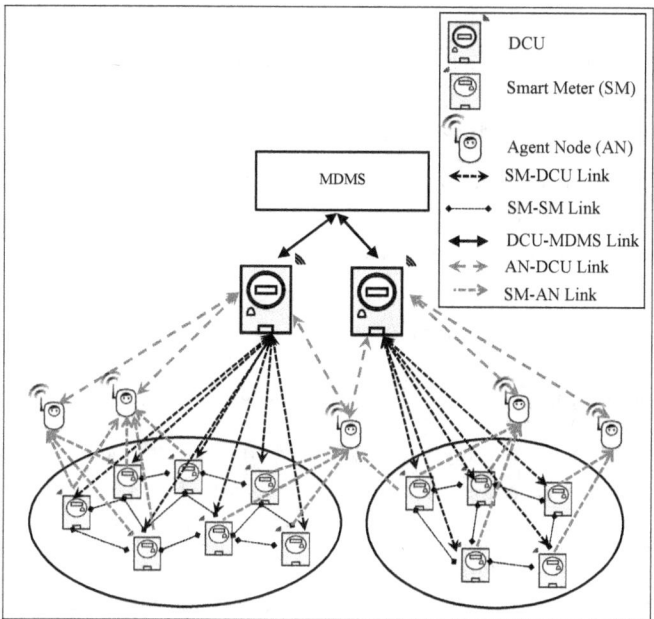

Figure 4.22: Agent based architecture of AMI.

any instructions to the smart meters. It can only read the data and transmit to the upper level DA or DCU.

Now, in order to implement our IDS, we assume that, an agent node A_0 calculates the trust value of its neighbouring smart meters. The neighbours of A_0 is a set of smart meters having one hop contact with A_0 and are represented as $N(A_0) = SM_1, SM_2, \ldots, SM_n$, where n is the total number of neighbour nodes for any agent node. Any node SM_i possesses a set of attributes denoted as $Att(SM_i) = A_1, A_2, \ldots, A_n$. Every agent node stores the attributes set of each of its neighbours. The attributes that are stored in the agent node for smart meter SM_i are :

- Packet Received (PR_t): denotes the number of packets received between the interval t-1 to t.
- Packet forwarded (PF_t): denotes the number of packets forwarded between the interval t-1 to t.
- Packet Generation Rate (PG_t): denotes the number of packets generated between the interval t-1 to t.

- Packet Transmission Pattern (PTP): denotes a sliding window of T time slots, where, T=$t_1, t_2, \ldots, t_n$ and number of packets transmitted at each time slot.

4.3.4 Information Stored at Smart Meters

Every smart meter keeps records of its own electricity usage, as well as maintains a list of its one hop neighbour smart meters and also tracks their electricity usage. The detail list of informations stored at smart meters are given in section 4.2.2.

Depending on this information, the DA, or the cluster head (CH) calculates the trust values for smart meter SM_i using algorithm 5.

4.3.5 Proposed IDS

Generally we can detect energy theft attacks using trust based methods, as the attackers act in standalone fashion. The rest of the nodes in the network can vouch for an attack or some misbehaviour within the network. However, in collaborative attacks, the attackers can cooperate. As a result, the neighbourhood of the attacker will have some other attacker nodes, and they can manipulate the decision of other trust worthy nodes, or can form a majority over false information and mask the attack.

Thus, in order to detect this type of attacks, we can use a function,

$$F_i = (TP, TA, HC) \tag{4.11}$$

which return a threshold value indicating whether a smart meter SM_i is an innocent node, attacker node or suspicious node.

F_i is a function of four parameters:
- TP denotes the trust value of SM_i depending on the data of its neighbour nodes.
- TA denotes the trust value of SM_i observed by an independent set of reliable monitor nodes or agents.
- HC denotes the overall trustworthiness of a cluster and is described as,
$$HC = (AR, SR)$$
where,
    - **AR** denotes the attacker node ratio of a cluster, i.e., (total number of attacker smart meters / total number of smart meters).
    - **SR** denotes the suspicious node ratio of a cluster, i.e., (total number of suspicious smart meters / total number of smart meters).

$\alpha, \beta, and \gamma$ are the respective weights for TP, TA and HC, where,

$$\alpha + \beta + \gamma = 1.$$

4.3.5.1 Working Principle

Determination of TA: Using the stored information, every agent node calculates the trust of its neighbouring smart meters as:

$$TA(SM_i) = ((PR_t/PF_t) + (PG_t/\xi) + \text{Variance of PTP}). \tag{4.12}$$

where, ξ = Average Packet Generation Rate (PG_t) for any smart meter SM_i at time interval t. ξ is a predefined value, measured by the DCU, depending on the functionalities of the cluster.

Variance in PTP is a measurement of relative deviation of the transmission pattern of a smart meter from the standard transmission pattern of the network.

Let, the standard transmission pattern fot $T=t_1, t_2, \ldots, t_n$ timeslot is $(x_1, x_2, \ldots, x_n)$ and transmission pattern for SM_i is $(x'_1, x'_2, \ldots, x'_n)$.

Then, variance in PTP can be calculated as-

$$\frac{\sqrt{\sum_{i=1}^{n}(x'_i - x_i)^2/n}}{\sum_{i=i}^{n} x'_i/n} \tag{4.13}$$

This metric helps to capture the consistency of any smart meter in the network.

Ideal Node Now we will discuss the notion of an ideal node. An ideal node is a node satisfying the following properties
- The number of packet forwarded is equal to the number of packets received, i.e, there is no loss. Therefore, for ideal node,
$$PR_t/PF_t=1.$$
- The packet generation is uniform and consistent with the given packet generation rate,i.e., ξ at every time interval. Hence,
$$PG_t/\xi=1.$$
- The variance in PTP is 0. That is the number of packets transmitted follows the defined transmission pattern of the network.

Even though, there is no existence of ideal node in real life scenario, we use this concept in our IDS for detection of suspicious nodes.

We consider that that 10% variation is considered normal for a node in a network. Therefore, a node is considered behaving normally if,

- Value of PR_t/PF_t may range between 0.9 and 1.1
- Value of PG_t/ξ may range between 0.9 and 1.1.
- Value of transmission variance is less than 0.1.

Therefore, TA of any innocent smart meter SM_i should lie betweena 1.9 to 2.3.

Determination of TP: Cluster Heads calculate TP for each smart meter SM_i depending on the information gathered from SM_i's neighbour nodes. The detailed procedure is already discussed in algorithm 5. Depending on that information a CH either marks a smart meter innocent and assigns a value 1, or as suspicious node and assigns a value 2.

Determination of HC HC is a function of AR and SR described as,

$$HC = 0.5*AR + 0.5*SR$$

where, AR = a/n and SR = s/n,

a = number of attacker nodes in a cluster,

s = number of suspicious nodes in a cluster,

n = total number of nodes in a cluster.

Suppose at the beginning, there are no attacker nodes or suspicious nodes in a cluster. Then the value of HC will be 0, as the value of a and s are 0, so do the values of AR and SR.

So, we will calculate the value of F_i for any SM_i as

$$F_i = 0.5 * TP + 0.5 * TA + 0$$

After this iteration, the cluster head can detect some nodes as attacker or as suspicious nodes within its cluster. As a result, it can calculate the value of HC . So, from the next iterations the value of F_i can be calculated as,

$$F_i = 0.33 * TP + 0.33 * TA + 0.33 * HC \text{ [equal weightage of all three parameters.]}$$

In an ideal situation, the value of HC will always be 0, i.e., no attacker or suspicious nodes in the cluster.

Otherwise,

- **Case 1:** if all the nodes of a cluster are attackers, then a = n, which implies AR = 1 and SR = 0.

    So, HC = 0.5*AR + 0.5*SR = 0.5*1 + 0.5*0 = 0.5.

- **Case 2:** if all the nodes of a cluster are suspicious nodes, then s = n, which implies AR = 0 and SR = 1.

  So, HC = 0.5*AR + 0.5*SR = 0.5*0 + 0.5*1 = 0.5.

- **Case 3:** if half of the total nodes of a cluster are attackers and half are suspicious, then a = s = n/2, which implies AR = 0.5 and SR = 0.5.

  So, HC = 0.5*AR + 0.5*SR = 0.5*0.5 + 0.5*0.5 = 0.5.

- **Case 4:** In all other cases a<n, s<n and a+s<=n, which implies 1>AR>=0 and 1>SR> = 0, and AR+SR<1.

  So, HC = 0.5*AR + 0.5*SR = 0.5*(AR+SR) < 0.5 as AR+SR<1

Thus, the value of HC lies between 0 to 0.5.

Calculating the Value of F_i: We have already calculated the range of TP (1.9 to 2.3), TA (1 for normal node, 2 for suspicious node) and HC(0 to 0.5).

Then the value of F_i can be calculated as,

$$F_i = 0.33*TP + 0.33*TA + 0.33* HC$$
$$= 0.33*1.9 + 0.33*1 + 0.33*0$$
$$= 0.957 \text{ [Lower limit]}$$
$$= 0.33*2.3 + 0.33*2 + 0.33*0.5$$
$$= 1.584 \text{ [Upper limit]}$$

Hence, if the value of any node lies between this, then its normal, otherwise, if the value lies between 0.8613 to 1.7424, i.e. 10% deviation of the threshold values then the node will be marked as suspicious node, otherwise, the node will be detected as attacker node.

4.3.6 Simulation Results

We have implemented the CET attack and the proposed IDS in Contiki-Cooja environment.

4.3.6.1 CET Attack Simulation

We have implemented the CET attack similar to that of DIET attack. We have considered varying node density of 5 to 30 nodes for our experiment. Data has been collected for every variation and then the averaged values are plotted in the graph. In order to implement CET attack, we assumed that each Cluster Head can have atmost 5 SMs

4.3. IDS for Detecting CET Attack

under its surveillance, and the energy supplied to these SMs is remained fixed at 10kW. δ is defined as 5% of supplied energy, i.e., 0.5kW.

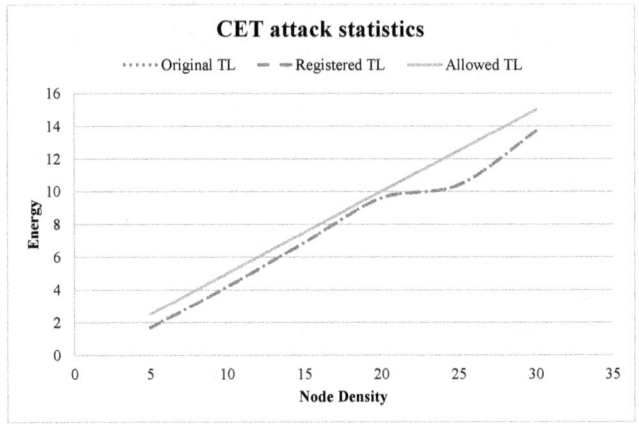

Figure 4.23: Original Technical Loss and registered Technical Loss for CET attack with varying node density.

As we already mentioned in CET attack description, in this attack types, the registered and original energy loss will remain same, as the attackers will maintain a equilibrium between these two values, such that it would be very dificult to detect this attack. In figure 4.23, describes the same situation, where the registered and original energy loss is same and lower to the allowed energy loss.

Compared to the DIET attack model, CET attacks are difficult to detect as the energy theft is not only below the allowed threshold value, but there is no significant variation between original and registered energy loss. These two characteristics help the attackers to successfully camouflaged the theft and apparently the whole network seems to working perfectly.

4.3.6.2 IDS Implementation

In order to evaluate the performance of our proposed algorithm, we have again considered three metrics: false positive, false negative and detection efficiency.

Figure 4.24(a) depicts the total percentage of false negatives against varying node density for two attack scenarios. Number of attackers in the system is also increased proportionally with the number of nodes. The false negative is null for the first instance.

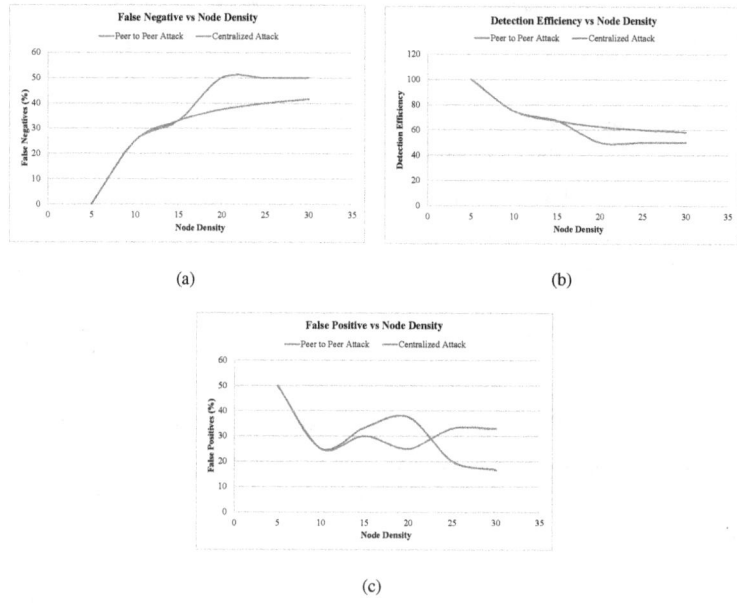

Figure 4.24: Various performance metrics of the IDS:(a) False Negative, (b) Detection Efficiency and (c) False Positive

However, it started increasing gradually thereafter, and reaches its peak when the node density is 30. Figure 4.24(b) depicts the total percentage of false positives against varying node density for two attack scenarios. The false positive values tend to vary within a range. Figure 4.24(c) shows the detection efficiency of our IDS. The detection efficiency for our proposed IDS remains 100% for smaller number of nodes (i.e., up to 5 nodes for our simulation scenario.). However, with increasing number of nodes and attackers, the detection efficiency tends to decrease gradually. The detection mechanism of our proposed IDS depends heavily on the anomalies in the data provided by SMs in a neighborhood. With fewer nodes in the scenario, it will be easier to analysis the data and hence the detection of an attacker. On the contrary, when the node density increases, it affects the complexity of data analysis and hence the detection efficiency.

4.4 Conclusions

Smart grid and especially AMI system enhances the efficiency, reliability, stability, security and economic facilities of traditional power grid systems. Advanced metering infrastructure (AMI) is arguably the most important and critical part of Smart Grid. AMI deals with the most sensitive informations in the Grid and transmits them through the network. There already exist a good number of security solutions for AMI. However the percentage of security attacks are also increasing day by day, and so does the innovative and intelligent ideas behind those attacks.

Energy theft is always a serious concern for power industry. With traditional power grid, tapping, physical tampering of meters are the common sources to theft. Smart Grid and AMI can mitigate these attacks, however, with the recent advancement in the technology, the attackers also invent newer and sophisticated ideas to attack the grid. In this chapter, we have proposed two new attack situations named, DIET attack and CET attack. Simultaneously, we have simulated these attacks and analyze the effect on the grid. In order to detect these attacks, we have proposed two advanced IDSs methods.

Our IDSs can successfully detect Type-1 and Type-2 attacks. Moreover, for some scenarios, the IDS cannot detect the attacker primarily, but it is been able to mark all of them as *Possible Attacker* and take precautionary measures against them. If those nodes continue to being malicious, then eventually the proposed IDS detect that node as attacker, otherwise, in case of a genuine node, the dependability factor will be increased with positive behavior Besides, there exists lots of works for detecting energy theft, many of them are only capable to detect whether a theft happened or not. On the contrary, the proposed IDS can not only identify an intelligent theft situation, but can detect the attackers and mark possible attackers in the network as well.

As a future extension of this work, we would like to merge our idea with some secure routing protocols as discussed in chapter 3, where trust based evolution of nodes are performed for route selection to ensure a secure communication system. The collaboration of the proposed IDS with this type of routing protocols will confirm security from DIET attack at transmission time and improve the performance of the system, in terms of detection efficiency and false negatives.

Section II - Load Forecasting in AMI

CHAPTER 5

STATE-OF-THE-ART FORECASTING MODELS FOR SMART GRID

One of the many improvements that Smart Grid offers over traditional power grid is a balanced supply-demand ratio. Now, as electricity is hard to store for future usage, it is important to be aware of the demand in order to generate enough electricity for uninterrupted power supply. The electricity demand management is a mechanism to motivate the electricity consumers to use less energy during the peak time so as to reduce the investment on electricity production and ensure a reliable supply. The typical measures for demand management are as follows [6, 112]:

- Incentive methods - The customers receive incentive for reducing their electricity usage during peak times. Alternately, the price of the electricity is made cheaper during the off peak.
- Direct load control - It is a load shedding mechanism managed where the utility reduces the energy consumption of home appliances by controlling its operation. The customers are offered incentives for helping relieve the local peak by cutting energy usage.
- Giving customers a better idea of their electricity usage. Smart meter offers in-home displays, so that consumers are able to follow their electricity consumption and have greater control over their electricity consumption during peak times.

- Promoting distributed generation solutions where electricity is produced near the customer premises, such as solar panels or wind turbines to minimize the local peak demand.
- Encouraging electricity customers to set up a power storage system along with their own solar panels which could meet the additional demand during the peak to avoid blackout in the grid.
- Load scheduling [113, 114] is another effective way to implement demand management at the customer side. It is an automated and intelligent method to shift a portion of the demand from peak to off peak, so that the demand curve is flattened.

Precise knowledge on the energy usage pattern of the consumers helps towards optimization of Demand Management. This is where the demand forecasting comes into play. Forecasting plays a vital role in Smart Grid. However, with various range of rapidly fluctuating influential parameters towards electricity consumption patterns, it is next to impossible to design a single forecasting model for different types of users. Typically, electricity usage depends on demographic, socio-economic and climate condition of any region. Besides, the dependencies between influential parameters and consumption vary over different sectors, like, residential, commercial and industrial.

In the next section we will review some existing works on forecasting in Smart Grids and discuss the inadequacy of these models on bigger geographical regions haviing diverse socio-economic and climate characteristics.

5.1 Variations of Forecasting Models

Forecasting models for Smart Grids can be categorized into three classes based on the prediction time period [96]: Short-term load forecasting (STLF) models; Medium-term load forecasting (MTLF) models; Long-term load forecasting (LTLF) models.

The STLF models are useful for power utilities towards planning demand response mechanisms and distributions scheduling for uninterrupted electricity flow. It aims at profitable and efficient management of the electricity utility. These models are good for studying electricity usage and various factors affecting them, including climatic changes, pricing, etc.

The MTLF models are generally used to find the peak load within a span of time. Besides, it can also be used to analyze the effect of different factors which have an impact on the electricity demand, such as - weather variations, advancement in the technologies used and modification of equipments in the industries, as well as in the households [97]. It is additionally used for testing events, commissioning and making any changes to the infrastructure in power utilities.

The LTLF models help the electricity utilities in planning the generation, transmission and distribution of the power system. These models are useful for modification or enhancement of utility assets to improve efficiency.

We have considered MTLF models as it gives us exact planning scenario, where changes in the pattern are neither abruptly frequent like STLF models, nor does it overlook some minute details like LTLF models. Additionally, MTLF models help in optimal utility planning for Smart Grid by considering seasonal changes, demographic pattern changes, identifying peak load curve, maintaining scheduling and component replacing or repairing [98]. Besides, monthly forecast of energy usage from such models can help the customers negotiate the electricity price and incentive schemes to maintain equilibrium in demand-production situation.

5.2 Mathematical Models for Forecasting

Generally the main aim of forecasting methods are to analyse the historic data and from that analysis infer some rules to predict the target value. This mapping between target variable and predictor variables are done using some mathematical models. Figure 5.1 depicts a simple and general diagram of any forecasting model.

It has two components:
- The Database consists weather related data, population density of that region, economical and social characteristics. Besides depending on the nature of predicted variable, the database may contain various predictor values.
- A mathematical model is used to find the relationship between predictor and predicted variables. The model must analyse the dependency of predicted variable on several predictor variables using the database and derives a relationship vector which can be used to future forecasting. The mathematical modeling combines abstraction and simplification. In the most cases the model is oriented to application, i.e., the model is built up for a special use.

The existing mathematical models can be classified based on these three criterias [111]:

– Type of the model function (linear / non-linear).

– Number of the influence variables (univariate / multivariate).

– General modeling aspect (parametric / non-parametric).

The separation between linear and non-linear methods depends on the functional relationship. A model is called univariate if only one influence factor will be regarded; otherwise it is of the multivariate type. Parametric models contain parameters besides the input and output variables.

The quality of the forecast methods mainly depends on the available historical data as well as on the knowledge about the factors influencing the energy demand.

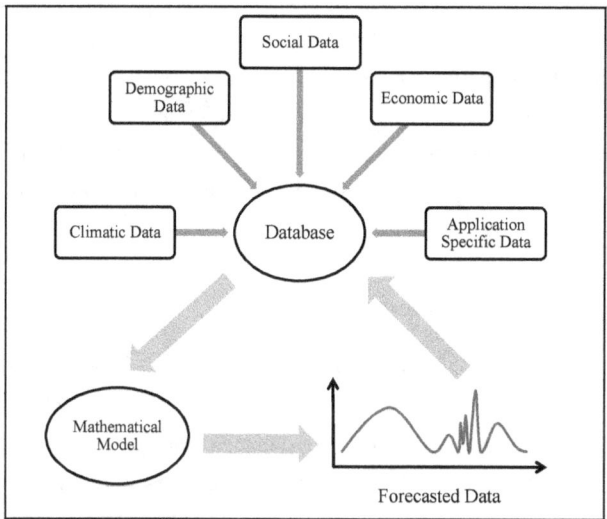

Figure 5.1: General diagram of a forecasting model

5.3 Limitations of soft computing based approaches

Different soft computing techniques, such as, fuzzy logic, ANN, genetic algorithms, etc. have received significant attention. Even though, some of these models are flexible and handle non-linearity in data, these often work as a black-box. Thus, it becomes quite difficult to interpret the relationships between predictor parameters and predicted result. Hence, it's quite a challenge to assess how sudden variations in predictor parameters affect the result. In this respect, statistical models clearly stand out as they allow interpretation of coefficients of the individual variables and due to the parametric assumptions of these models, inferences can also be drawn regarding the significance of certain variables in prediction or classification problems.

One of the important limitations of neural networks [99–101] is that the determination of various parameters like number of hidden layers or number of nodes in hidden layer is not straightforward and finding the optimal configuration of neural networks is a very time consuming process. It is difficult to conclude that one has developed the best possible neural network for a particular application given multiple training algorithms available and the empirical nature of model development. Another limitation of neural networks is over-fitting. The ability of a neural network to model interactions and nonlinearities implicitly may also be a disadvantage as it can lead to over-fitting a training data with poor performance in external test datasets.

Random Forests (ensembles of decision trees) offer another powerful prediction model. These are indeed very fast to train, but quite slow to create predictions once trained. More accurate ensembles require more trees, which inturn decreases the prediction time of the model.

5.4 Regression based models

The quality of time series based demand forecast methods depends significantly on the availability of historical consumption data as well as on the knowledge about the main influence parameters on the energy consumption. Any statistical model trains and learns quantitative relationships between the target variables (variables that have to be predicted) and the predictor variables are determined from historical data. Thereafter a mathematical model is determined from these example dataset and this model can then be used to compute the values of the target variables as a function of the predictor variables for periods for which only the predictor variables are known.

Regression based models can provide both accuracy and interpretability at the same time. Performance of regression models depends on the quality of data sets and the computing capability of machines [102–104]. Our main objective is to develop a generalized forecasting model by analyzing the dependency of energy usage upon different parameters and how this dependency level changes with the changing socio-economic environment. Thus, we choose regression based data mining techniques. Although there exist several regression based forecasting models, their applicability to MTLF is quite limited.

For example, authors in [12] examined two kernel based intelligent regression methods: Gaussian Process Regression (GPR) and Relevance Vector Regression (RVR), and showed that RVR delivers more accurate monthly forecasting results than GPR for the New England data set in the U.S.

In [105], authors proposed three models: linear, polynomial and exponential, based on multivariable regression to predict hourly electricity load. They also claimed that the linear model performs better than the other models and suits the needs of the National Electric Power Company of Jordan. However, these models were trained using previous year's hourly load only. No other information, like weather and socio-economic data were considered in the forecasting process.

MTLF and STLF approaches presented in [13] are based on semi parametric additive regression method. The proposed models consider the load collected every 10 minutes by the French manager of the public electricity distribution network at 2260 substations located at the frontier between the high voltage grid and the distribution network in France. Each of the substations are associated with approximately 40 big customers- (e.g., industries and supermarkets) and over 16,000 small customers- (e.g., residential or small businesses). These models estimate the relationship between load and the explanatory parameters, such as, temperatures, calendar variables, etc. However, the same model is used for all types of customers irrespective of their diverse requirements.

In [106] has proposed a fuzzy regression technique to efficiently forecast long-term energy consumption in the industrial sector of Iran. They have introduced four independent variables such as energy price, energy intensity, gross domestic production, and employment as inputs to the model. The prediction accuracy is better than traditional ANOVA and ARIMA model.

A short-term load foresting model based on wavelet decomposition and the random forest has proposed in [107]. The traditional data mining algorithms have some drawbacks, viz. They can fall into local optimum or they have poor generalization capability. Wavelet decomposition algorithm is a valid method to extract the load of the different components as the training set and random Forest regression algorithm suffers less from the problem of overfitting and determining the difficulty of model parameters.

5.5 Research Gaps

There exist many good works on demand forecasting [106–110] which propose various methods to forecast future energy usage in residential, commercial and industrial sectors. Majority of these did not consider sudden and abrupt changes in parameter values while predicting power demand. Our proposed model is on how to forecast the monthly electricity demand of an area (e.g., a state, a county etc.) depending on some effective parameters that influence electricity usage, even if the parameters behave abnormally. In order to achieve this, we have analysed combinations of monthly user data and other predictor parameters of different states of U.S. to find some decision-making information to validate our models. This is used to find the coefficient for each parameter corresponding to different type of users to optimize the predicted demand. Similarly, if we consider the data of a different region, then the coefficient database will be different from the proposed one. Thus, the scope of our models is not limited to one US state only. We can apply these models on any county or region, which have similar characteristics.

CHAPTER 6

MID-TERM LOAD FORECASTING MODELS FOR SMART GRID

Smart Grid can be defined as an electrical power system that provides autonomic services to enhance efficiency of power delivery and cost of operation [96]. Besides, the grid should be flexible enough to be responsive to certain events, such as- rapid change in requirements (e.g., due to certain events, like natural disaster, festivals, sports events, political summits etc.). Unlike many other commodities, electrical power cannot be stored efficiently. Therefore, the generation, transmission, and distribution of electrical power are all processed simultaneously [115]. The relevant infrastructure for each aspect is built to meet the peak demand which can be more than double of the average demand on a typical day [7]. Thus high peak values contribute to the biggest portion of electricity price. If demand could be controlled during peak time, there could be a substantial reduction in infrastructure requirement, which will dramatically reduce the cost [116]. Thus, prediction of power demand and its potential fluctuation in a given period is highly important towards the stability and economic efficiency of any power system.

6.1 Motivation

Historical data show that the peak demand may rise excessively a few times each year, e.g., on extremely hot summer days or in extremely cold weather. In both cases, when the demand exceeds the generation capacity, it can lead to power outages and catastrophic failures in the grid. Demand management is a mechanism to motivate the consumers to use less energy during the peak time so as to reduce the investment on electricity production and ensure a reliable supply. Typical measures for demand management include incentive methods, direct load control policies and different load scheduling techniques to shift a portion of the demand from the peak to off peak [117]. Besides, precise knowledge of consumers' energy usage pattern helps towards optimization of demand management.

The primary motivation behind this work is to develop a generalized version of mid term electricity forecasting system which offers flexibility to accommodate any behavioral changes in pattern of influence parameters under consideration while forecasting energy demand. Another desired property of the model is the applicability of the model over a large geographic area, consisting several regions with diverse range of values for influence parameters.

There already exists a lot of forecasting models based on both regression methods and ANNs. However, the purpose of this work is to check, whether a particular model, trained on a dataset of a particular region, can be applied directly on any other region? If not, then why and how can we modify the situation so that one particular forecasting model can be used for any region.

Energy usage of any region is depended on several parameters, which in turn represent the characteristics of that region. If we can identify the effective parameters and quantify their effect on energy usage then we can easily predict the energy demand of any region. However, this apparently simple conclusion needs several complex questions to be answered. Firstly, which parameters to chose? Secondly, What are the domain of those parameters? and finally, how to quantify the effects of those parameters?

Now, there are several parameters that influence the energy usage of any region. Besides, the number of parameters also varies with the geographic location. Generally, we found that, weather related parameters like maximum and minimum temperature, precipitation, demographical parameters, such as, population density, per capita income etc and other socio-economic parameters, like GDP, number of holidays, price of electricity, types of users are the main factors that influence energy usage. Besides, there still exists a lot of situational factors that are location specific and application specific, such as, certain localities have increased demand during their festivals, famous tourist spots have a very different set of parameters depending on the peak value of incoming tourists, energy usage in industrial sectors depend on the type of energy, availability of resources, water supply etc. It will be quite cumbersome to incorporate all these parameters into one single model. Thus, we have chosen only those parameters, which mostly influence the usage of residential and commercial users.

Next, as it is a data driven, empirical model, the domain of each parameter will depend on the data set that is used to build that model as well as the range of value of that parameter for the target regions. As an example, in our model, we have selected population density as an influencing parameter and our target region (i.e., states in U.S.) exhibits a range of 1 person per sq. meter (Alaska) to 1218 person per sq. meter (New Jersey) [118]. Hence, we can quantify the effect of population density on energy usage for this particular domain, because we have calculated the coefficients depending on the data between this range. Some states of India have population density of more that 2500 person per sq. meter (Uttar Pradesh, Bihar, West Bengal etc.) [119] and also the types of gadgets and electrical equipments used by residential users are drastically different from the residential users of U.S. Thus, this model can not perform accurately for Indian states, as it is not equipped enough to analyse the electricity usage pattern of this country. Though we have shown that for some states, which obtain similar characteristics of our target regions, the model can perform well enough.

The electricity demand of any region can be described as

$$y = F(X, C) \tag{6.1}$$

where, the function F describes the influence of the input vector X on the output variable y by determining the coefficient vector C. Using the given measurements of the input X and the output y calculate the coefficients C so that the model fits the relation between X and y in a best way.

The equation 6.1 can be extended as,

$$y = F(X, C) = c_0 + c_1 x_1 + c_2 x_2 + \ldots + c_m x_m \tag{6.2}$$

$$y = \begin{Bmatrix} y_1 \\ y_2 \\ \vdots \\ y_n \end{Bmatrix} \quad C = \begin{Bmatrix} c_0 \\ c_1 \\ \vdots \\ c_m \end{Bmatrix} \quad X = \begin{Bmatrix} 1 & x_{11} & \cdots & x_{1m} \\ 1 & x_{21} & \cdots & x_{2m} \\ \vdots & \vdots & \vdots & \vdots \\ 1 & x_{n1} & \cdots & x_{nm} \end{Bmatrix} \quad (6.3)$$

where the vector y contains the measurements of the output variable, C represents the vector of the regression coefficients, and the matrix X contains the measurements x_{ij} of the ith observation of the input x_j.

Over the years, different forecasting techniques have been developed to model the electricity load, using both time series [12, 105, 120] and machine intelligence [99, 121] frameworks. However, very few of these aim to quantify the effects of various control parameters towards forecasting power demand. Some good works on load forecasting are based on specific cities [12, 100, 121]. As, the time series based models calculate the demand based on statistical models describing the influence of climate factors, socio-economic parameters and demographic information, it is difficult to build up a single forecasting model for the electricity demand of a vast region. The existing works provide accurate results only when the control parameters behave steadily. However, it is quite difficult to predict if one or more of these parameters shift from its normal profile. As an example, if a city is organizing a big sports tournament or is affected by some natural disaster, then its demographic and weather related control parameters will change drastically in a short period of time. Consequently, the existing forecasting models may fail to predict the change in demand correctly.

Now, a good model should have the ability to learn from the dataset and adjust accordingly to predict demand under any circumstances. However, in order to become a 'good' model, it requires a large number of datasets, containing significant variations of influence parameters to trained on. Somehow we can manage to prepare this type of dataset for a small region, but for a large geographic area, it will be very difficult. These problem can be simplified if we can find the value of C vector for every variations of vector X. Then we can predict the demand for any region directly by just picking the appropriate coefficients for the given variations of control parameters, i.e.,

$$\hat{C} = \begin{Bmatrix} c_0 \\ c_1 \\ \vdots \\ c_m \end{Bmatrix} \text{ for every set of } \hat{X} = \begin{Bmatrix} 1 & x_{11} & \cdots & x_m \end{Bmatrix} \quad (6.4)$$

We can have the desired demand for that particular region by simply multiplying these two vectors. This model can help us to skip the process of data collection, preprocessing and training for each region.

Thus, the problem is to identify the variations in control parameters influencing load forecasting and how to quantify the coefficients of these parameters. This motivates our work.

6.2 Challenges

Predicting the future usage of electricity in the Smart Grid is quite challenging. Still, there exist quite a good number of works that came up with novel methodologies in order to address this issue. However, as we discussed earlier, a generalized forecasting model covering a diverse demographic region and applicable to a greater number of customers coming from various socio-economic background is still an open research problem. The challenges arise mainly due to the following reasons:

- **Huge amount of data:** Smart Grid systems deploy smart meters as a last mile device to bridge the communication between users and utilities. Smart meters provide readings at every 15 minutes for each user to the Data Collection Units (DCU), thus producing a huge amount of data about customers' usage pattern [96]. Using predictive analytics on these data, not only is accurate forecasting possible, but also a correlation between different parameters with forecasted result can be derived.

- **Mixed group of customers:** A localized area may contain a hybrid group of users, consisting of residential and commercial sectors. Each of them has different requirements and usage pattern. Thus it becomes quite difficult to identify the factors responsible for energy consumption and quantify those factors to optimize forecasting value.

- **Dynamic behavior:** In Smart Grid, the usage pattern changes over time. Besides the distributive nature of energy generation, storage and renewable energy sources is increasing unpredictability. Thus, a forecasting model should consider sufficient parameters that cover the effect of different socio-economic, demographic and weather scenarios to capture the dynamic behavior of users.

6.3 Contributions

The main objective of ours is to develop a data-driven, generalized medium-term dynamic load forecasting model for Smart Grids, based on the geographic, socio-economic and weather conditions of different regions. In order to achieve this, we consider three major aspects:

- Identify the nature of dependencies among predictor parameters and predicted demand (linear or non-linear).
- Compare different data mining techniques and analyse the results to select the most suitable one to analyze time series data of energy usage and associated parameters.
- Develop a coefficient database to quantify the effect of predictor parameters.
- Experimental study is conducted using electrical usage history of various states in U.S.

The novelty of this framework is that it proposes a generic, medium-term forecasting model for energy demand in smart power grid which,

- is applicable on different type of users, e.g., residential and commercial.
- works on various geographical locations (e.g., a state in U.S), having different socio-economic, demographic and weather conditions.
- predicts accurately even if one or more control parameters change abruptly and shift from its normal profile. As an example, if a city is organizing a big sports tournament or is affected by some natural disaster, then its demographic and weather related control parameters will change drastically in a short period of time.

We have used additive regression [122, 123] based data mining algorithms as an underlying methodology for our proposed energy forecasting model. Using this model we can predict monthly electricity usage of different types of customers in a large geographic region like a U.S. state. The justification behind selection of additive regression based algorithms are given in Section III-D. The quantification of factors affecting electricity load is based on an iterative approach of training the model, fitting this into different data sets of various regions, interpreting the results, and finally testing the model. We validated the proposed model using real life data available from the U.S. Energy Information Administration (EIA) [32]. We have further compared our work with several significant works in this domain [12–14].

6.3. Contributions

The block diagram for the construction of coefficient database for this framework is given in figure 6.12:

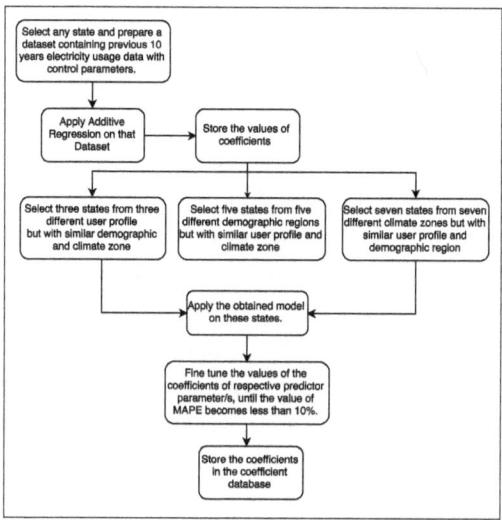

Figure 6.1: Block diagram for construction of coefficient database.

In this project, we have worked with a decade long data set of monthly electricity usage for more than 18 U.S states of both residential and commercial users. Now, these states exhibit a dynamic range of characteristics in terms of its socio-economic, demographic and weather related predictor parameters. Some of these states like New Jersey, Rhodes Island, Connecticut have approximately ninety percentage usage divided almost equally among residential and commercial users. Whereas, in New York and South Carolina commercial usage occupies the largest share in electricity usage. Similarly, New Jersey and Rhodes Island have very high population density (more than 1000 person/sq. mi), Connecticut has high population density (less than 1000, but more than 500 persons/ sq. mi), Florida, California have moderate population density (less than 500, but more than 250 persons/ sq. mi), North and South Carolina, Michigan have low population density (less than 250, but more than 100 persons/ sq. mi) and Missouri, Arizona, Kansas have very low population density (less than 100 persons/ sq. mi). Besides, these states belong to different climate zones, e.g., Connecticut and New York have cold climate, Florida and Louisiana have hot-humid climate, New Jersey and North Carolina has mixed-humid climate. Thus, we can claim that our data set tackles the dynamic nature of mixed group of customers in the Smart Grid.

The motivation behind this work is to develop a generic model to forecast the energy usage that works beyond geographic barrier. In order to fulfill our purpose, we have selected three different and distinct set of parameters that influence energy usage and depending on which, we can classify a large geographic region in small clusters. Moreover, variations in each set of parameters significantly identifies key characteristics of these regions. The proposed model can be further extended, by incorporating more parameters, that in turn help us to analyse the energy usage pattern from other aspects and with more detailing. As an example, our model only concentrates on two types of users: residential and commercial. However, some regions may have a majority of industrial users or agricultural users. In order to analyze the energy usage of these users, we have to include certain parameters that influence their usage, such as, type of soil, availability of water resources, types of corps produced etc. (for agricultural users) and types of industries, transportation system, utilization of heavy machinery etc.(for industrial users).

The proposed model is an application specific solution. The empirical model that is proposed is for smart grid only and based on the electricity usage data of several states across U.S. In another application domain, such as - predicting sales for a company or economic forecasting of a country, similar models may be developed using data pertaining to that specific domain. However, as it is a data driven approach, the proposed model for Smart Grid will not work for other domains, e.g., the data mining algorithms that we found fits well for smart grid scenario, may not be effective for disaster recovery projects. However, the idea and methodology can be applicable to similar situations, only the underlying data mining algorithm may change based on the nature of data.

6.4 Proposed Methodology

This section describes the detailed procedure for the following tasks and selection of the appropriate data mining technique.
1) Selection of predictor parameters for energy forecasting.
2) Data Collection.
3) Analyzing the relationship of predictor parameters with predicted value using scatterplots.

4) Comparison of different data mining techniques in an open source machine learning software Waikato Environment for Knowledge Analysis (WEKA) [134] and analyze results for different metrics.

5) Verifing the result with electricity usage data for 2016.

The modeling and analysis methodology is detailed in this section. The assessment is based on the actual data.

6.4.1 Selecting Predictor Parameters for Energy Forecasting

Electricity demand can be defined as a function of several circumstantial factors that manipulate the quantity of electricity usage. Our first objective is to find those predictor parameters that have a significant effect on electricity demand and classify them in equal intervals using the lower and upper bounds on those parameters.

We have to find n equally distributed intervals, for parameter x_k, as:

$$n = \frac{x_{k\_upper} - x_{k\_lower}}{h} \quad (6.5)$$

where, x_{k_lower} and x_{k_upper} are the lower and upper bound on the parameter, and h is the interval length. We have to choose h carefully in order to distinguish the variance of effect of that parameter on the predicted value.

Sometimes, a group of parameters can construct a single profile which affects the predicted value. In such cases, we need to identify those parameters and try to classify that profile using appropriate intervals of those parameters, such that every interval can have distinct effect on the predicted value.

We have considered nine predictor parameters for monthly electricity forecasting of a particular region:

(i) Usage history (average of 10 years' data)

(ii) Gross Domestic Product (GDP) growth rate

(iii) Monthly average maximum temperature

(iv) Monthly average minimum temperature

(v) Monthly average precipitation

(vi) Price of electricity (cents/kilowatt-hour)

(vii) Residential/commercial load utilization (indicates the percentage of electricity usage)

(viii) Population density (persons/sq. mi)

(ix) Monthly holidays.

6. MID-TERM LOAD FORECASTING MODELS FOR SMART GRID

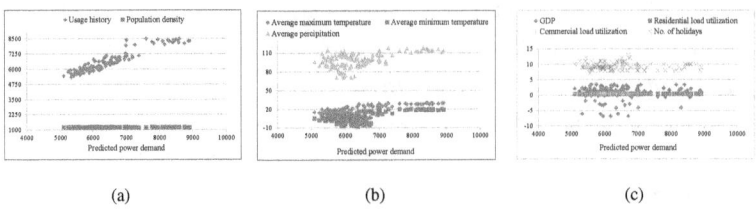

Figure 6.2: Scatterplots for predicted power demand vs. (a) usage history, population density; (b) average maximum temperature, average minimum temperature, average percipitation; (c) GDP growth rate, number of holidays and residential and commercial load utilization respectively.

6.4.2 Data Collection

Our experiment is based on the data from different states in U.S. They include state wise energy usage data, price of electricity/kilowatt-hour and load utilization factor for both residential and commercial sectors from the U.S. Energy Information Administration (EIA) [32]. The GDP data are extracted from different white paper documents of the Bureau of Economic Analysis and the U.S. Department of Commerce [33]. The information about population density and holidays are collected from different U.S. websites. In order to train our data mining models and predict monthly electricity demand of a state, we have arranged a 12 year long dataset, i.e., from 2004 to 2015, with actual monthly usage data and corresponding values of the predictor parameters for that state. Majority of the existing literature in this field did not consider on such large dataset. They mostly focused on a city where the data follow some particular pattern and hardly vary abruptly.

6.4.3 Relationship of Predictor Parameters with Predicted Value

To identify the appropriate data mining technique for our proposed model, it is necessary to analyze the relationships between the predictor parameters and the predicted value. Hence, we use scatterplots, which provide a good visual representation of the association of two parameters.

After analyzing the scatterplots in Figures 9.8(a) to 9.7(c), we conclude that some of the predictor parameters, such as- average usage history, population density, precipitation, residential and commercial load utilization have linear relationships with forecasted data and rest of the parameters have non-linear relationships. Thus, we analyze four data mining techniques: two linear and two non-linear for our experiments.

6.4.4 Comparative Analysis of Data Mining Techniques

Data mining techniques allow us to extract useful information from a large dataset that can be used to find inherent relationships and patterns among data and also to predict future values by analyzing the trends [122]. Initially we have considered four regression based linear and non-linear data mining techniques: *Multiple Linear Regressions (MLR); Additive Regression; M5 based model tree (M5P) and Reduced Error Pruning Tree or (REPTree)*.

MLR is one of the most used and comparatively simple method for forecasting as compared to other models. It seeks to establish a relationship between a dependent parameter (e.g., energy consumption) and two or more independent parameters (e.g., predictor parameters) in the form [124]:

$$Y = b_0 + b_1 x_1 + b_2 x_2 + \ldots + b_n x_t + \epsilon \tag{6.6}$$

In this equation ($b_0 \ldots b_n$) are regression coefficients to be estimated by curve fitting, based on the least square method with the aim of minimizing the difference between observed and estimated values. Here ϵ is referred as the residual.

Additive regression generates predictions by combining contributions of a collection of different models. This method starts with a base model (linear or non-linear) and adds new models sequentially [122]. M5P trees are ordinary decision trees [125] with linear regression models at the leaves that predict the value of observations [126]. REPTree uses the regression tree logic and creates multiple trees in different iterations based on the information gain or reducing the variance. Then it selects the best one from all generated trees [126].

6.4.4.1 Experimental Setup

The experiments are performed with WEKA 3.8 [134]. Initially, we developed four monthly electricity forecasting models with four regression based data mining techniques. The predictive effectiveness of these models are measured using [127]: Correlation Coefficient (CC), Mean Absolute Error (MAE), Root Mean Squared Error (RMSE), Relative Absolute Error (RAE), Relative Root Squared Error (RRSE), and Mean Absolute Percentage Error (MAPE). Each model is verified against the dataset of 2015 of New Jersey. Finally, we predict the monthly usage of 2016 using the most effective model.

6. MID-TERM LOAD FORECASTING MODELS FOR SMART GRID

If a_i and f_i denote the actual and forecasted value of ith set of data, and $i = 1, \ldots, m$, where m is the total number of observations, then we can define the above mentioned comparison metrics [127] as in Table 9.2.

Table 6.1: Definition of Comparison Metrices

Comparison Metrices	Formula
Correlation Coefficient	Where, $S_{FA} = \frac{S_{FA}}{\sqrt{S_F S_A}}$, $S_{FA} = \frac{\sum_{i=1}^{m}(f_i - \bar{f})(a_i - \bar{a})}{m-1}$ $S_F = \sqrt{\frac{\sum (f_i - \bar{f})^2}{m-1}}$, $S_A = \sqrt{\frac{\sum (a_i - \bar{a})^2}{m-1}}$, $\bar{f} = \frac{\sum_{i=1}^{m}(f_i)}{m}$ and $\bar{a} = \frac{\sum_{i=1}^{m}(a_i)}{m}$
Mean Absolute Error (MAE)	$\frac{\sum_{i=1}^{m} |f_i - a_i|}{m}$
Root Mean Squared Error (RMSE)	$\sqrt{\frac{\sum_{i=1}^{m}(f_i - a_i)^2}{m}}$
Relative Absolute Error (RAE)	$\frac{\sum_{i=1}^{m} |f_i - a_i|}{\sum_{i=1}^{m} |a_i - \bar{a}|}$
Relative Root Squared Error (RRSE)	$\sqrt{\frac{\sum_{i=1}^{m}(f_i - a_i)^2}{\sum_{i=1}^{m}(a_i - \bar{a})^2}}$
Mean Absolute Percentage Error (MAPE)	$\frac{\sum_{i=1}^{m} |\frac{f_i - a_i}{a_i}|}{m}$

At first, these four regression based data mining techniques are applied to the dataset of New Jersey for quantative comparison. The results of this experiment are given in Table 6.2.

Subsequently, we analyzed these data and found that additive regression with MLR as a base model performs better than the other three methods for all five comparison metrics. This motivates us to use additive regression to build our load forecasting model for Smart Grid.

Table 6.2: Performance of Regression based Data Mining Techniques on New Jersey

Regression Techniques	Correlation Coefficient	MAE	RMSE	RAE	RRSE
Additive Regression	0.9612	194.5984	253.0627	27.28%	27.43%
M5P	0.8952	359.2849	469.8586	50.37%	50.92%
MLR	0.9505	196.7033	253.5909	27.58%	27.48%
REPTree	0.9126	262.7237	373.6709	36.83%	40.50%

However, we observe that the values for MAE and RMSE are still on the higher side. To improve these values, we categorize the users into two types: residential and commercial users. In this study, we limited our scope to only these two types of users, and develop separate datasets for each type of users. Next, we have applied the above four data mining techniques to these two separate datasets, the results of which are given in Table 6.3.

Table 6.3: Regression based techniques for residential and commercial sector of New Jersey

Regression Techniques	Correlation Coefficient	MAE	RMSE	RAE	RRSE
Residential Sector					
Additive Regression	0.9632	110.3634	137.8228	23.07%	25.01%
M5P	0.9238	1934235	268.611	42.48%	46.88%
MLR	0.9447	135.4228	187.9549	29.74%	32.80%
REPTree	0.9618	111.1383	156.9591	24.41%	27.39%
Commercial Sector					
Additive Regression	0.9672	58.2744	79.0858	24.80%	26.19%
M5P	0.9266	109.2733	143.4863	46.50%	47.52%
MLR	0.9423	77.5911	101.101	33.02%	33.48%
REPTree	0.9551	67.5571	91.18	31.02%	32.49%

6.4.5 Verification of the Proposed Model

In order to evaluate the accuracy and effectiveness of the proposed model, we have tried to forecast monthly energy usage for both residential and commercial sectors for 2016 and compared our results with the actual usage data.

Table 6.4 provide the MAE and MAPE for each applied technique. Figures 6.15(a) and 6.15(d) present the actual usage data versus the predicted electricity usage for both user types for the year of 2016 in New Jersey.

The above results clearly confirm that additive regression is a better choice for predicting electricity demand.

Table 6.4: Mean Absolute Error and Mean Absolute Percentage Error

Regression Techniques	MAE		MAPE	
	Residential	Commercial	Residential	Commercial
Additive regression	97.475	58.646	5.965	3.576
MLR	270.876	193.139	10.376	7.461
M5P	352.333	210.525	14.317	8.989
REPTree	478.938	271.573	19.121	10.423

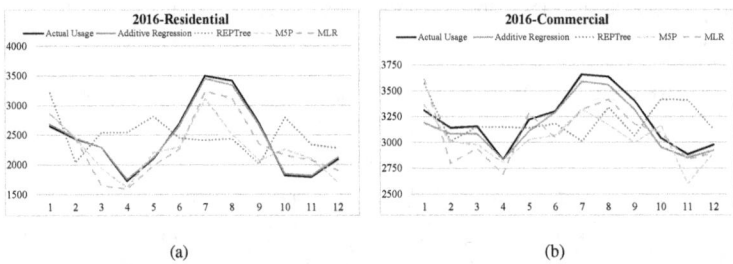

Figure 6.3: Actual usage vs. prediction values in (a) residential sector and (b) commercial sector, using four data analysis techniques for 2016

6.5 Constructing Coefficient Database

The ultimate objective of our approach is to propose a generalized load forecasting model for Smart Grids that will predict monthly load of any region based on its geographic, socio-economic and weather conditions. In order to achieve this, we have applied the proposed model as discussed in Section III to different states of U.S. to check if the same model can be applied to different states. If not, then what variations should the model require?

Figure 6.4 shows the comparison of actual usage data and predicted power demand in the residential sector for the year of 2015 in Lousiana. Here, we have put residential data of Lousiana in the model for New Jersy. We observe that the patterns for both

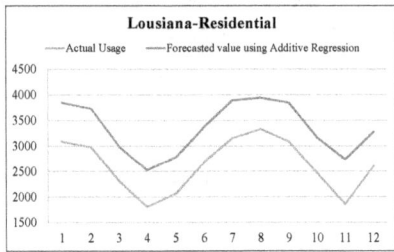

Figure 6.4: Actual usage vs. predicted value for residential sectors of Louisiana.

curves (actual usage and predicted demand), are similar in nature, but magnitude is different. This confirms that our model performs well to forecast energy demand of a particular state based on the specified parameters, but fails to provide accurate results for different states. We also performed this experiment on three other states (New York, South Carolina and Rhodes Island) and all of them show similar results. However, it

6.5. Constructing Coefficient Database

is not easy to develop a single model for all states. Hence, we propose to group the states with similar characteristics and try to build a database storing coefficients for parameters that suits the uniqueness of each group.

Using population density [118], we can classify the demographic profile as:
- Very high (more than 1000 persons/sq. mi).
- High (less than 1000, but more than 750 persons/ sq. mi).
- Upper medium (less than 750, but more than 400 persons/ sq. mi).
- Moderate (less than 400, but more than 250 persons/sq. mi).
- Lower medium (less than 250, but more than 150 persons/sq. mi).
- Low (less than 150, but more than 50 persons/sq. mi).
- Very low (less than 50 persons/sq. mi).

We have considered two types of Smart Grid users- residential and commercial. Thus, using load utilization factor, we classify all U.S. states for three different types of user profile:
- States with almost equal share of each type of users, i.e., almost equal percentage of residential, commercial and industrial load.
- States with either residential or commercial dominance.
- States with dominating sector other than residential or commercial.

Besides, using average maximum and minimum temperature, average precipitation we can classify seven different climate zones [128] as: Cold; Very cold; Mixed humid; Hot humid; Mixed dry; Hot dry; and Marine.

In order to construct the proposed model we have to find the coefficients of predictor parameters which define these zones. As an example, the coefficient for population density will be different for seven demographic regions. Similarly, residential/commercial load utilization and weather parameters will have three and seven set of values, respectively. Thus, the base algorithm of additive regression model, i.e., the MLR model can select the appropriate coefficients depending on the values of the predictor parameters, from the database. And the additive regression model then predicts the monthly electricity demand using the following base model as equation (6.2) and (6.3):

$$Y = c_0 + \sum_{i=1}^{t}(c_i x_i) + \epsilon \qquad (6.7)$$

where, Y is predicted electricity demand; c_0 is the intercept value, such that, c_0 is the expected mean value of Y when all $x_i = 0$; t is the number of predictor parameters; x_i is

ith predictor parameter; and c_i is the coefficient for parameter x_i. ϵ is the error term, which points out the difference between original data and predicted value. Our aim is to find the coefficients, i.e., c_is, for all variations of x_is such that it optimize the ϵ for each data set.

For this model $t = 9$, and values of c_i's can be selected from the coefficient database. The step wise procedure for configuration of the coefficient database is given in algorithm 6.

Algorithm 6: Configuration of the Coefficient Database

1 initialization;
2 Initially build a model by applying additive regression with MLR as a base algorithm, on a data set of residential sector for a selected state;
3 Store derived coefficients for each predictor parameter;
4 Select five states from seven different demographic regions but with similar user profile and climate zone;
5 Apply the obtained model in (Step 1) on those seven states;
6 Fine tune the values of the coefficients of identified predictor parameters, which define demographic region, until the value of MAPE becomes less than 10%;
7 Store the coefficients in the coefficient database;
8 Repeat Steps 3 to 5 for three different states representing three distinct user profiles, and for seven different states with different climate zones;
9 Repeat Steps 1 to 7 for commercial sector;

Outputs of the algorithm 6 are listed in Tables 6.5 through 6.8.

Table 6.5: Predictor Variables on Weather Profile for Residential and Commercial sector

Commercial Sector	Cold	Very Cold	Mixed Humid	Hot Humid	Mixed Dry	Hot Dry	Marine
Average Maximum Temperature	-4.66	-19	-3.5	7.5	3	3	-3
Average Minimum Temperature	7.5	22	5.5	3.5	-12	-12	-0.5
Average Rain	0.45	-(Average Rain/5)	-8	-7	10	10	-2
Residential Sector							
Average Maximum Temperature	11	-1	10	25	5	5	3
Average Minimum Temperature	-11	2.5	1.5	25	-5	-5	-7.5
Average Rain	-0.25	-(5% of Average Rain)	20	8.5	0.5	0.5	-0.75

Table 6.6: Values of Population Density for Residential and Commercial Sector

Demographic Profile for Commercial Sector	Very High	High	Upper Medium	Moderate	Lower Medium	Low	Very Low
Population Density	-(Average Commercial usage/ Population density)+1	-(Average Commercial usage/Population density)+1.25	-(Average Commercial usage/Population density)+4.25	-(Average Commercial usage/Population density)+1.25	-(Average Commercial usage/Population density)+4	-(Average Commercial usage/Population density)+6	-(Average Commercial usage/Population density)+14
Demographic Profile for Residential Sector							
Population Density	-(Average Residential usage/ Population density)+2.5	-(Average Residential usage/ Population density)+2	-(Average Residential usage/ Population density)+3.5	-(Average Residential usage/ Population density)+2	-(Average Residential usage/ Population density)+1.52	-(Average Residential usage/ Population density)+1.75	-(Average Residential usage/ Population density)+2.5

Table 6.7: Values of Load Utilization Factor for Residential and Commercial Sectors

Commercial Sector	Equal Sharing of each Sector	Two strong Sectors with one Minor Sector	One Dominating Sector with two Minor Sectors
Load Utilization	-(27% of Average Commercial usage)	-(69% of Average Commercial usage)	-(91% of Average Commercial usage)
Residential Sector			
Load Utilization	-(17% of Average Residential usage)	-(80% of Average Residential usage)	-(95% of Average Residential usage)

Table 6.8: Remaining Predictor Variables for Residential and Commercial Sectors

Predictor Variables	Commercial Sector	Residential Sector
Average Usage History	0.6326	0.985
GDP Growth rate	3	5
Price of Electricity	29	-1.27
Number of Holidays	-4	27
Intercept Value	1.9*Average Usage History	36% of Average usage History

6.6 Results

We have applied our proposed forecasting model to predict electricity usage of various states of U.S. and compared the obtained results with the actual usage data of 2016, as recorded in [32]. We have selected the states in such a manner that the whole selection can reflect the variations in the control parameters for electricity usage. Table 6.9 shows the variations of states according to their control parameters, i.e., climate, population density and electricity usage.

Figure 6.5 shows the comparison results for three states: commercial sectors of New Jersey and Arizona, and residential sector of North Carolina. Besides, MAPE is calculated for these states and compared to the results, obtained by different forecasting models. Figure 6.6 presents the comparisons of MAPE for monthly forecasting using different models. The kernel based forecasting model in [12] is based on the datasets

Table 6.9: US states according to climate, population density and electricity usage.

State	Climate	Population Density	Ratio of Residential, Commercial and Industrial electricity usage
New Hampshire	Cold	Lower Medium	0.41 : 0.41 : 0.18
Wisconsin	Very Cold	Low	0.32 : 0.34 : 0.34
North Carolina	Mixed Humid	Lower Medium	0.44 : 0.36 : 0.2
Lousiana	Hot Humid	Low	0.36 : 0.28 : 0.36
Arizona	Mixed Humid	Low	0.43 : 0.39 : 0.18
Oregon	Marine	Very Low	0.41 : 0.34 : 0.25
South Carolina	Mixed Humid	Lower Medium	0.38 : 0.27 : 0.35
Wyoming	Very Cold	Very Low	0.16 : 0.23 : 0.61
New York	Cold	Upper Medium	0.35 : 0.53 : 0.12
Connecticut	Cold	High	0.44 : 0.45 : 0.11
Missouri	Cold	Low	0.43 : 0.37 : 0.2
New Jersey	Mixed Humid	Very High	0.39 : 0.51 : 0.1
Rhode Island	Cold	Very High	0.4 : 0.49 : 0.11
Kansas	Cold + Mixed Humid	Very Low	0.34 : 0.39 : 0.27
Illinois	Cold + Mixed Humid	Lower Medium	0.33 : 0.36 : 0.31
Minnesota	Cold + Very Cold	Low	0.33 : 0.34 : 0.33
Albama	Mixed + Hot humid	Low	0.36 : 0.25 : 0.39
New Mexico	Hot dry + Mixed dry	Very Low	0.29 : 0.39 : 0.32

of New England, and establishes the fact that MTLF models are best suited for Smart Grid. The semi parametric based forecasting model in [13] is one of the most cited paper in AMI forecasting. It emphasizes on the interpretability of predictor parameters and forecasted values and shows that the effect of changes in the parameters (such as, temperature and calender variables) can be easily distinguished and estimated. Finally the ARMA model in [14] is one of the pioneer and highly cited paper in this field. Thus we have decided to compare our work with these papers. The results clearly confirms that our proposed model performs better than these forecasting models using GPR and RVR [12], ARMA model [14] and Semi Parametric Additive Models (SPAM) [13]. Thus, we can claim that our proposed model offer more reliable and accurate forecasting results without being location specific. Besides, it is more stable than other models, as it incorporates the changes in socio-economic, demographic and weather informations of any region and forecasts accordingly.

Besides, while analyzing the characteristics of different states, we notice that some states belong to more than one climate zones, mentioned in section 4. Thus, if we choose the coefficients for one climate zone, then it might not give us the accurate prediction for that state.

In order to justify this statement, we pick two states: Kansas and Illinois. Both of this satates have a combination of cold and mixed humid climate across the state. At first, we have applied the coefficients for cold climate, then we tried to predict the usage

6.6. Results

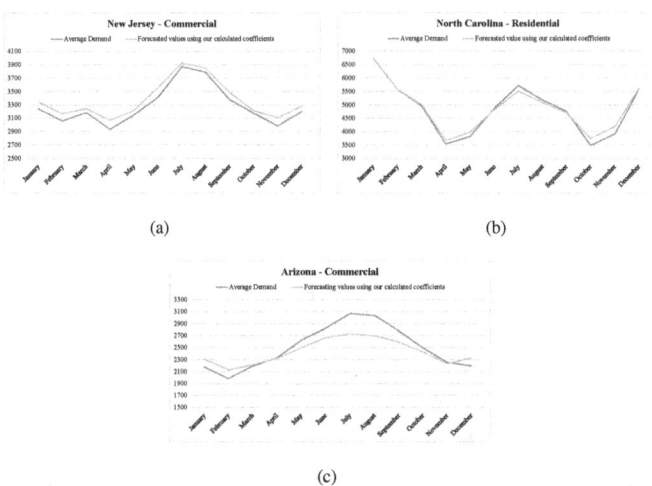

Figure 6.5: Actual usage vs. prediction data using proposed model for 2016 of [a] New Jersey-commercial, (b) North Carolina-residential, (c) Arizona-commercial.

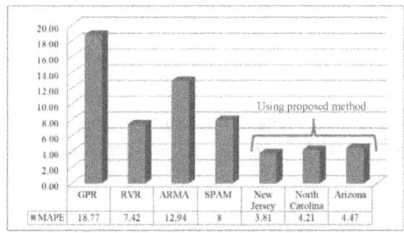

Figure 6.6: Comparison of different forecasting models using MAPE.

using coefficients for mixed humid climate, and calculated the MAPE value for both scenarios. The MAPE is on the higher side for both the cases, which inspired us to fine tune the weather related coefficients and we discover a new coefficient set, that works well for states having a combination of cold and humid climates. These new coefficient sets are mentioned in table 6.10 and figure 6.7 and 6.8 depicts the variations in predicted usage as well as MAPE values for this experiment.

This proves that this model can be extended to cover more variations in the control parameters, so that it can predict electricity usage of new regions.

Finally, figure 6.9 describes the obtained MAPE for both residential and commercial sector, for 18 different states in U.S. using our forecasting model. The average values of

Table 6.10: Coefficients of weather related predictor variables for Residential and Commercial sectors

	Cold + Mixed Humid climate zone		
	Average Maximum Temperature	Average Minimum Temperature	Average Rain
Commercial Sector	3	-4.5	7.5
Residential Sector	5	10	-10.5

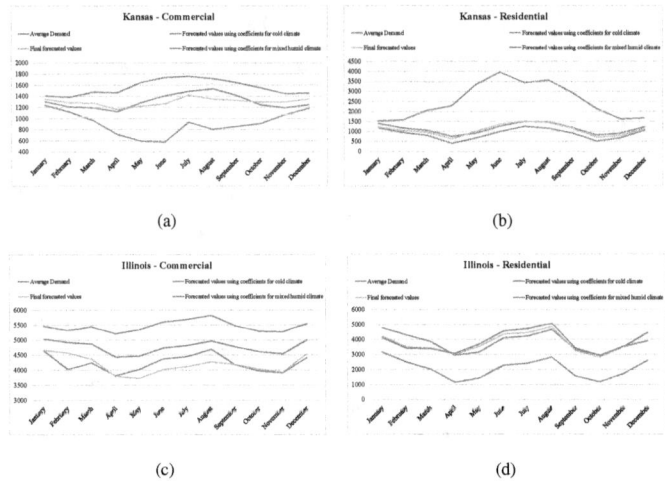

Figure 6.7: Variation of predicted usage data using different coefficient sets for weather related control parameters for (a, c) commercial and (b, d) residential sectors of Kansas and Illinois respectively.

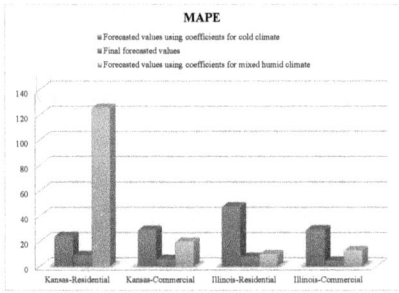

Figure 6.8: Variation of MAPE using different coefficient sets for weather related control parameters for commercial and residential sectors of Kansas and Illionois.

MAPE are found to be **6.83** and **5.63** for residential and commercial sectors respectively.

6.6. Results

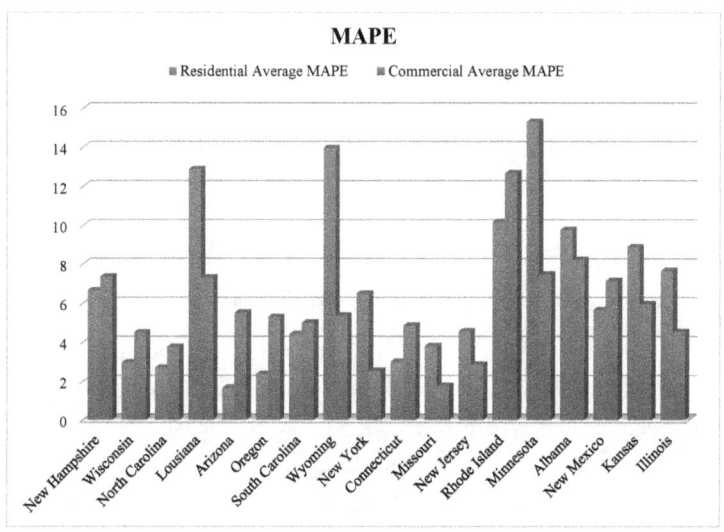

Figure 6.9: MAPE values for different states in both residential and commercial sector, using proposed forecasting model.

6.6.1 Applicability of The Model on Other Regions

We applied our model on the commercial sector of Himachal Pradesh, a state in India, which has very different socio economic background. While analyzing the characteristics of Himachal Pradesh, we find that, the population density of Himachal Pradesh is *low* and its climate resembles the *cold* climate zone of U.S. Thus, with the help of appropriate parameters we predict the energy usage of 2016 and compared it with the actual usage. In figure 6.10, the dashed line, i.e., *predicted usage 1* depicts the comparative result with the MAPE value 7.3%.

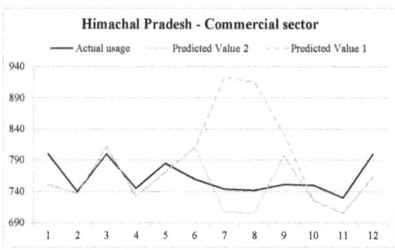

Figure 6.10: Actual usage vs predicted value in Himachal Pradesh - 2016.

119

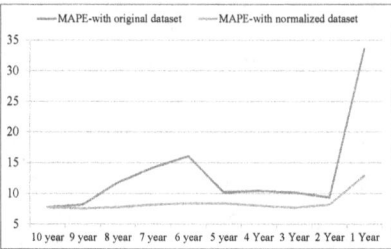

Figure 6.11: Variations in MAPE for original and normalized dataset.

Now, from figure 6.10, it is clearly visible that our model works quite well except for 7th, 8th and 9th month. Actually these three months represent rainy season in India and Himachal Pradesh experiences heavy downpour in this time, which is quite different from the *cold* climate zone, on which we select our coefficients. Thus, we pick the weather coefficients from *Hot Humid* zone for these three months, i.e., for July, August and September. Besides, due to this weather conditions, the number of tourists also decrease significantly during these months, which affects the population density. Thus we modify the coefficient for *population density* from *low* to *very low* for these three months and then calculate the predicted energy for 2016. This modified result is represent by the dotted line as *Predicted Usage 2*. The MAPE value is also decreased to 3.77% for this results.

Thus, we can say that our model will work on any region, state or territory having similar climate, demography and socio-economical environment like our target regions. And we can extent the applicability of this model by adding granularity and more loaction specific parameters.

6.7 Some Interesting Facts

Initially we trained our model using previous 10 years of data and gradually decreasing the training period by one year to notice the variations. Figure 6.11 shows that MAPE in original dataset initially increases as we decrease the training period. However, after 6 years, the trend suddenly shifts in opposite direction, and MAPE value is lower for 5 years than 6 years. Besides, for 5, 4 and 3 years MAPE remains almost constant. While analyzing this trend, we noticed some facts:

- Electricity price for residential sector was increased by 1.7% and 1.5% respectively in 2007-08 and 2006-07.

- The population growth of New Jersey was increased by more than 4.7% over the time period of 2004-2014.

Due to these factors average electricity usage also increased over the years. Forecasted demand is a function of all predictor parameters. Some of these parameters experience a noticeable variation during last 10 years, which again affect the average usage history. Figure 9.8(a), shows a very strong linear relationship between the average usage history and predicted demand. When we consider 10 years of data to train our model, the recent trends of parameters (for last 5 years) and the distant histories (trends before last 5 years) maintain a balance in their weightage to influence the forecasted value. Thus the model delivers accurate forecasting results.

Consequently, when we decrease the training period, balance between recent trends and distant history become quite unstable, which is reflected in the forecasting result. However, when we consider last five years of data to train, the recent trends have almost 100% weightage in forecasting results, implying better performance. In order to justify this explanation, we normalize the values for those parameters, which have significant variations over the years. We have replaced all the values under each parameter by the arithmetic mean of the data, i.e., if $(x_1, x_2, \ldots, x_n)$ are n distinct values under parameter X, then we replace each x_i with $(\sum_{i=1}^{n} x_i)/n$. This process helps us to remove the variations for each parameter in the dataset. Figure 6.11 includes the variations in MAPE after modification in the dataset.

6.8 Applicability of the Model on Industrial Sector

The above mentioned forecasting model can be applied to various geographical regions, having different socio-economic, demographic and weather parameters. However, on industrial sector, it was not performing as expected. Upon analyzing the results further, we have found that the energy demand in industrial sector is guided by a different set of parameters than the other two sectors. Besides, even the common influential parameters have different effects on these sectors. As an example, weather variations and festivities do not affect the energy usage of the industrial sector as much as from residential sector. U.S. Energy Information Administration (EIA) categorized the industrial sector in three distinct industry types [129]:

- *energy-intensive industries*, generally consist of iron and steel manufacturing, petrolium refineries, nonferrous metals and nonmetallic minerals industries.
- *nonenergy-intensive industries* including various pharmaceuticals, electronic and electrical gadget manufacturing industries.
- *nonmanufacturing industries*, such as agricultural, forestry, fishing, construction etc.

The energy demand in the industrial sector varies across regions and countries, depending on the level and mix of these above types of industries. Hence, we have selected industrial energy usage as the primary driving factor, that can be used to distinguish different regions for our proposed model. The purpose of this model is to predict quarterly energy demand of any large geographic region e.g., a state of a particular country. We have used six different data mining techniques and identified the most suitable one depending on the results. Then we have tried to find a multiplier variable which can be multiplied by the forecast value to introduce accuracy in prediction. Here, we have categorized different geographical regions, based on their average electricity usage in the industrial sector and for each region we have tried to find out a range of multiplier.

6.9 Proposed Methodology

The construction of our proposed model generally consists of two primary phases:
1) **Select underlying data mining algorithm:** using **training** and **testing** of various data mining algorithms and comparing the results.
2) **Construct multiplier database:** this phase helps us to generalize our proposed model so that we can apply it on a large geographical region.

Figure 6.12 depicts the basic block diagrams for the two phases separately.

In order to justify the correctness of our multiplier values, we have tried to predict the multipliers and compared the obtained values with our calculated multipliers and found that they actually belong to the same range.

6.9.1 Select Underlying Data Mining Algorithm

The following series of steps will describe briefly the methodology of selecting proper data mining techniques for predicting industrial electricity usage.
- 1. Selection of the predictor variables for industrial sector.
- 2. Data collection

6.9. Proposed Methodology

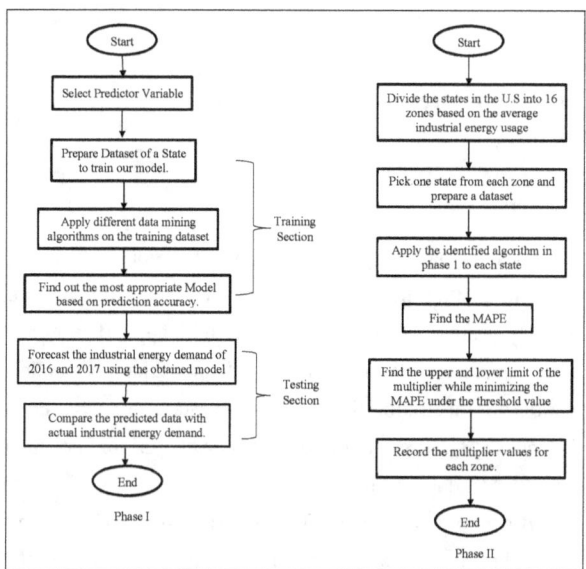

Figure 6.12: Block diagram for proposed forecasting model.

- 3. Data Preprocessing.
- 4. Experimental Setup and results
- 5. Verify the result using the data of 2015.
- 6. Predict the quarterly demand for energy for the year of 2016 and 2017.

6.9.1.1 Selection of the predictor variable for the industrial sector:

We have selected 10 industry related influential parameters as follows:

1) **Previous quarterly energy usage(Thousand megawatts) history**, an average of 10 years' usage data for each quarter.
2) **Number of Energy Intensive Industry**, Here we mainly focused on petroleum refinery, heavy metal, and manufacturing industries.
3) **Number of Energy Non-intensive Industry**, consists of mainly wood, plastic, rubber, computers and electronic equipment manufacturing etc.
4) **GDP growth rate** for each quarter of each state.
5) **Population density** of each state for each quarter.
6) **Average Maximum Temperature** of each state.
7) **Average Minimum Temperature** of each state.
8) **Average Mean Temperature** of each state.

123

9) **Industrial load share**, determines what percentage of electrical energy is used for industrial sector amongst all sector.
10) **Retail sale of energy(cents per kilowatt-hour)** for each quarter to industries of each state.

6.9.1.2 Data Collection :

The next important task is to develop datasets on which various data mining techniques can be applied. All dataset has been prepared on the basis of different states of the U.S. We have collected 15 years long quarterly data. We have applied different data mining techniques on these datasets. Data for parameter 1, 9 and 10 has been collected from US Energy Information Administration (EIA) [32]. The establishment of energy intensive and nonintensive industry has been collected from Bureau of Labor Statistics (BLS) [130]. The GDP and population data has been collected from Bureau of Economic Analysis (BEA), U.S. Department of Commerce [33] and [131] respectively. Parameter 6, 7 and 8 have been collected from national centers for environment Information(NOAA) [132]. We have prepared 7 decade long datasets, i.e.: 2000-2009, 2001-2010, 2002-2011, 2003-2012, 2004-2013, 2005-2014, 2006-2015 for different states of USA.

6.9.1.3 Data Preprocessing :

It is a common requirement for many machine learning estimators to standardize datasets. Here we scale features to lie between a range of 0 to 1. In this case, the data representing each predictor variable x_i for i = 1, 2, ..., n are normalized using the following equation 6.8.

$$x_i\_norm = \frac{(x_i - x_i\_min)}{(x_i\_max - x_i\_min)} \qquad (6.8)$$

where, x_i_max and x_i_min are the maximum and minimum values for the vector x_i, and x_i_norm is the resultant normalized vector. n is the total number of predicted variables.

6.9.1.4 Experimental Setup and Results :

All experiments have been performed on WEKA: Waikato Environment for Knowledge Analysis [134]. It is a suite of machine learning software written in Java to perform data mining tasks.

6.9. Proposed Methodology

6.9.1.4.1 *Selection of appropriate data mining algorithms :* We have selected 6 regression based data mining approach to identify which approach gives better result than other methods. These algorithms are :

Additive Regression, Least median Square Regression, Random Forest, M5P Tree, MLP Regressor and SMO

We have taken a decade-long training dataset (2006-2015) of North Carolina. Each year has been divided into quarters. We have applied 6 different regression techniques on the training dataset to produce models. We have compared the performances of these models based on 7 metrics, [122] such as Correlation Coefficient (CC), Mean Absolute Error (MAE), Root Mean Square Error (RMSE), Relative Absolute Error (RAE), Relative Root Square Error (RRSE), Mean Absolute Percentage Error (MAPE) and we have used R^2 value for model testing. The results of our experiments are given in table 6.11. After analyzing all these data and taking consideration of every comparison metrics we have found that Random Forest gives better accuracy in forecasting amongst regression techniques.

Table 6.11: Performance of Different Regression Methods

Regression Technique	Correlation Coefficient	MAE	RMSE	RAE (%)	RRSE (%)	MAPE	R2 Value
Additive Regression	0.9693	34.25	45.498	23.40	24.94	4.131	0.94
LeastMedSq	0.8944	50.661	84.239	34.62	46.17	3.741	0.87
Random Forest	0.9914	26.195	33.506	19.90	18.36	3.349	0.96
M5P Tree	0.9718	34.45	43.21	23.54	23.68	3.686	0.85
MLP Regressor	0.9719	34.91	43.05	23.86	23.60	3.739	0.95
SMO	0.9238	44.57	71.9	30.46	39.13	3.516	0.80

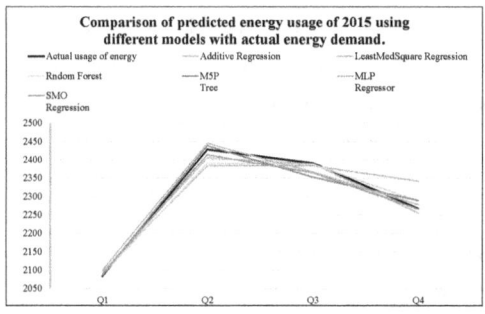

Figure 6.13: Energy demand prediction for North Carolina - 2015.

6.9.1.5 Verification of the proposed model :

We have forecasted the quarterly usage of energy in the industrial sector for the year 2015 using these regression models and compared our prediction results with the actual energy usage. The results are given in figure 6.13. Analyzing these results, we can conclude though every model has the similar pattern with the actual value, the performance of Random Forest is quite better than the others.

6.9.1.6 Predict quarterly usages of energy for the year 2016 and 2017 :

Here we have tried to predict the quarterly energy usage in the industrial sector of North Carolina for the year 2016 and 2017 using the model based on Random Forest. We have compared our results with the actual energy usages. Figure 6.14 shows the comparison of actual and predicted usages of energy. The pattern of prediction curve has similarity with the actual curve.

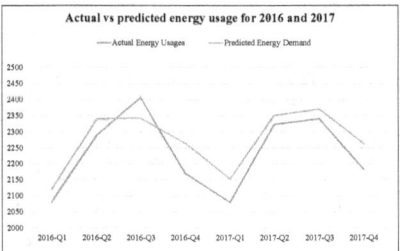

Figure 6.14: Comparison results using Random Forest for North Carolina.

6.9.2 Construct Multiplier Database :

In this section 6.9.1, we have created a model based on Random Forest to forecast the energy usages of North Carolina. Here we will measure the performance of the proposed model using the datasets of different geographic region of the same country, which have same socio-economic parameters. We have studied 15 years long quarterly data for average energy usages in the industrial sector of all states of the U.S then we have divided the country into 16 regions, based on average industrial energy usage. This division is given in Table 6.12.

We have selected datasets of at least one state from each region and have applied our proposed model on them. We have selected New Hampshire, New Jersey, New

6.9. Proposed Methodology

York, Wisconsin, Lousiana, Michigan, Indiana, Ohio and Texas from zone A-I and P respectively. Figure 6.15(a)-(d) shows the comparison between actual quarterly energy usages and predicted quarterly energy demand for the year 2014 and 2015. It has been observed from figures 6.15(a)-(d) that for all states, the prediction is in the range of 2000-3000. However, interestingly there is some similarity in patterns. Most of the cases the actual energy usage curve and the prediction curve are similar. Thus, the work reduces to find a constant to be multiplied by the predicted value to improve prediction accuracy. In the next section, we will produce a multiplier database which we have calculated after doing experiments on states of the different region. We have also predicted multiplier for each quarter of the year 2015 for a state and verified it with its multiplier range. There is an upper and lower limit of multiplier for each region. By using appropriate multiplier from this range we can improve the accuracy of the predicted result.

Table 6.12: Division of region based on Average energy usage in previous 15 years

Region	Average industrial energy usage (Gigawatt)	States
A	0-500	Maine, New Hampshire, Rhode Island, Vermont, North-Dakota, South Dakota, Delware, Montana, Alaska, Hawaii
B	500-1000	New Jersey, Kansas, Nebraska, Idaho, New Mexico, Utah, Wyoming
C	1000-1500	Massachusetts, New York, Missouri, Florida, Virginia, West-Virginia, Mississippi, Arkansas, Oklahoma, Arizona, Colorado, Nevada, Oregon
D	1500-2000	Wisconsin, MInnesota
E	2000-2500	North Carolina, South Carolina, Tennessee, Louisiana
F	2500-3000	Michigan, Georgia, Alabama
G	3000-3500	Illinois, Kentucky
H	3500-4000	Pennsylvania, Indiana, California
I	4000-4500	Ohio
J, K, L, M, N, O	4500-....-7500	NIL
P	>7500	Texas

6. MID-TERM LOAD FORECASTING MODELS FOR SMART GRID

Figure 6.15: Actual vs. Predicted energy usage for different U.S.A. States

6.9.2.1 Multiplier database :

Here, our objective is to find a multiplier database, which can be used to improve the accuracy and scalability of our proposed forecasting model. We have applied our model on the datasets of each state representing each zone and calculated MAPE from the predicted and the actual energy usage. If the value of MAPE is less than 10 then we can say that prediction has higher accuracy. If the MAPE is not below 10 then we have to minimize the value of MAPE by changing the predicted value. Here our main objective is to find out a range of multiplier say x for each zone. Algorithm 7 describes the procedure for finding x, for which the minimum value of MAPE is less than 10. Using algorithm 7 in various states, we have found the upper and lower limit of the multiplier. The results are given in table 6.13 and figure 6.16

Table 6.13 clearly shows that Louisiana-North Carolina, and Indiana-California both are from region E and H respectively and both of them have similar multiplier range. So by calculating the average of individual multiplier limits of all states belonging to the same region, we can produce the approximate range of multiplier for that region. It has also been observed from figure 6.16 that actual energy usage curve belongs within

Algorithm 7: Find Multiplier

Input: Quarterly data of Predicted and Actual usages of energy.
Output: mul_L and mul_U: Lower and Upper limit of multiplier respectively.

1 Start;
2 let x = 0, min_mape = 0, flag = 2;
   /* flag determines the upper and lower limit of the multiplier.   */
3 **while** $(flag \neq 0)$ **do**
4     $min\_mape = \frac{\sum_1^n abs((actual_i - x \times predicted_i)/actual_i)}{n} \times 100$;
5   **if** $(min\_mape < 10 \ \&\& \ flag == 2)$ **then**
6         $mul_L = x$;
7   flag = 1;
8   **else**
9   **if** $(min\_mape \geqslant 10 \ \&\& \ flag == 1)$ **then**
10            $mul_U = (x - 0.001)$;
11   flag = 0;
12   **end**
13   **end**
14   x+ = 0.001;
15 **end**
16 End;

Table 6.13: Upper and Lower Limit of Multiplier for different states

Region	State	Upper limit of Multiplier	Lower limit of Multiplier
A	New Hampshire	0.06	0.08
B	New Jersey	0.28	0.31
C	Florida	0.57	0.7
C	New York	0.52	0.7
D	Wisconsin	0.77	1
E	Louisiana	0.9	1.1
E	North Carolina	0.9	1.1
F	Michigan	1.01	1.2
H	Indiana	1.4	1.7
H	California	1.5	1.8
I	Ohio	1.7	2.1
P	Texas	3	3.7

the prediction range.

We have done another experiment on multiplier range. We have taken 7 decade-long datasets of Ohio from the region I and has found that both upper and lower limits are almost same for all dataset. Figure 6.17 depicts the results.

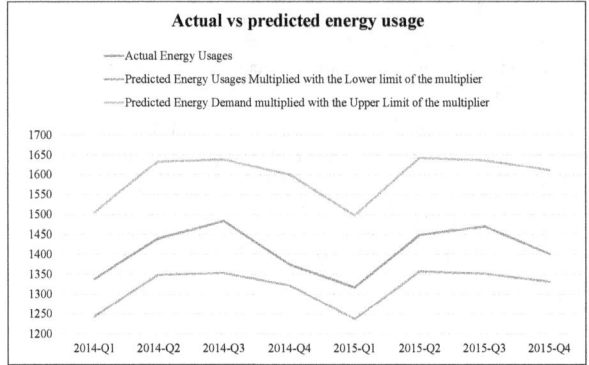

Figure 6.16: Actual vs predicted energy demand of Florida (2014-15)

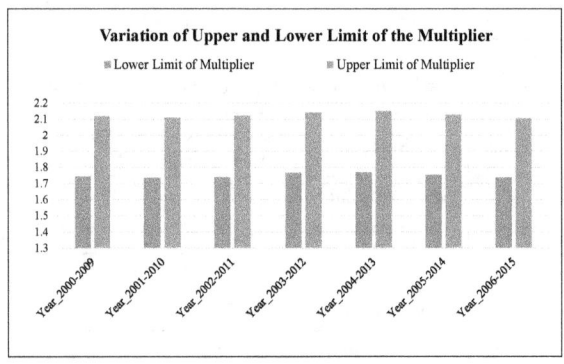

Figure 6.17: Variations of Upper and Lower limits of multiplier for Ohio

6.9.2.2 Forecasting Multiplier:

In the previous section we have discussed the process of finding multiplier range for the different region. Here we have tried to predict the multiplier for a state and compared it with our calculated values. We have collected 15 years long quarterly data which contains actual energy usage for each quarter and predicted energy demand for each quarter which has been calculated by applying the proposed model, discussed in [133]. We have selected the dataset of Florida for experimental purpose and calculated the

6.9. Proposed Methodology

multiplier for each quarter where MAPE is minimum. The result has been shown in table 6.14.

Now we have done time series forecasting in WEKA [122] using these obtained multiplier values in table 6.14. In time series forecasting we have applied Random Forest as a base learner and Maximum Lag creation is 12. We have forecast energy usage for each quarter of 2015 for Florida. The output of predicted multiplier has given in table 6.15. It has been observed that predicted multipliers are in the range of region C as mentioned in table 6.13 in section 6.9.2.1. These results, in turn, justify the effectiveness and correctness of our multiplier database, as well as, our proposed forecasting model.

Table 6.14: Minimum MAPE and corresponding Multiplier (Florida 2000-2014).

Year with Quarter	Actual Energy Usages	Predicted Energy Usages	Multiplier	Minimum MAPE
2000-Q1	1527.33	1526.16	0.578	0.077
2000-Q2	1578.33	1579.34	0.584	0.064
2000-Q3	1575.33	1576.51	0.577	0.075
2000-Q4	1502.33	1503.61	0.577	0.085
...	...	...	...	...
2014-Q1	1338	1338.56	0.618	0.042
2014-Q2	1440.33	1439.21	0.622	0.078
2014-Q3	1483.67	1482.65	0.637	0.069
2014-Q4	1374.33	1374.44	0.613	0.007

Table 6.15: Multiplier prediction and Actual vs. Predicted energy usage (Florida)

Year with Quarter	Predicted Multiplier	Actual Energy	Predicted Energy
2015-Q1	0.615	1317.33	1334.4
2015-Q2	0.621	1448.67	1478.697
2015-Q3	0.624	1470	1479.654
2015-Q4	0.619	1400.33	1445.74

6.10 Conclusions

Accurate load forecasting model in Smart Grid works as a supporting tool to optimize demand scheduling. This chapter proposes two accurate energy forecasting models that optimize reliability and stability, while minimizing processing and computational load. In particular, we analyzed combinations of monthly user data and other predictor parameters to find some decision making information. This is used to find the coefficient for each parameter corresponding to different types of users to optimize the predicted demand. Besides, we also identify that additive regression based models are best suited for both residential and commercial sectors.

As part of future work, we plan to develop an autonomic and dynamic forecasting tool based on our proposed approach that would use additive regression technique to generate the meta-model using previous 10 years' data. Existing models are mostly static, built using a fixed set of data, and are quite inaccurate in predicting electricity usage for future years. The proposed tool will automatically regenerate the forecasting model for every year using recent past data as sliding window of 10 years. As an example, for predicting monthly forecasting of 2016, the tool will build the forecasting model depending on the past trends during 2006-2015. However, for 2017, the model will rebuild automatically using the past data of 2007-2016. This would help us capture the recent trends of electricity usage of a region towards effective prediction of the near future electricity usage more accurately.

SECTION III - DESIGN ISSUES IN IOT BASED AMI

CHAPTER 7

EXISTING SOLUTIONS TOWARDS SECURITY IN IoT BASED AMI

IPv6 is a new technology which gained a massive attention, as a supporting layer in smart grid communication. The huge address space of IPv6 supports the network architecture of the smart grid communications. Besides, features like stateless address auto configuration (SLAAC) and IPSec support makes IPv6 more suitable for smart grid. IPv6 also supports prioritization of messages and different Quality of Service models, which complements several smart grid applications [20]. Therefore, the US National Institute of Standards and Technology (NIST) framework for Smart Grid interoperability [21] explicitly encourages the use of IPv6 for Smart Grid installations. However, like any new technology, IPv6 too comes with a bunch of issues on which more work needs to be done. One of these is address configuration for Smart Grid components. IPv6 has a huge address space. However, the challenge is to use these addresses efficiently. Another challenge of incorporating IPv6 in Smart Grid is: Security. IPv6 is exposed to various attacks, such as header modification attack, fragmentation attacks, reconnaissance attack etc. [156, 157] In this chapter, we focus on some of the possible ICMPv6 attacks that are particularly relevant in the context of building networking infrastructure between Smart Meters (SM), Data Collection Units (DCU) and Meter Data Management System (MDMS).

7.1 Addressing Format of IPv6

The scope of a global address is the entire IPv6 Internet [147]. The general format for IPv6 Global unicast address [148] is presented in figure 7.1 The structural formats are

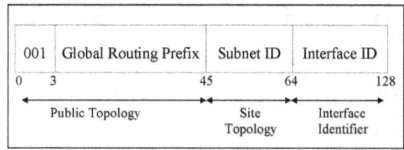

Figure 7.1: The structure of Global Unicast Address.

described here:
- **The three high-order bits** are fixed and set to 001.
- **Global Routing Prefix** indicates the global routing prefix for a specific organization's site. The combination of the three fixed bits and the 45-bit Global Routing Prefix is used to create a 48-bit site prefix, which is assigned to an individual site of an organization.
- **Subnet ID** used within an organization's site to identify subnets within its site. The size of this field is 16 bits. The organization's site can use these 16 bits within its site to create 65,536 subnets or multiple levels of addressing hierarchy and an efficient routing infrastructure.
- **Interface ID** indicates the interface on a specific subnet within the site. The size of this field is 64 bits, allowing up to 2^{64} possible hosts on the same subnet.

The fields within the global address create a three-level topological structure. The public topology is the collection of larger and smaller Internet Service Providers (ISPs) that provide access to the IPv6 Internet. The site topology is the collection of subnets within an organization's site. The interface identifier specifies a unique interface on a subnet within an organization's site [148].

However, the above mentioned general format will not be suitable of every application scenarios. In this format, 64 bits are allocated as Interface ID, which can uniquely identify 2^{64} distinct nodes in a single level of hierarchy. However, 2^{64} is a huge address space and the proper utilization of this space is required to maximize the benefits of IPv6 addressing structure. It is rarely possible to allocate 2^{64} nodes without using hierarchical structure. Projects like, Smartdust, where thousands of sensor nodes are distributed over a region to collect data, may properly use these 64 bits. But some applications would not support so many nodes at a single level. Rather, they would prefer a multi-level hierarchical structure where the total number of nodes of the entire organization will be huge, but only some few hundred nodes will be present at a single level of hierarchy.

In Smart Grid communication architecture, there exist at least a three level of hierarchies in every organization including MDMS(Meter Data Management System), DCU(Data Collection Unit) and Smart Meters. Besides, the level of hierarchies will change dynamically with the density of Smart Meters in a particular area. In a very densely populated area, with a large number of high rises and shopping malls, each high-rise and malls may contain more than 1000 SMs. So the utility have to allocate a DCU for each building to collect the data, resulting in a large number of DCUs in a very small geographical area. This again calls for an upper level of DCUs in the hierarchy for collecting the data from the lower level DCUs and so on. On the contrary, in a sparsely populated area, a DCU may cover a large geographical area without exceeding the maximum number of Smart Meters registered under it. So, depending on the density of SMs, a modification in the level of hierarchies in the architecture is needed. And practically, it is not possible to allocate 2^{64} numbers of Smart Meters under a single DCU. Each DCU can collect and process the billing information from maximum 1000 SMs. Therefore, if 64 bits are allocated for Interface ID, then almost 54 bits will be wasted for each DCU. Hence, a flat addressing structure will not be appropriate to support such applications.

Some of these limitations may be resolved only if the IPv6 addressing format is especially tailor-made for Smart Grid. Some works have already been reported on the addressing format of IPv6 for Smart Grid and address configuration of nodes [143–146] The primary and common motivation for all of these existing works is to efficiently utilize the available 128 bits of IPv6 address space so that large number of devices can be addressed in the hierarchy of electrical smart grid.

7.1.1 Existing Works

Authors of paper [143] proposed IPv6 address configuration scheme called Multi-Projection IP address Assignment (MPIPA) to assign each sensor node a unique, spatial IPv6 address using three-dimensional locations coordinates and based on grouping methods and scan-line scheme. Also, Assignment Success Rate (ASR) is used in this paper to evaluate the probability that assigns unique IP address to nodes successfully.

The proposed scheme divides the network into several groups depending on nodes location information. Then all nodes are projected into the planes corresponding to their groups, and then each plane adopts SLIPA-Q to assign an IP address to each projection sensor node.

SLIPA-Q [165] is an improved version of Scan Line IP address Assignment (SLIPA). SLIPA-Q utilizes location information, equal-quantity partition, and scan-line scheme to ensure that not only each node is to be assigned a unique IP address, but also the spatial relation between nodes is maintained. According to C. Y. Cheng et. al. [143], the IPv6 address has been divided in five parts: first 64 bits are global routing prefix and the next 64 bits are again divided into: PAN ID, group ID, zone ID and member ID. PAN ID uniquely identifies a Personal Area Network and has only one IPv6 gateway. Group Id, zone Id and member ID are made up of r bits and derived from nodes location information. The global routing prefix is same for all the nodes in the WSN. It is the first paper where three dimensional location coordinates are used to obtain the IPv6 address of a node. Since it is a location based addressing scheme, the address of neighbor nodes reflect a spatial relationship, which provides an ideal situation for deployment of an efficient geographic routing protocol.

C. Y. Cheng et. al., have proposed another IPv6 address configuration scheme [144] called distributed spatial IP address assignment (DSIPA). The main idea of DSIPA is that nodes with IP address are responsible for assigning IPv6 address to its neighbors based on neighbors' location coordinates. And each node's IP address is determined by transferring their physical location coordinates to logical location coordinates. Therefore, the spatial relation among nodes can also be maintained to support developing geographic routing protocol.

In DSIPA, the IPv6 address is divided in three parts. The first 64 bits are global routing prefix, the second part is PAN ID and the third part consists of X coordinates, Y coordinates and inner ID. X and Y coordinates are both s bits long and derived from a particular nodes' location information. Size of inner ID is i bits and it represents the maximum number of nodes under each Location Area (LA). The size of PAN ID is (64-2s-i) bits. The value of s and i is dependent on the density of sensor nodes and the size of the WSNs.

X. Wang and S. Zhong [145] have proposed a hierarchical IPv6 address configuration algorithm based on the cluster-tree architecture for all-IP WSN, where a sensor node has a globally unique IPv6 address and uses the IPv6 protocol to perform the point-to-point communication with the Internet. They claimed that the proposed architecture is consistent with the IPv6 network architecture and also the IPv6 address configuration delay is shortened due to the simultaneous configuration of cluster members of different clusters. They also proposed a hierarchical routing based on the same architecture.

According to the authors in paper [145], the new addressing format for IPv6 includes two parts. The first part is global routing prefix, which is identical for all nodes and the second part is sensor node ID, consists of PAN ID, cluster head ID and cluster member ID. PAN ID uniquely identifies one PAN. PAN IDs of all nodes in one PAN are identical. Cluster head ID uniquely identifies a cluster in one PAN. Cluster head IDs of all cluster members in one cluster are identical and Cluster member ID uniquely identifies a cluster member. The global routing prefix is 80 bits long and the rest of three parts are 16 bits each in length.

In another paper [146], X. N. Wang and H. Y. Qian, proposed an IPv6 address auto configuration scheme for wireless sensor networks, based on a new IPv6 addressing structure. Authors claimed to reduce the address configuration cost and shortened the configuration delay by controlling the transmission scope of the control packets within one-hop scope and restricting the recording of the address assignment states and duplicate address detection for the assigned addresses.

According to authors in paper [146], an IPv6 address includes two parts. The first part is global routing prefix which uniquely identifies a particular sensor network and is (64+n) bits long. The second part is interface ID which identifies a sensor node in WSN and is made up of gateway node ID and sensor node ID. Gateway node ID uniquely identifies a gateway node in WSN and Sensor node ID uniquely identifies a sensor node in WSN. Gateway ID and Sensor node ID are i and (64-n-i) bits long respectively. Values of n and i can be determined by the density of sensor nodes and the scale of the WSNs.

7.1.2 Research Gaps

Thus we find that in [143–146], different authors proposed different IPv6 addressing structures, mainly for sensor nodes. Some of these [143, 144] are proposed specifically for sensor nodes in Smart Grid environment. However, both of these papers proposed address configuration schemes based on location information and did not consider the inherent dynamic, hierarchical architecture of Smart Grid. Consequently, a large no of bits are allotted for interface identifier, whereas, it is quite evident that a DCU can handle at most some hundreds of Smart Meters to work properly. The additional bits in the interface identifier are thus wasted.

Besides, in [143] nodes themselves assign their IPv6 address and in [144] neighbor nodes assign IPv6 address for a node. In both the cases, providing security and maintaining privacy is a problem. Besides, Smart Meters are installed in public places. This makes them easily accessible [166]. Thus, we could not apply these methods directly to Smart Grid Network. Essentially, Smart Gird networks adopted a dynamic hierarchical clustering architecture. The levels of hierarchy in a Smart Grid Network may vary depending upon the demographic information of localities. Thus a fixed hierarchical structure is not suitable for Smart Grids.

7.2 ICMPv6 Abuses in IPv6

IPv4 networks often filter ICMP messages to avoid security concerns. However, for IPv6, this is not possible. ICMPv6 is used for basic functionalities and used by other IPv6 protocols like Neighbor Detection Protocol (NDP). Neighbor Discovery Protocol (NDP) is a protocol used with IPv6 to perform various tasks like router discovery, auto address configuration of a node, neighbor discovery, Duplicate Address Detection, determining the Link Layer addresses of other nodes, address prefix discovery, and maintaining routing information about the paths to other active neighbor nodes [149]. Thus, the implementation of IPv6 in Smart Grid needs some serious care to protect from the security vulnerabilities of the ICMPv6 protocol. NDP uses five ICMPv6 messages. These are:

- **Router Solicitation (RS) message:** Hosts send RS message to enquire about a legitimate router on the link.
- **Router Advertisement (RA) message:** Routers send RA message, either periodically or in response to RS message.
- **Neighbor Solicitation (NS) message:** Hosts send NS message to determine the link layer address of a specific node, and also to verify whether an address is already present on link or not.
- **Neighbor Advertisement (NA) message:** Hosts send NA message in response to the NS message.
- **Router Redirect (RR) message:** Routers send RR message to inform a host about a better router on its link.

Some work has been done to secure smart meters and communication network of Smart Grid or SCADA systems [24]. An IPv6 based moving target defense system is provided in [150] to secure the communication between hosts. Most of the network attacks target some specific addresses, so, moving the target address will prevent hosts from being located for an attack. [143, 144, 151] explains different techniques for IPv6 address configuration schemes for smart grid. However, security solutions for specific IPv6 problems, like ICMPv6 attacks, for Smart Grid environment are still need to be addressed. In [152], a distributive, trust based approach to detect attacks in Duplicate Address Detection (DAD) phase was proposed. However, this concentrates only on one type of attack in DAD. In [153], the requirements and practical needs for monitoring and intrusion detection in AMI are discussed. In [154], a layered combined signature and anomaly-based IDS for HAN was proposed. This IDS was designed for a ZigBee based HAN which works at the physical and medium access control (MAC) layers. However, the work only considers the HAN part of AMI. In [155], a specification-based IDS for AMI is proposed. While the solution in [155] relies on protocol specifications, security requirements and security policies to detect security violations, it would be expensive to deploy such IDS since it uses a separate sensor network to monitor the AMI.

7.3 Configuration and Compliance Issues in AMI

Smart Grid can be referred as an upgrade to the already existing power grid. Thus, it will not be appropriate to use traditional system development methods to build Smart Grid. Instead, Component Based System Design (CBSD) strategies will suit it better.

The differences between Traditional Software Development (TSD) approaches and CBSDs [136, 137] are listed in Table 7.1. In CBSD, the management of different components and their versions is one of the most challenging tasks [138]. To achieve this configuration management is used. Configuration management is the task of managing the configuration of different components in a system so that the system operates seamlessly. For a large and complex system, a systematic use of configuration management is used to maintain the correct operability of the components. Authors of paper [162–164] have discussed the various challenges of configuration management in CBSD. They also suggested that run time configuration is needed for CBSD and proposed a model for it. In [158], authors propose a component based configuration management model, where the components are the integral logical constituents of

Table 7.1: Difference between TSD and CBSD

Property	TSD	CBSD
Development Style	Each software is developed from scratch.	Already existing components are assembled to build new software. Reusing of software components are the main theme of CBSD.
Life Cycle	In TSDS the different activities are, requirement analysis, feasibility study, design, coding, testing, maintenance etc.	Life cycle in CBSD consists of, finding components, selecting those that fit the requirements, adapting them, and replacing them with modified versions.
Languages	Programming languages are used to implement the system.	Primitive components are implemented using programming languages, and composite components are built using component description languages and architecture description languages.
System Construction	The system is usually implemented by a group of source code files which can be compiled and linked together to form the final system.	System construction is a recursive process, in which, primitive components are used to construct composite components. Both primitive and composite components are used to construct larger composite components
Working Team	There are engineering teams, which provide all the functionalities during the life cycle of software and end-users.	There are component producer teams developing components; consumer teams developing software reusing components and hybrid teams that are both consumer, producer, and end-users.

the system. The model analyzes the relationship among the components and the configuration management part is dependent on that analysis. A model based on the component system and layered architecture is proposed in [159]. Authors claimed that this layered architecture improves reusability and maintainability of configuration management in CBSD. Another distributive, component based layered model for configuration management in CBSD is proposed in [160]. The layered architecture makes this model easily adaptive, dynamic to changes and also brings down the coupling of the system. In [161], dependency graphs identify different types of dependencies among components and analyze them. The graphs are used to facilitate maintenance by identifying differences, i.e., deviations of a configuration from a functioning reference configuration. Based on the unique features of CBSD, we summarize new requirements of CM for CBSD as follows:

- For component based software development, the first step is to select a component from the existing component database. The owners of the database may update the components periodically. If there are more than one versions of a component between two baselines, then there will be two aspects for version management: either store the older versions in the repository, or replace the older versions by the new version. For the first case, the user can use older versions of a component if they want to. However, for the next situation, users are forced to accept the new versions of the components. In figure 7.2, two versions of component 1 exist between two baselines. If a user wants to use version 3 of component 1, then, it will allow doing so, if the older versions of the component are stored in the repository. Otherwise, it has no choice, but to work with the new version of component 1.

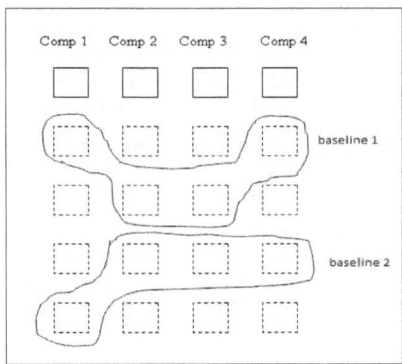

Figure 7.2: Version management problem in CBSD.

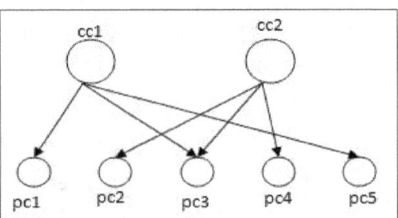

Figure 7.3: Dependency between components.

- Suppose two composite components cc1 and cc2 are dependent on primitive components pc1, pc3, pc5 and pc2, pc3, pc4 respectively, as in figure 7.3. Let us update primitive components pc2, pc3, pc4 and form a new base line for composite component cc2. Now, composite component cc1 is also dependent on primitive component pc3. So, for cc1 there exist two scenarios: Fig. 1.
    - If older versions of primitive components are replaced by the new versions of those components, then cc1 has to adopt itself with the new version of pc3. And also the other primitive components of cc1, such as pc1 and pc5, may also need some up gradation to comply with the new version of pc3.

Thus the modification of one component can lead to modification of several components, which may or may not be directly linked with that component.
– If older versions of primitive components are kept in a repository, then for a given time instant (for a baseline), the two composite components of a system will have two different versions of the same primitive components. This may lead to a compliance error.

Compliance often refers to the validation of a system against some legal policies, internal policies or some basic design facts [142]. Compliance checking can be of two types: compliance by detection and compliance by design. In Compliance by detection method, the existing system is checked thoroughly to detect whether it violates any rules or not. If it does not comply, then corrective measures are taken to make it compliant. In Compliance by design method, the system is developed, by taking into account the business rules. Thus, the system is designed in such a way, that it can comply with the rules [139]. In CBSD, the system is not developed from scratch [137]. Thus, the Compliance by design method does not suit CBSD. Hence, in CBSD, Compliance by detection method is more appropriate to use.

Architectural Compliance is a one of the most important concern for CBSD. To ensure architectural compliance, the system designer has to guarantee proper transformation of architectural rules in the design and implementation of a system. The architecture of a system should provide information regarding the design issues of the system, i.e., the component structures, relationship between components, functional and non functional requirements to comply with the policies and regulations of the organization etc [140, 141] In CBSD, developers import the components from outside. This makes them vulnerable for violating the architectural rules of a system.

Since, Smart Grid is built on an already existing and functioning system, it is necessary to verify the compliance issues before integrating a component in the system. Compliance by detection method checks for compliance violation only after integration of components. Thus, for systems like Smart Grid Compliance by Verification is the most appropriate method for compliance checking.

7.3.1 Research Gaps

There exists some research work on configuration management in CBSD, but neither of them incorporates the idea of compliance management with that. Compliance is a very important factor in CBSD because the developer imports the components from outside. This makes them vulnerable for violating the business terms and policies of an organization.

CHAPTER 8

IMPLEMENTING COMMUNICATION NETWORK USING IPv6

Smart Grid (SG) is an intelligent and adaptive energy delivery network that combines the traditional power grid and IT communication network. It aims to provide more efficient, better fault-resilient and reliable energy support. Robust communication architecture is the key that differentiates Smart Grid from the traditional energy delivery system. The backbone of the Smart Grid will be its communication network. This network is to connect the different components of the Smart Grid together, and provide two-way communication. IP enabled devices are necessary to build such network spread over a large geographic region and connecting devices starting from common household electrical appliances up to power generation units. With the huge number of devices including the smart electrical appliances, increasingly being used in homes, IPv6 become an obvious choice for Smart Grid for its bandwidth. IPv6 is a new technology which gained a massive attention, as a supporting layer in smart grid communication. The huge address space of IPv6 supports the network architecture of the smart grid communications. Besides, features like stateless address auto configuration (SLAAC) and IPSec support makes IPv6 more suitable for smart grid. IPv6 also supports prioritization of messages and different Quality of Service models, which complements several smart grid applications [20].

However, like any new technology, IPv6 too comes with a bunch of issues on which more work needs to be done. In this chapter we have focused our research towards the implementation of Smart Grid communication network using IPv6.

8.1 ICMPv6 Vulnerabilities

In this thesis, we focus on some of the possible ICMPv6 attacks that are particularly relevant in the context of building networking infrastructure between Smart Meters (SM), Data Collection Units (DCU) and Meter Data Management System (MDMS). Three main functions of NDP: Router Discovery, Duplicate Address Detection and Neighbor Discovery are discussed with respect to Smart Grid environment. We first consider the normal procedure for executing each phase, and then discuss the possible attacks. Finally a prevention procedure is given to secure the system. The proposed work considers multiple security breaches on Smart Grid and provides an IPS to prevent these attacks in Router Discovery and Updation phase as well as in Neighbor Discovery and DAD phase. This, in turn, helps preventing several attacks on ICMPv6 protocol, like DoS, man-in-the middle attack, spoofing attacks efficiently. It is also light weight and does not burden the system with unnecessary packet overhead.

IPv4 networks often filter ICMP messages to avoid security concerns. However, for IPv6, this is not possible. ICMPv6 is used for basic functionalities and used by other IPv6 protocols like Neighbor Detection Protocol (NDP). Neighbor Discovery Protocol (NDP) is a protocol used with IPv6 to perform various tasks like router discovery, auto address configuration of a node, neighbor discovery, Duplicate Address Detection, determining the Link Layer addresses of other nodes, address prefix discovery, and maintaining routing information about the paths to other active neighbor nodes [149]. Thus, the implementation of IPv6 in Smart Grid needs some serious care to protect from the security vulnerabilities of the ICMPv6 protocol. NDP uses five ICMPv6 messages. These are:

- Router Solicitation (RS) message: Hosts send RS message to enquire about a legitimate router on the link.
- Router Advertisement (RA) message: Routers send RA message, either periodically or in response to RS message.
- Neighbor Solicitation (NS) message: Hosts send NS message to determine the link layer address of a specific node, and also to verify whether an address is already present on link or not.

- Neighbor Advertisement (NA) message: Hosts send NA message in response to the NS message.
- Router Redirect (RR) message: Routers send RR message to inform a host about a better router on its link.

8.1.1 Router Discovery

When a SM X is installed in a subnet, it should find a DCU to bind with. The Smart Meter X will continue to communicate through that DCU, until it receives any ICMPv6 Router Redirect (RR) message from the previous DCU.

8.1.1.1 Normal Procedure for Router Discovery

Normally Smart Meters discover their router or DCU through the following steps,
- First, X sends an ICMPv6 Router Solicitation (RS) message to locate a DCU in its local link.
- A legitimate DCU then responds with an ICMPv6 Router Advertisement (RA) message, with a 64 bit prefix address for its subnet.
- Then X registers that DCU as its default router in the link, and auto-configures a global unicast address based on the received prefix.

8.1.1.2 Attacks in Router Discovery phase

The most prominent attack in this phase occurs if an attacker falsely claims to be a DCU. It can spoof an RA message from a legitimate DCU and send it to the Smart Meter, with or without altering the prefix address for that subnet. In either case, the newly installed Smart Meter registers the attacker as its DCU. If the adversary alters the prefix address, then the Smart Meter will auto-configure its global address based on a wrong prefix. As a result, the Smart Meter will get blocked in the subnet and will not be able to communicate with any other Smart Meter or DCU except the attacker. The situation becomes a bit more complex when the adversary sends the RA message without changing the prefix. In this situation, the Smart Meter can communicate within its subnet. However, it becomes quite impossible for the Smart Meter to communicate beyond its subnet as the registered DCU for the Smart Meter is an attacker who is not recognized by other Smart Meters in the Neighborhood Area Network.

Once an adversary successfully convinces a newly installed Smart Meter of being its valid DCU, it can launch a myriad of conventional network attacks on the Smart Grid.

It can launch a man-in-the-middle attack by intercepting packets from the Smart Meters or from the DCUs and suitable changing the Source and Destination address fields such that neither of these two entities are aware of the presence of an attacker in between. The attacker can also tweak the data contained in the intercepted packets. Another traditional network attack is the Denial-of-Service attack. The attacker can overload the network resources by generating spurious packets having the newly installed Smart Meter address as the Source Address.

8.1.2 Duplicate Address Detection

After auto configuring the address for itself, the Smart Meter X will want to know whether the address is available for use. The following steps are used for duplicated address detection.

- Smart Meter X, sends an ICMPv6 Neighbor Solicitation message for the address it wants to claim.
- If any Smart Meter on that subnet already has that address, then it sends an ICMPv6 Neighbor Advertisement message.
- If X does not receive any NA messages stating that the address has been taken, then X is able to use that address.

8.1.2.1 Attacks in Duplicate Address Detection phase

An intruder can prevent a Smart Meter from acquiring any auto-configured address, by sending an NA for the corresponding address in every NS message sent out by the Smart Meter. As a result, the Smart Meter will not be able to communicate within the network. Besides, an intruder can block a NA message from an authentic SM. This results in two or more SMs using the same address within a network. As a result of this attack, a legitimate SM can be accused of identity spoofing. Also, more than one assignment of the same address within a network can cause improper functioning during the routing phase. In order to detect these kinds of attacks, we propose a modified version of the Duplicate Address Detection phase,

- SM X sends an ICMPv6 NS message for the address it wants to acquire.
- On receiving the NS message, every Smart Meter scans its neighbor cache information for that address. If they find the address in their cache, then they send a reply to the X.

8.1. ICMPv6 Vulnerabilities

- If any Smart Meter on that subnet already has that address, then it sends an ICMPv6 NA message.
- If the X receives neither any NA messages stating that the address has been taken nor receives any messages from its neighbors stating that the address is present in their cache, then X is able to use that address.

If X receives only the NA message from another Smart Meter but no neighborhood information about that address is received, it implies that such an address the address is not in existence within the subnet and some attacker is trying to prevent X from acquiring that address. If X does not receive any NA message, but its neighbors reply with their cache information stating that the address is present in their neighborhood, then the X concludes that an attacker has intercepted the NA message from the target Smart Meter and has dropped it. Thus, X is able to use an address only when it neither receives the NA nor any neighborhood cache information from its neighbors.

If the attacker is intelligent enough, it can send both the NA message and also spoof some reply messages from other Smart Meters and change their contents. In that case, SM X will not be able to detect the attack. So, to detect this kind of attack, if a Smart Meter exists with the same address, it not only replies with an NA message but also sends its neighborhood information to X. SM X then sends unicast queries to each of the neighbors found in the reply message to verify the existence of such a Smart Meter. In this way, X can be assured whether he is being duped or whether the particular address is really being used within the subnet. However, since the reply message can also be intercepted by the attacker, it must be broadcast within the network. This will assure the delivery of the reply message to X.

8.1.3 Neighbor Discovery

Once the Smart Meter acquires a unique global address, then it can start communication through the DCU. It can also communicate with the other Smart Meters, both in its subnet and in other subnets. Smart Meters on the same subnet can communicate directly with each other without using any router or gateway when a SM has link layer addresses of other neighboring SMs. Thus it is important to store the link layer addresses of the neighboring SMs in the local cache of every SM. Neighbor Discovery facilitates the same.

8.1.3.1 Normal Procedure for Neighbor Discovery

In order to communicate with a SM B on its own subnet, a Smart Meter A has to perform the following steps,
- First, the SM A sends an ICMPv6 NS message requesting the link-layer address of B.
- If B is present in that subnet, then it replies with an ICMPv6 NA message. SM A knows the MAC address of B from this NA message.
- SM A then creates a neighbor cache entry for B that binds the MAC address of B to its IPv6 address.

8.1.3.2 Attacks in Neighbor Discovery phase

The attacks of this phase are similar to the attacks of the Duplicate Address Detection phase. Here also an intruder can try to impersonate B, and intercept all packets that are destined to B, or an intruder can block a NA reply from B so that A thinks that B is not present in the network.

8.1.4 Proposed Intrusion Prevention System

Figure 8.1 shows a high level view of intrusion detection in Router Discovery and Updation phase, when an attacker spoofs a RA message from DCU and sends it to a Smart Meter X without changing the 64 bit prefix address. In the first half of the figure, an attacker spoofs a RA message and sends it to the newly installed Smart Meter X. In the second half of the figure, an attacker broadcasts a RA message to all the working Smart Meters. Figure 8.2 shows a high level view of intrusion detection in Duplicate Address Detection phase, when X verifies the presence of another SM in the subnet, with same address. An attacker blocks an NA message from an authentic SM X. Figure 8.3 shows a high level view of intrusion detection in Neighbor Discovery phase, when DCU X wants to communicate with Z, but attacker tries to impersonate Z.

8.1.5 Results

Negative occurs when a system cannot detect an attack. False negatives are often a greater threat than false positives. If there wasn't an attack and the system makes a false detection, it can affect the throughput at most. However, if there was an attack and the system is not able to detect it, then it may be disastrous. However, in our proposed IPS,

8.1. ICMPv6 Vulnerabilities

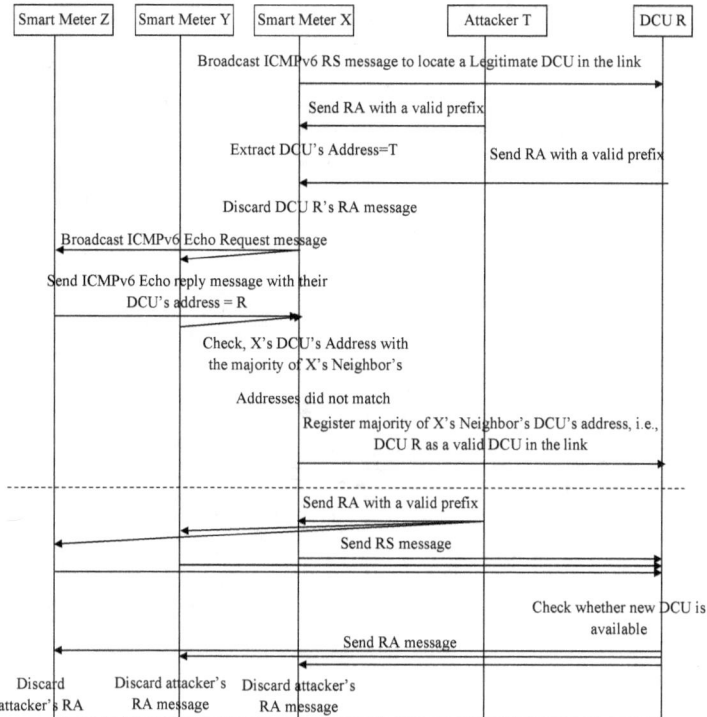

Figure 8.1: High level view of Intrusion Prevention in Router Discovery and Updation phase.

there are no false positives for relatively smaller number of intruders. However, the IPS suffers from false negatives with increasing percentage of malicious nodes. Figure 6 shows that there are no false negative for 2, 4, or 6 malicious nodes out of 50 nodes. The false negative increases with increasing number of malicious nodes. Figure 8.4 and 8.5 show the effect on false negatives with a linear percentage of malicious nodes. The experimental results are in line with reality where any IPS system fails when majority of nodes become compromised.

8. IMPLEMENTING COMMUNICATION NETWORK USING IPv6

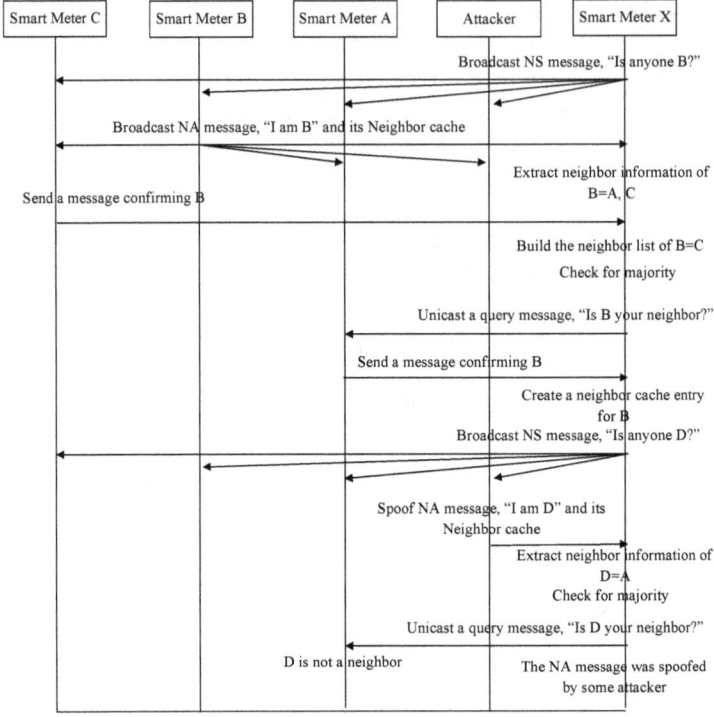

Figure 8.2: High level view of Intrusion Prevention in Duplicate Address Detection phase.

8.2 Address Configuration

Another concern of using IPv6 is the addressing structure for proper utilization of 128 bits for Smart Grid components. Smart Grid relies on a hierarchical architecture and the topology of every layer of hierarchy is different. The level of hierarchies will change dynamically with the density of Smart Meters in a particular area. A new IPv6 address configuration schema for Smart Grid has been proposed. The proposed schema is consistent with the demands of large, dynamic, hierarchical smart grid network. The schema improves accessibility and scalability in terms of configuring a huge number of devices in the smart grid, thereby, fully extracting the potential of 128-bit IPv6 addressing mode.

8.2. Address Configuration

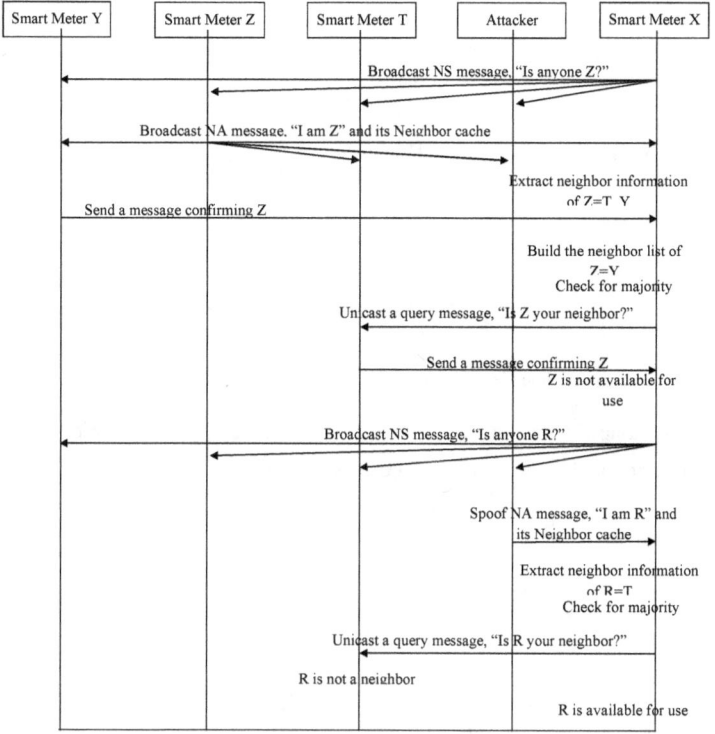

Figure 8.3: High level view of Intrusion Detection in Neighbor Discovery phase.

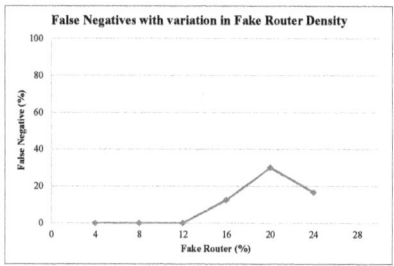

Figure 8.4: False Negative vs. Number of Malicious DCUs.

155

8. Implementing communication network using IPv6

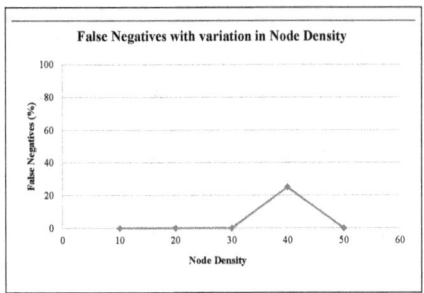

Figure 8.5: False Negative vs. Node density.

8.2.1 Proposed Addressing Format

We propose a new addressing format for IPv6, suitable for the dynamic hierarchical communication architecture of Smart Grid as in figure 8.6.

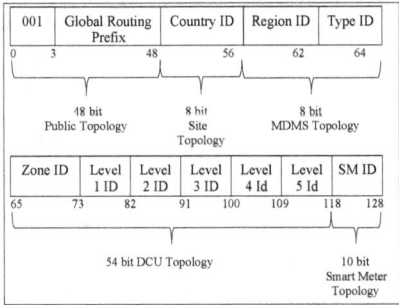

Figure 8.6: Proposed IPv6 addressing structure.

- **The three high-order bits** and **Global Routing Prefix** fields are same as the Global Unicast address format [148].
- **Country ID** is used within an organization's site to identify different countries within its site. The size of this field is 8 bits. Country ID is identical for every MDMS, DCU and Smart Meter within a country.
- **Region ID** is used within a country's site to identify different regions within the country. The size of this field is 6 bits. Every region should have a MDMS. Region ID is identical for every DCU and Smart Meter within a Particular region, i.e., under a all DCUs and Smart Meters under a specific MDMS will have the same Region ID.

8.2. Address Configuration

- **Zone ID** is used within a region's site to identify different zones within the region. The size of this field is 9 bit. Every zone should have a DCU and these DCUs are called to be the Level-0 DCU. Zone ID for each zone is identical, i.e., all DCUs and Smart Meters under a specific zone or Level-0 DCU will have the same Zone ID.
- **Type ID** identifies whether an address specifies a DCU or Smart Meter or MDMS. It consists of 2 bits. If its a MDMS then Id=11, if a DCU then Type ID=01 and for Smart Meter, Type ID=10.
- **Smart Meter ID** Last 10 bits of the address are used to identify individual Smart Meters. Therefore, maximum of 2^{10} SMs can be accommodated under a DCU.
- **Level x ID** We can divide the rest 45 bits in 5, 9 bit groups. Each group denotes a certain level of hierarchy. With this structure, we assume that maximum of 29 DCUs can be allocated under its upper level DCU. If the number goes beyond that, then we have to build a new DCU in the hierarchy. For all Level x DCUs, under the same zone, all the previous Level IDs, i.e., Level x to Level 1 will be identical.

The public topology and site topology are same as the Global Unicast address format [148]. MDMS topology is the collection of MDMSs within a country of an organization. DCU topology is the collection of DCUs under a particular MDMS of a region. Smart Meter topology specifies a Smart Meter in the zone.

The proposed algorithms for address configuration of a Smart Meter and DCU are given in figure 8.7 and 8.8 respectively.

8.2.2 Performance analysis

In this section, we will discuss the performance of the proposed address configuration scheme for IPv6. A couple of aspects on which the performances are estimated are mentioned below.

8.2.2.1 Accessible from wider internet:

In the proposed addressing scheme, the first 48 bits of the 128 bit IPv6 address is unaltered. According to the general format for IPv6 Global unicast address [148], the combination of first 48 bits, i.e., the three fixed bits 001 and global routing prefix is used to create a site prefix. These 48 bits are unique for each organization. Rest of the 80 bits may be used to configure the subnets in a manner such that the accessibility increases

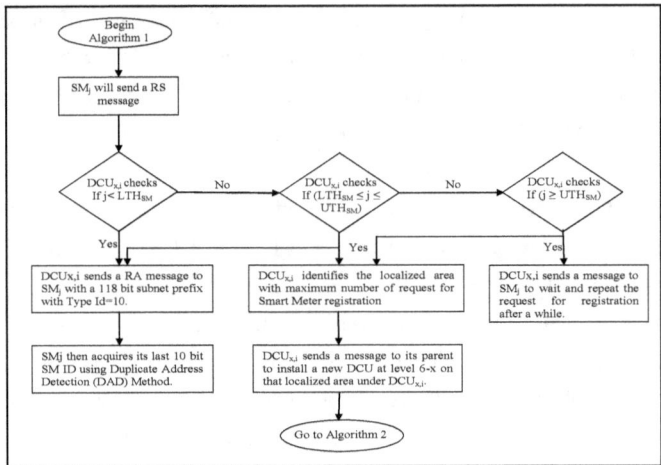

Figure 8.7: Flow chart for address configuration of a Smart Meter.

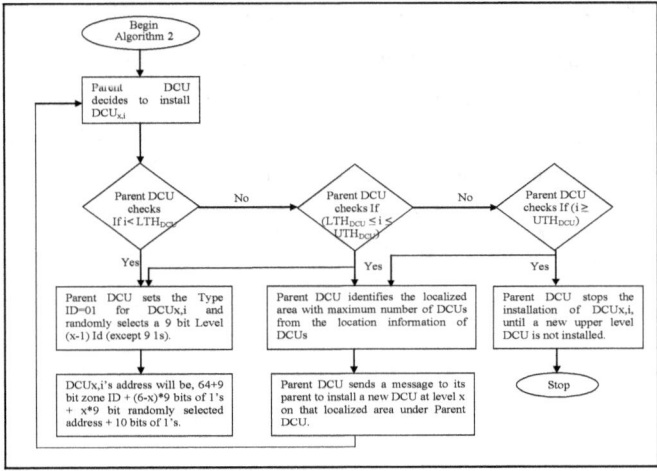

Figure 8.8: Flow chart for address configuration of a DCU.

for specific application domains [143, 144]. Again, it will not be a problem to connect with the wider internet as the first 48 bits are not modified.

8.2. Address Configuration

8.2.2.2 Scalable:

As par the general format of the IPv6 address, a specific organization can have at most 2^{16} subnets and each subnet can accommodate 2^{64} nodes. This gives total $2^{(16+64)}$, i.e.

$$2^{80} \text{ unique addresses for each organization.}$$

However, in Smart Grid environment, there already exist a three level hierarchy of MDMS, DCU and Smart Meters and it is not possible to allocate that huge number of SMs under a DCU. Every DCU can communicate with not more than 1000 Smart Meters for a Smart Grid network. Now, 10 bits will be enough to accommodate 1000 SMs, the rest of 54 bits will be left unused. i.e., maximum $2^{(10+16)} = 2^{26}$ SMs can be allocated in the network. This gives only,

$(2^{26}/2^{80}) * 100\% = 5.55 * 10^{-15}\%$ usage of the total address space for an organization.

Now, according to our proposed addressing format described in figure 8.6, every organization can spread its business across 2^8, i.e., 256 countries. Every country can be divided in maximum 2^6, i.e., 64 regions. Every region will have a MDMS. Each region can be further divided into maximum 2^9, i.e., 512 zones. Each zone is headed by a DCU. So, at the beginning, every organization can set up this primary infrastructure for providing Smart Grid facilities. In this framework, it is assumed that, each DCU can have at most 900 Smart Meters under it. If the number of SMs exceeds 900 then a new DCU will be established by the utility and the load will be shifted to the new DCU. Now, 10 bits will be enough to accommodate 900 SMs, the rest of 45 bits will be left unused. Thus, to properly utilize the address space, a 5-level hierarchy is proposed. This hierarchy ensures that maximum of $2^{(10+8+6+9*6)}$ SMs can be accommodated in the network. This gives,

$(2^{78}/2^{80}) * 100\% = 25\%$ usage of the total address space for an organization.

Figure 8.9 states the usage of total address space under each organization for different addressing formats. The address space utilization for our proposed method is almost $4.5 * 10^{15}$ times greater than the number of SMs used using general IPv6 format. The usage percentage is also 25% for each organization, which is much better compare to the other formats. Thus, this architecture can increase the scalability of the network.

8. Implementing communication network using IPv6

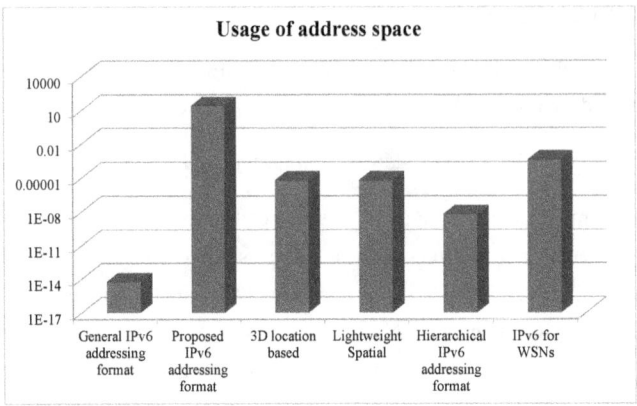

Figure 8.9: Address space utilization for various addressing formats.

8.3 Conclusions

Integrating IPv6 with Smart Grid is quite natural, as only IPv6 could match the size of Smart Grid network. The large address space, auto configuration of addresses, QoS support technology helps Smart grid to construct a large network with a unique address specified for each and every device, efficient routing, end-to-end security. However, smart grid has very high security demand that needs to be considered before deploying IPv6 towards building Smart Grid. In this chapter, the problems of using ICMPv6 in NDP and the possible effects of these problems on Smart Grid are considered. Besides, a new address format of IPv6 Global Unicast addressing towards supporting the dynamic hierarchical communication architecture of Smart Grid Network and address configuration methods for both Smart Meters and DCUs are proposed.

Three main functions of NDP: Router Discovery, Duplicate Address Detection and Neighbor Discovery are discussed with respect to Smart Grid environment. We first consider the normal procedure for executing each phase, and then we discuss the possible attacks. Finally a prevention procedure is given to secure the system. This intrusion prevention system helps preventing several attacks on ICMPv6 protocol, like DoS, man-in-the-middle attack, spoofing attacks efficiently. It is also light weight and does not burden the system with unnecessary packet overhead. The proposed work considers multiple security breaches on Smart Grid and provides an IPS to prevent these attacks in Router Discovery and Updation phase as well as in Neighbor Discovery and

DAD phase.

The proposed addressing schema is better than the general IPv6 addressing structure, in terms of better utilization of address space and supporting the dynamic hierarchical architecture of Smart Grid. Besides, it also helps Smart Grid to become more scalable. This method reduces the address configuration delay, as the configuration process done locally. Besides it also reduces the burden of MDMS for configuring the address of each DCU under it. in this method each DCU can configure the address of its children DCUs. The proposed methodology builds the foundation for several meaningful extensions in future. In continuation to the proposed work, it would be interesting to develop a new routing protocol for the last mile communication in Smart Grid.

CHAPTER 9

CONFIGURATION AND COMPLIANCE MANAGEMENT FRAMEWORK

In order to overcome the problems identified in chapter 7, we propose a new framework for providing configuration and compliance management of components of a system. This model consists of three layers: component management, configuration management and compliance management. The component management layer deals with the selection of components and assembling them. It also modifies and replaces components if necessary. The configuration management layer keeps tracks of the dependencies and relationships between the components. It also analyzes them for achieving maintainability. The compliance management layer is responsible for compliance checking of each component, as well as the total system. We also propose an algorithm to find the effect propagation within a system, when a primitive component is modified. The algorithm is able to identify sets of primitive and composite components, which may get affected with the modification of a certain primitive component. Thus, it helps to configure a system properly. Thus we propose a layered model which incorporates configuration management and compliance checking with CBSD.

9.1 Working Principle of the Proposed Framework

In this section, we proposed a new framework for configuration of components of a component based software with run time compliance checking. The proposed model

has three different parts:
1) Component Management
2) Configuration Management
3) Compliance Management

9.1.1 Component Management

The Component management part basically deals with the selection of composite and primitive components and maintains their relationships in the form of a list. The functions of the Component management are:
- Select Components: The component manager first identifies the composite components of the system. Then for each composite component, primitive components are selected from the component repository.
- Modify Components: It is not always possible to find the exact component, which meets the requirements of the system. So, then the Component manager modifies the components according to the requirements and adapts them to the system.
- Integrate Component: After collecting all the primitive components, the component manager integrates those primitive components to develop a composite component. The interconnections and dependencies between the composite components are also maintained by the component manager.
- Replace Component: The component manager also replaces the older versions of a component by the newer and upgraded versions of that component.

Component layer stores the architectural design of the whole system.

Architectural Design of The System Main objective of architecture is to define the structure and behavior of the system. Besides, the architectural design includes *Pre_Compliance_Rules* and *Post_Compliance_Rules*. The compliance rules are derived from the design documents of the system. For any sub-system S its corresponding Architectural Design can be defined as

$$AD = (C, \Delta_i, \delta_o, \Gamma_{Post}, \Gamma_{Pre})$$

where,
1) C defines the total number of components in the system. In context of this framework, a component is a task specific modular part of a system, which provides interfaces to other components for data communication. A component

may be replaced by one or more off the shelf components while building the system, which again may be replaced by multiple primitive components if satisfies their integrated requirements.

Besides a component can be defined by its properties as,
$$C = (I_{in}, I_{out}, F)$$
Where,

- I_{in} = Number of components from which it takes inputs.
- I_{out} = Number of components to which it sends it outputs.
- F = set of specific functions or tasks. Each fuction is expressed as a set of atomic propositions, where an atomic proposition is defined as a declarative sentence that is either true or false and cannot be simplified further without modifying the logical equivalence of the proposition. Each atomic proposition is expressed in First Order Logic (FOL).

2) Δ_i is the interface matrix. It defines the relation between components with respect to interfaces. Δ_i can be expressed as an (m*m) matrix, where m is the total number of components in the system.

$$\Delta_i[p][q] = 1, \text{ if } C_p \text{ and } C_q \text{ are connected through an interface (either } I_{in} \text{ or } I_{out})$$
$$= 0 \text{ otherwise.}$$

3) δ_o can be defined as a function, mapping (c*Φ) to (s), where

- c ∈ C and denotes all the components which have an interface to other existing sub systems in the system.
- s ∈ S and denotes all the existing sub systems of the system which are connected to this component.
- Φ denotes the set of events, which triggers the data and control information interchange.

δ_o describes the degree of backward compatibility of a system. It denotes the dependency between newly installed components with pre existing sub systems within the system.

4) Γ_{Post} defines a set of *Pre Compliance Rules* for each component.

Pre Compliance Rules are requirements and constraints that the system should achieve before the execution of that component. These rules are prerequisite for each component. A component cannot function accordingly and provide the desired goal if the system violates any of these rules.

5) Γ_{Pre} defines a set of *Post Compliance Rules* for each component.

Post Compliance Rules for each composite component defines the requirements and constraints that the system should achieve after the execution of that component. The end results of an individual component must satisfy these rules to ensure stability, maintainability and proper synchronization of the system.

Both of these sets of rules, i.e., Γ_{Post} and Γ_{Pre} are expressed as a set of atomic propositions, where an atomic proposition is defined as a declarative sentence that is either true or false and cannot be simplified further without modifying the logical equivalence of the proposition. Each atomic proposition is expressed in First Order Logic (FOL).

9.1.2 Configuration Management

The configuration management part deals with the version management of each primitive components and how it affects the whole system. Since primitive components are interrelated, modification in one primitive component leads to the modification of its dependent components.

The functions of Configuration Management are:

- Monitor: the configuration manager monitors the whole system to assure that its working properly and consistently.
- Select a component for modification: While monitoring the system, the configuration manager also maintains a database for storing the versions of each component. If a new version of a component arrives in the market, then the configuration manager identifies that component for modification.
- Identify all the related components: Modifying one primitive component at run time may affect all the other primitive components related with that component, and also the composite components which are associated with them. So to maintain consistency it is necessary to modify all the other components. Configuration manager uses an algorithm, depicts in 9, to identify the related components of an primitive component.
- Modify: After identifying the components, the configuration manager modifies the components accordingly.
- Report to Component management: Then configuration manager reports to the component manager about these modifications. The component manager then

9.1. Working Principle of the Proposed Framework

checks the newly modified components and sends them to compliance manager to make sure that they comply with the business rules of the company.
- Store: after the compliance checking of the modified components, the configuration manager stores the new versions of those components in a database.

Besides, we propose two algorithms: i) the first algorithm selects the minimal set of primitive components to achieve the functionalities of each composite component, considering architectural compliance with the system and ii) the second algorithm finds the effect propagation within a system, when a primitive component is modified. This algorithm is able to identify sets of primitive and composite components, which may get affected with the modification of a certain primitive component. Thus, it helps to configure a system properly.

In order to verify the compliance for each component as well as the whole system, we propose a two tier compliance verification model. The first tier works with individual component integration. The primary job of this tier is to ensure that a composite component is integrated using only those primitive components whose combined effects comply with the pre defined semantic effects of the activity as well as the compliance rules.

The second tier of compliance verification works with individual traces of the BPMN diagram and it concerns with the compliance through the execution trace of an individual component, that is, the cumulative compliance checking for each component. This phase ensures that the integrated component is consistent with its previous components.

The workflow diagram of our proposed framework is depicted in figure 9.1.

Configuration management layer maintains two arrays:

P_{Array}- for storing primitive components, which are related to a particular primitive component P_i.

C_{Array}- for storing the Composite Components, which are related with a particular Primitive Component P_i.

Suppose a primitive Component P_j has been modified and a new version of P_j, i.e. $P_{j.1}$ is introduced. The purpose of algorithm 9 is to identify the related primitive as well as composite components.

Let us assume that a system has 8 composite components. Figure 9.2 describes the structure for 8 composite components. Suppose primitive component P5 has been modified due to some reasons. Therefore a new version of P5 is introduced as P5.1. In order to maintain the concurrency and compatibility, we must check the other primitive

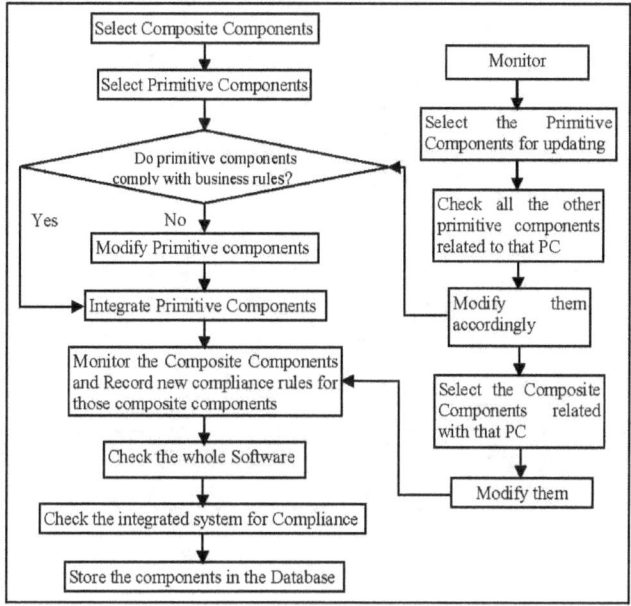

Figure 9.1: Workflow diagram of proposed framework.

Algorithm 8: Algorithm for identifying dependent components

1　Start;
2　**for** $i = 1$ *to* n **do**
3　　check the list for each C_i;
4　　**if** P_j *is in the list of* C_i *and* C_i *is not in* C_{Array} **then**
5　　　put C_i in a C_{Array};
6　　　**for** *other primitive components in the list of* C_i **do**
7　　　　**if** *they already exist in the* P_{Array} **then**
8　　　　　break;
9　　　　**else**
10　　　　　put the primate component in P_{Array};
11　　　　**end**
12　　　**end**
13　　**end**
14　**end**
15　End;

---

components that are related to P5. In cascade, the Composite Components which depends on those primitive components will also be checked.

9.1. Working Principle of the Proposed Framework

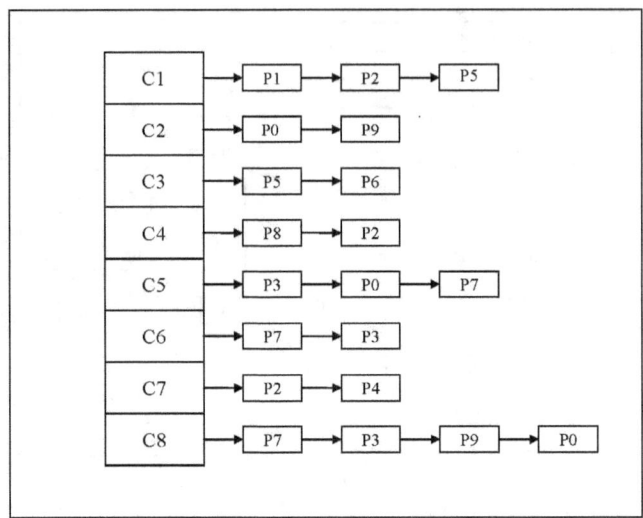

Figure 9.2: Component relation structure.

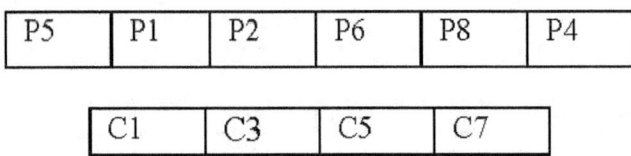

Figure 9.3: Content of C_{Array} and P_{Array}.

First, we find P5 from the component table. It has been found in the list of C1. Then C1 is added in the C_{Array}, and all other primitive components of C1, i.e. P1 and P2 are added in the P_{Array}. Next, P5 is also in the list of C3. So we put C3 in C_{Array} and P6 in P_{Array}. P5 is not connected with any other composite component. So we take the second element from the P_{Array}, i.e. P1, and repeat the same procedure. P1 is not connected with any other composite component, so we move on to the next primitive component in P_{Array}, P2. P2 is in the list of C4 and C7. So we put both of them in C_{Array}, and add their primitive components, i.e. P8 and P4 in P_{Array}. The next primitive components in P_{Array} are P6, P8 and P4. Since they are not in the list of any other composite components, the procedure is terminated. Figure 9.3 shows the content of P_{Array} and C_{Array}.

9.1.3 Compliance Management

The compliance management layer is responsible for checking the compliance of each individual component and as well as the whole system. It also records new compliance rules through the development process of the system. The functions of this layer are described in the next section.

9.1.3.1 Compliance Checking

In order to verify the compliance for each component as well as the whole system, we propose a two tier compliance verification model. The first tier works with individual component integration. The primary job of this tier is to ensure that a composite component is integrated using only those primitive components whose combined effects comply with the pre defined semantic effects of the activity as well as the compliance rules.

The second tier of compliance verification works with individual traces of the BPMN diagram and it concerns with the compliance through the execution trace of an individual component, that is, the cumulative compliance checking for each component. This phase ensures that the integrated component is consistent with its previous components.

First Phase - Compliance for Component Integration Let us assume that we want to develop composite component B. Now, we already know that, B has to comply with *Compliance Rules*: $C(x) \wedge C(y) \wedge C(z)$ and the effects should match with the Compliance Effects: {p, q, r, s}. [As Comply (t1, 2) = C (x) C (y) C (z) and Effect (t1, 2) = p, q, r, s].

We may have multiple primitive components available off the shelf that satisfy some subset of these conditions as well as some additional constraints. For example, let P1, P2, P3, P4 be four such off-the-shelf components that satisfy the effects (p, q, $\neg t$), (r, s, t), (p, r), and (q, s), respectively. In order to build the entire system, we have to integrate only those primitive components which satisfy two conditions: Entailment and Consistency [172].

Entailment The combined *Pre Compliance Rules* and *Post Compliance Rules* of primitive components should satisfy the *Pre Compliance Rules* and *Post Compliance Rules* of the entire composite component.

9.1. Working Principle of the Proposed Framework

For example, primitive components P1 and P2 can be combined to satisfy all the four conditions (p, q, r, s). Similarly, P3 and P4 can also be combined to satisfy the system conditions. Thus,

$$(p, q, \neg t) \wedge (r, s, t) \vdash (p, q, r, s, \neg t, t).$$
$$(p, r) \wedge (q, s) \vdash (p, q, r, s).$$

Suppose composite component C is developed by integrating primitive components P1, P2... Pn, then,

$$(P1.\textit{Post Compliance Rules} \wedge P2.\textit{Post Compliance Rules} \wedge \ldots \wedge$$
$$Pn.\textit{Post Compliance Rules}) \vdash C.\textit{Post Compliance Rules}$$

and

$$(P1.\textit{Pre Compliance Rules} \wedge P2.\textit{Pre Compliance Rules} \wedge \ldots \wedge$$
$$Pn.\textit{Pre Compliance Rules}) \vdash C.\textit{Pre Compliance Rules}$$

Consistency The combined effect of the primitive components should be logically consistent, i.e., they should not derive falsity.

For example, P1 and P2 satisfies all the system constraints but are mutually inconsistent as

$$(p, q, \neg t) \wedge (r, s, t) \models F$$

On the other hand, P3 and P4 are mutually consistent and entail the system conditions as well.

$$(p, r) \wedge (q, s) \models T$$

Thus, we can generalize this as,

$$(P1.\textit{Post Compliance Rules} \wedge P2.\textit{Post Compliance Rules} \wedge \ldots \wedge$$
$$Pn.\textit{Post Compliance Rules}) \not\models F$$

and

$$(P1.\textit{Pre Compliance Rules} \wedge P2.\textit{Pre Compliance Rules} \wedge \ldots \wedge$$
$$Pn.\textit{Pre Compliance Rules}) \not\models F$$

Minimality The minimality criterion tries to extract that particular set of primitive components that minimize a certain criterion or soft goal. Soft goals usually represent QoS parameters. To evaluate the minimal combination of primitive components, we need to annotate each primitive component with respect to that particular soft goal.

Once this is done we find out all combinations of primitive components that satisfy Entailment and Consistency and select that particular combination which minimizes the selected soft goal. Then the compliance manager reports to the component management layer, and the component management layer integrates those primitive components.

Second Phase To ensure compliance through an entire execution trace in the BPMN diagram we have to ensure that the post execution effects of each component is consistent with the previous components in that trace. i.e., the immediate effects of component H should be consistent with the cumulative effects of H for every traces with H in it. As an example, H is a part of three traces in the diagram: t_1, t_2 and t_3.

Besides, it may sometime possible to invoke some extra compliance rules and effects while integrating primitive components. In such cases, it is necessary to validate these new rules with respect to the cumulative rules and effects of each trace in which the components participate.

Thus the immediate effect of H should be consistent with the cumulative effects of (A, B, C, H), (A, B, D, F, H) and (A, B, D, G, F, H).

Now, the cumulative rule and effect of each trace can be calculated using the union of individual rules and effects of each components in that trace. Thus we can verify the compliance of the whole system by ensuring that the immediate effects and compliance rules of the collective primitive components are consistent and entailed with the cumulative rules and effects of the trace.

Algorithms Algorithm 9 describes the process of primitive component selection for a particular composite component C. Suppose the algorithm takes N primitive components as input and considering Entailment, Consistency and Minimality criteria, gives the best set of primitive components to achieve the functionality of C.

Algorithm 10 finds all possible subsets over Pi's (for all i=n) which satisfies the Entailment criteria and gives *Entailed_Components* set and algorithm 11 provides the lists from *Entailed_Components* set which satisfy the Consistency criteria. Finally

9.1. Working Principle of the Proposed Framework

Algorithm 9: $Compliance\_Checking(C, P_1, P_2, \ldots, P_n, N)$

Input: C: Structure of the composite component C.
$P_1, P_2, \ldots, P_n$: Structure of N primitive components.
N: number of primitive components to be considered.

Output: $Primitive\_Component$: Best set of primitive components for composite component C.

1 initialization;
2 $Entailed\_Components = Entailment\_Checking(C, P1, P2\ldots Pn, N)$;
3 $Consistent\_Components = Consistency\_Checking\ (Entailed\_Components)$;
4 $Primitive\_Component = Minimality\_Checking\ (Consistent\_Components, M_1, M_2, \ldots, M_t, t)$;
```
/* Record new compliance rules                              */
/* "-" denotes the set difference operation.                */
```
5 $Additional\_Pre\_Compliance\_Rules = (C.Pre\_Compliance\_Rules - Primitive\_Component.Pre\_Compliance\_Rules)$;
6 $Additional\_Post\_Compliance\_Rules = (C.Post\_Compliance\_Rules - Primitive\_Component.Post\_Compliance\_Rules)$;

---

12 identifies the best possible set of primitive components, that satisfies all of the three criterias, i.e., entailment, Consistency and Minimality.

Algorithm 10: $Entailment\_Checking(C, P_1, P_2, \ldots, P_n, N)$

Input: C: Structure of the composite component C.
$P_1, P_2, \ldots, P_n$: Structure of N primitive components.
N: number of primitive components to be considered.

Output: $Entailed\_Component$: Structure of sets, contains the union of two or more primitive components which holds the entailment criteria.

1 initialization;
2 Find all possible subsets from $(P_1, P_2, \ldots, P_n)$, excluding the null set 0 and all the singleton sets, i.e., $P_1, P_2, \ldots, P_n$;
3 $t = 2^N - N - 1$;
4 **for** $i = 1$ *to* t **do**
5 $\quad (Pre\_Compliance\_Rules) = \forall(\text{primitive components in ith subset}), \cup_i P_i.Pre\_Compliance\_Rules)$;
6 $\quad (Post\_Compliance\_Rules) = (\forall(\text{primitive components in ith subset}), \cup_i P_i.Post\_Compliance\_Rules)$;
7 **end**
8 **if** $C.Pre\_Compliance\_Rules \in (P_i.Pre\_Compliance\_Rules))\ \&\&\ (C.Post\_Compliance\_Rules \in (Subset\_Pi.Post\_Compliance\_Rules)$ **then**
9 $\quad Entailed\_Components_k := Subset\_P_i$;
10 $\quad k=k+1$;
11 **end**

---

9. Configuration and Compliance Management Framework

Algorithm 11: $Consistency\_Checking(Entailed\_Components)$

Input: $Entailed\_Component$: Structure of sets, contains the union of two or more primitive components which holds the entailment criteria.

Output: $Consistent\_Component$: A structure of sets contains the union of two or more primitive components which holds both the entailment criteria and consistent criteria.

1 initialization;
2 count = number of elements in $Entailed\_Components$;
3 **for** $i = 1$ *to* count **do**
4   **if** $(\forall i, \wedge_i Entailed\_Components_i.Pre\_compliance\_Rules) \not= F$ &&
     $(\forall i, \wedge_i Entailed\_Components_i.Post\_compliance\_Rules) \not= F$ **then**
5        $Consistent\_Components = Entailed\_Components_i$;
6   **end**
7 **end**

Algorithm 12: $Minimality\_Checking(Consistent\_Components)$

Input: $Consistent\_Component$: Structure of sets, contains the union of two or more primitive components which holds the entailment and consistent criterias.
$M1, M2...MT$: QoS parameters of individual primitive components.
$\delta M1, \delta M2...\delta MT$: System Tolerability for each QoS parameter. It defines the level up to which the system can perform efficiently without compromising the Quality of Service.

Output: $Primitive_Component$: The best possible combination of primitive components which satisfies Entailment, Consistency and Minimality.

1 initialization;
2 count = number of elements in $Consistent\_Components$;
3 temp = 0;
4 **for** $i = 1$ *to* count **do**
5   **for** $j = 1$ *to* T **do**
6        $\lambda j = \delta M j - M j$ $//\lambda j$ gives the difference between system's tolerance and component's value for a QoS parameter.
7        $Consistent\_Components_i.Minimality\_Score+ = \lambda j$;
8   **end**
9   // sort the components according to their Minimality_Score. **if** $Consistent\_Components_i.Minimality\_Score > temp$ **then**
10        $temp = Consistent\_Components_i.Minimality\_Score$;
11        $Primitive\_Component = Consistent\_Components_i$;
12   **end**
13 **end**

9.1.3.2 Record New Rules

While integrating the primitive components, it is sometimes necessary that the components, both primitive and composite, should comply with some new rules for successful

9.1. Working Principle of the Proposed Framework

execution. Thus, another function of compliance manager is to record new compliance rules at run time and keep the business rule database up to date with each change in the system.

9.1.3.3 Monitor The Integrated System for Compliance

Compliance of each primitive and composite component does not always imply that the whole system is also compliant with the business rules. Therefore, after checking the primitive and composite components for compliance, the compliance manager monitors the whole integrated system for compliance. A baseline is approved only when the system is compliant with the business policies.

9.1.4 System Design

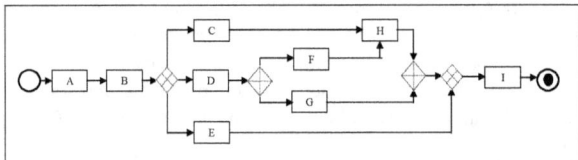

Figure 9.4: Business Process diagram.

In order to describe our framework, we used Business Process Modelling Notation (BPMN) to design the system. Figure 9.4 describes an example of a BPMN, which is a graphical design document that helps a business organization to model different activities during system design phase. Generally a simple BPMN diagram consists of two types of objects:

- Flow objects and
- Connecting objects.

The combination of flow and connecting objects defines the possible ways in which a process can be executed. Where a possible execution is called process trace or simply trace.

BPMN is an internationally accepted, model-independent tool, which can create a bridge to reduce the gap between business processes and their implementations by providing a unified and standardized graphical representation of any business model. Thus, as a basis of our proposed framework, we use BPMN, to graphically describe smart meter systems, and analyze the effect of component changes on the whole system.

When a change request is placed, then the aftereffects of the change for each individual component, as well as the cumulative effect on the whole system is analyzed using semantic effect annotations [168]. This helps identifying the affected components through change propagation and also how the system can be re-configured for a particular change request. The objective is to compare the results produced by the proposed algorithm vis-à-vis finding from BPMN.

Now, compliance rules are an integral part of business process development. By combining compliance rules in BPMN, we can be able to generate a system design document that will be compliant with the rules and regulations of the organization. In order to achieve this, we have associated a data file with each activity in the system, called Compliance Rules and followed by semantic effect annotations, which describes the outcome of the execution of that activity or compliance Effects. Our purpose is to select appropriate components for each activity such that the cumulative effects confirm the associated compliance rules as well as achieve the desired objectives.

Let us assume, *Voltage Step Down* is an activity, associated with the following Compliance Rule:

$$\text{Upper\_Threshold (t)} \land \text{Lower\_Threshold (t)} \land \text{Noise (n)} \land \text{Heat (h)}$$

where,
- Upper_Threshold (t): Output Voltage t is greater than X kW.
- Lower_Threshold (t): Output Voltage t is less than Y kW.
- Noise (n): Noise n is less than N.
- Heat (h): Generated heat during the process is less than H.

And the Effects are (t, n, h), where,
- t: Output Voltage
- n: Noise Level in the output voltage.
- h: generated heat during the process.

Each Compliance Rules is expressed in conjunctive normal form, i.e. each rule is a conjunction (logical "and") of clauses, where each clause is a disjunction (logical "or") of literals. Literals are predicate symbols that may be positive or negative. Each literal can contain variables. These variables denote the semantic effects of each activity and can be expressed as atomic propositions, where an atomic proposition is defined as a declarative sentence that is either true or false and cannot be simplified further without modifying the logical equivalence of the proposition. All these propositions and

9.1. Working Principle of the Proposed Framework

predicate symbols are quantified universally, and range over the entities of interest at process execution time. Each clause is a constraint on the activities that are desirable as per the norms and regulations of the system; if the effects of any activity do not satisfy the rules, then that state is noncompliant. Due to the outer conjunction, all clauses must be satisfied.

Thus, we can annotate the compliance rules and effects for each activity in a BPMN diagram activity can be represented formally as-

Now Let, T is the set of traces in a BPMN diagram, T= $t_1, t_2...t_n$, where

n is the total number of traces and each t_i consists of activities in sequential order and represents a unique trace.

Then, we can write the functions as:

$$\text{Comply: } T \times \mathbb{N} \rightarrow \wedge_\lambda$$
$$\text{Effect: } T \times \mathbb{N} \rightarrow 2^\tau$$

where, λ is the set of clauses of predicate logic used to model the compliance rules and τ is the set of variables of propositional language used to model the semantic effects.

The function Comply returns a conjunctive normal form of compliance rules that an activity in a trace has to fulfil to comply with the rules and regulations of the organization.

On the other hand, the function Effect gives the effects of an activity that should confirms the compliance rules.

Consider the BPMN diagram of Figure 9.4,

$T = t_1, t_2, t_3, t_4$, where
$t_1 = A, B, C, H, I$
$t_2 = A, B, D, F, H, G, I$
$t_3 = A, B, D, G, F, H, I$
$t_4 = A, B, E, I$

Now,

$$\text{Comply }(t_1, 4) = C(x) \wedge C(y) \wedge C(z) \text{ and}$$
$$\text{Effect }(t_1, 4) = p, q, r$$

describes that fourth activity in trace t_1, i.e., H has to comply with Compliance Rules: C(x), C(y) and C(z) and as a result of their association the output of that activity should match with the effects: {p, q, r}.

9. Configuration and Compliance Management Framework

Our main objective is to build a system using component based software development strategy, that ensures compliance checking while integrating components. For that, we assume each activity in the BPMN diagram as a composite component and every composite components is developed using one or more primitive components such that the new developed component can fulfil the desired objectives as well as comply with all the normative requirements of the organization.

When a change request is placed, then the after effects of the change for each individual component, as well as the cumulative effect on the whole system is analyzed using semantic effect annotations of BPMN. This helps identifying the components affected by the change and also how the system can be re-configured for a particular change request.

9.1.5 Verification of the Configuration Management Layer

We assume that, there are 5 basic services provided by a smart meter. We consider these five services as five composite components and each composite component further decomposed into several primitive components.

Table 9.1: Coefficients of weather related predictor variables for Residential and Commercial sectors

Composite components	Primitive Components
C1: Generate the total electricity consumption of a user.	P1: Decode Receive message from DCU.
	P2: Collect the total unit of usage.
	P3: Generate the bill.
	P4: Send message to DCU.
C2: Send SMS, if the consumption unit of a user exceeds its previous bill.	P5: check the current unit of usage, with previous bill.
	P6: Generate an alert message for excess bill amount.
	P7: Generate a intermediate bill.
	P8: Send message to the user.
C3: Alert user before power cuts.	P1: Decode Receive message from DCU.
	P8: Send message to the user.
	P9: Generate an alert SMS for power cut.
C4: Services provided for users, who generate electricity in their own houses.	P10: Check the electricity generation of a home.
	P11: Draw current from home electricity source.
	P12: Draw current from outside electricity source.
	P13: Check if, generated electricity is sufficient for the home.
	P14: calculate the amount of surplus energy and generate a message.
	P4: Send message to DCU.
C5: take necessary actions, if DCU reports a power shortage.	P1: Decode Receive message from DCU.
	P8: Send message to the user.
	P15: Generate an alert SMS for power shortage.
	P16: cut off electricity to some appliances after certain time period.

Table 9.1 provides a detail list of the entire composite and their primitive components for a smart metering System. Now we apply the proposed algorithm on this system and analyze the effect of changing a primate component on the system.

According to algorithm 9 if, primitive component P5 is modified, then the contents of P_{Array} and C_{Array} will be, P_{Array} = P6, P7, P8, P1, P9, P15, P16, P2, P3, P4, P10,

P11, P12, P13, P14. C_{Array} = C2, C3, C5, C1, C4.

Thus, if P5 is modified, then we have to check all the primitive and composite components to check who also need modification. Figure 9.5 shows the BPMN diagram of the smart meter system. BPMN provides a graphical diagram of how different objectives can be achieved in a business process, with enough information, so that the process can be analyzed, simulated and executed. There are different elements in BPMN - activities, events, gateways and connectors. A connector links activities, events and gateways and shows the control flow relation. An event can be a start event (start of the process), end event (end of the process), or an intermediate event, that can either be some messages or a timer or error. An activity or a task is an atomic activity and stands for work to be performed within a process. Gateways determine the branching, forking, merging and joining of paths [168, 169].

Immediate effects can be described as the outcome of execution of an activity. This model requires the designers to provide the immediate effects of each activity. Then the cumulative effect of each component can be calculated by accumulating the immediate effects [170, 171].

In figure 9.5,
- e1 to e16 are the immediate effect of primitive components P1 to P16 respectively.
- CEC1 to CEC5 are the cumulative effect of composite components C1 to C5, respectively. The arrows towards CEC1 to CEC5 mark the points where the cumulative effects have been calculated.
- Cumulative effect of C1 (CEC1) = $(e1 \wedge e2 \wedge e3 \wedge e4)$
- Cumulative effect of C2 (CEC2) = $(e5 \wedge e6 \wedge e8) \vee (e5 \wedge e7 \wedge e8)$
- Cumulative effect of C3 (CEC3) = $(e1 \wedge e9 \wedge e8)$
- Cumulative effect of C4 (CEC4) = $(e10 \wedge e12) \vee (e10 \wedge e11 \wedge e13 \wedge e14 \wedge e4) \vee (e10 \wedge e11 \wedge e13 \wedge e12)$
- Cumulative effect of C5 (CEC5) = $(e1 \wedge e15 \wedge e16 \wedge e8) \vee (e1 \wedge e15 \wedge e8 \wedge e16)$

Again, if a change request for P5 is made, then from the diagram and the cumulative effects, we can conclude that,
- Cumulative effect of C2 may get affected, as well as the immediate effect of other primitive components of C2, i.e., e6, e7, e8, and the immediate effects of P6, P7, and P8 respectively.
- Now, P8 is further used in C3 and C5. Hence, if the immediate effect of P8 changes, due to P5, then it may also affect the immediate effects of P1, P9, P15, and P16.

9. CONFIGURATION AND COMPLIANCE MANAGEMENT FRAMEWORK

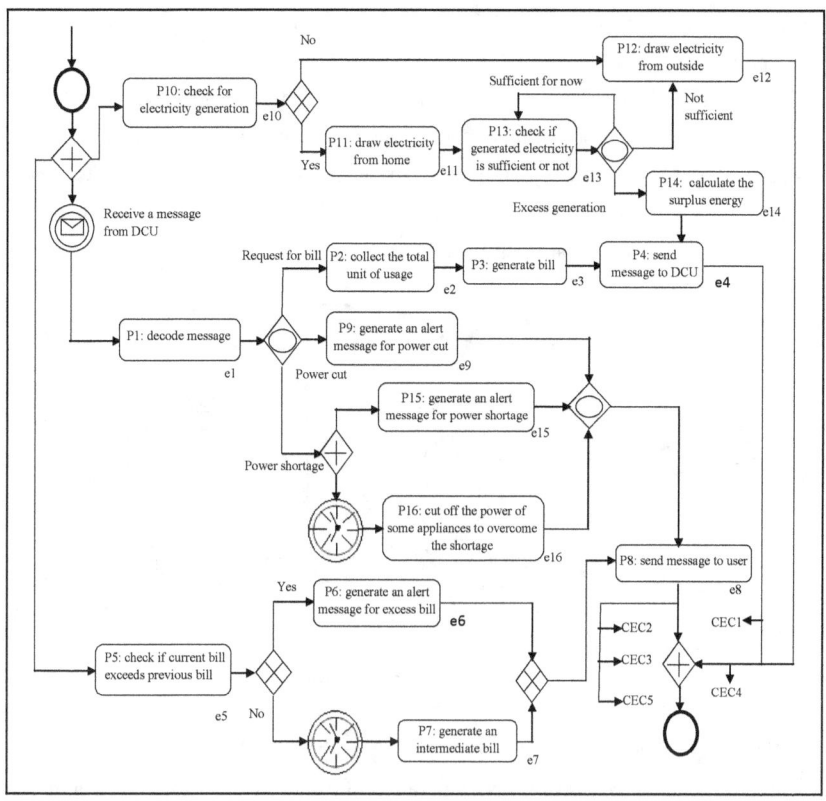

Figure 9.5: BPMN diagram of a smart meter.

- Again P1 also had contributions in the cumulative effect of C1. Thus, P2, P3, P4 might be affected.
- P4 is also used in C4. So, P10, P11, P12, P13, P14 might also be affected.

Hence, we may conclude that, the BPMN with semantic effect annotation confirms the result of our algorithm.

9.1.6 Verification of the Compliance Management Layer

In this section, we have considered the application of distributed generation system in the AMI. Now let us explain this application briefly. Suppose, some customers produce electiricity in their homes, using solar pannel or small bio electricity generation systems etc. Now, the customers will use this electricity for their daily usage, and if they produce

9.1. Working Principle of the Proposed Framework

excess electricity then they can sell it to the grid. Figure 9.6 describes the working of this application.

Since, Smart Grid is an extension of the existing electrical grid, it will have to add new components to properly implement such applications. As an example, the smart meter has to add a additional component to predict hour ahead demand of its owner based of some parameters, the smart meter should also have a switch to toggle between two incoming electricity source: grid and home etc.

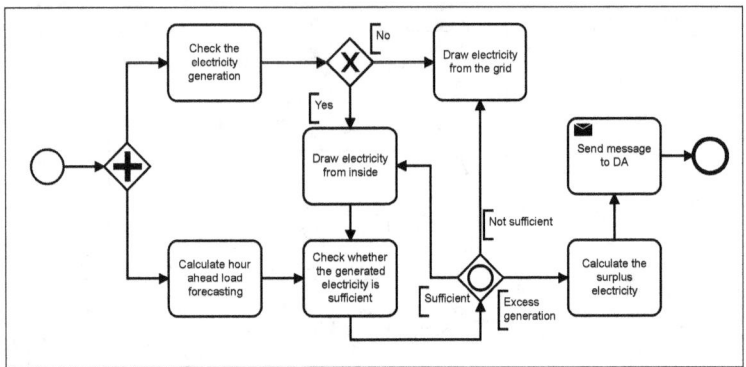

Figure 9.6: BPMN diagram for the distributed generation in AMI.

Now, all of these components must comply with the architectural compliance of the existing system. Moreover, The integration of IoT makes this scenario a bit more complex.

Inorder to verify our proposed framework, we have used Event-B modelling [173], which is a formal approach towards system-level modelling and analysis. Here, at first we have identified the functional and non functional requirements of the complete composite component and model that system using Event-B. After that we have disintegrated the composite component into several primitive components using our algorithms, and tried to model those collective primitive components so that the new system can comply with the old system. We have used Rodin modeling tool [174] which is an Eclipse-based IDE for Event-B that provides support for refinement and proof for system modeling.

We have considered the application described in section 9.1.5 as an example.

181

Table 9.2: Components of Smart Meter

Components	Responsibilities
Forecasting device (F)	Forecast the hour ahead demand of the household
Calculating device (C)	Calculate the capacity of the distribured electricity generation source
Monitor (M)	Controls the flow of electricity and the two different channels.
Sensors (S1 & S2)	Enable the channels

9.1.6.1 Phase 1

First of all make a list of basic functional and non-functional requirements and check their correctness with Event B modelling.

Functional Requirements

- **FR_1:** The smart meter need to/must differentiate between the electricity coming from grid and that is coming from the solar panel.
- **FR_2:** The system must be able to monitor the electricity generation and thus check whether it is sufficient or not.
- **FR_3:** The system should be enabled to calculate the day ahead demand of a household.
- **FR_4:** If the power coming from solar panel is not enough the house can then buy electricity from the grid.
- **FR_5:** If there is excess power at the end of the day the system should be able to sell.

Non-Functional Requirements

- **NFR_1:** Data integrity should be maintained.
- **NFR_1:** The system should maintain the relation between grid, generation unit and home owner.
- **NFR_1:** As the first source of electricity is Solar Panel, if for some reason the panel gets damaged the system should be able to sense that and provide recovery measures by switching to the grid electricity immediately.

Now, table 9.2 lists all the components that are required for the proper execution of this application.

Now let us take the following assumptions:

9.1. Working Principle of the Proposed Framework

- The average demand of household is y
- The capacity of the distribured electricity generation source is x
- Usually x ≥ y

When for some reason y increases to 'y + d', then following two scenarios can happen:

1) $x > (y + d)$: electricity from distribured electricity generation source is enough.
2) $x < (y + d)$: shortage of electricity.

Following is the actions taken for both of the scenarios.

- Step 1: If 'y' increases to 'y + d', M sends a request to Grid.
- Step 2: Check the status between 'x' and 'y'.
- Step 3: If $x > (y + d)$, M kept the grid channel disabled.
- Step 4: If $x < (y+d)$, M disable the channel from distribured electricity generation source and enables the channel from Grid.

In case of second scenario the requirement F1 is needed and for that we first define a context with the set STATUS defining the two different statuses of the channels: enable and disable.

- Set: STATUS
- Constants: enable and disable
- Axioms & invariants:
    - $axm\_1 > Status$= enable, disable
    - $inv\_1 > S1.enable$ if and only if S2.disable and vice versa.

Axioms defines the context, whereas invariants are conditions which are remain true despite the changes over in time. Now we take three variables:

- *channel_sensor_sp*
- *channel_sensor_grid*
- *monitor_control*

In this connection, the monitor acts as an action, whereas the channel acts as a reaction. As we know the reactions of the channels are strongly synchronized to the action of the monitor. Table 9.3 describes the patterns which are used to instantiate the situation:

This leads to the list of events as shown in figure 9.7, which are supposed to represent the reactions of the channels and from that we can show that the smart meter can differentiate between electricity coming from different sources.

Table 9.3: List of patterns

a	monitor_control
r.s	channel_sensor_sp
r.g	channel_sensor_grid
0	disabled
1	enabled
a_on	monitor_enable_channel
a_off	monitor_disable_channel
r.s_on	sp.channel_enabled
r.s_off	sp.channel_disabled
r.g_on	grid.channel_enabled
r.g_off	grid.channel_disabled

```
r.s_on
    when
        r.g = 0
        a = 1
    then
        r.s = 1
end
sp.channel_enabled
    when
        channel_sensor_grid = disabled
        monitor_control = enable
    then
        channel_sensor_sp = enable
end
```

(a) Event 1: When channel coming from solar panel is enabled

```
r.s_off
    when
        a = 1
        r.g = 0
    then
        a = 0
        r.s = 0
        a = 1
        r.g = 1
end
sp.channel_disable
    when
        monitor_control = enable
        channel_sensor_grid = disable
    then
        monitor_control = disable
        channel_sensor_sp = disable
        monitor_control = enable
        channel_sensor_grid = enable
end
```

(b) Event 2: When the solar panel channel is disabled

```
r.g_on
    when
        r.s = 0
        a = 1
    then
        r.g = 1
end
grid.channel_enabled
    when
        channel_sensor_sp = disabled
        monitor_control = enable
    then
        channel_sensor_grid = enable
end
```

(c) Event 3: When Grid channel is enabled

```
r.g_off
    when
        a = 1
        r.s = 0
    then
        a = 0
        r.g = 0
        a = 1
        r.s = 1
end
grid.channel_disable
    when
        monitor_control = enable
        channel_sensor_sp = disable
    then
        monitor_control = disable
        channel_sensor_grid = disable
        monitor_control = enable
        channel_sensor_sp = enable
end
```

(d) Event 4: When Grid channel is disabled

Figure 9.7: List of Events

9.1.6.2 Phase 2

Suppose we have 4 primitive components to construct a composite component. Table 9.4 describes the functional and non-functional requirements of each primitive components. Now we can observe that none of the primitive components are self sufficient to full

9.1. Working Principle of the Proposed Framework

Table 9.4: List of Primitive Components and their functional and non-functional requirements

Primitive Components	Functional requirement	Non-functional requirement
PM1	{F1, F2, F3}	{NF1, NF2}
PM2	{F4, F5, ^F2,F6}	{NF1, NF3, Nf4}
PM3	{F4, F5, F7}	{NF3, NF4}
PM4	{F2, ^F5, F3}	{NF3, ^NF2}

fill all the requirements. From the above 4 PCs we can construct $2^4 = 16$ possible combinations of promising candidates: [PM1, PM2, PM3, PM4, PM1,PM2, PM1, PM3, PM1, PM4, PM2, PM3, PM2, PM4, PM3, PM4, PM1,PM2,PM3, PM1,PM2,PM4, PM1, PM3,PM4, PM2, PM3,PM4, PM1,PM2,PM3,PM4. Out of these 16 subsets only PM1, PM3 is the valid candidate.

9.1.6.3 Phase 3

From the above phase we got our valid candidate but it comes with two new requirements: F7 and NF4. Now these two new requirements are included along with the valid candidate component and thus we need to validate these two against our existing system. We can perform the validation process/we can prove the validation by modelling them with Event B.

Let's us take requirement NF4 which is an important requirement for PM3 that ensures the security of the excess electricity i.e. the excess electricity cannot be sold outside without the consent of DA of that smart meter. This requirement limited the access of the excess electricity. Now in our basic requirements of the existing system we don't have any security requirements like this. Hence, let's refine our integrated system with its new component and new requirement.

The first new component (Excess Electricity Detector or EED) has two parts: sender and receiver. The sender part works as an alarm. When the smart meter has excess electricity that alarm is triggered and all smart meters within one hop distance receive that signal. The DA under which that smart meter is registered also receives this signal. Thus the information of excess electricity is known in the neighbourhood. Now as soon as DA receives this signal, it sends another signal to the sender smart meter with timestamp. In the meantime other smart meters within one hop distance also send signals to this smart meter for buying the electricity. Now the second new component is an array (A) where the first field contains the amount of total excess electricity and fields from that contains the ids of all requesting smart meters. Within that timestamp from DA the smart meter holding excess electricity, sends a response to the DA along with the array. If the DA got the response within the defined timestamp it determines the price of that electricity and also the smart meter to sell. Then it sends another signal to the smart meter along with a packet containing the price and id of the buyer smart meter. If the DA didn't get a response from the sender smart meter within the timestamp, it assumes that smart meter is selling the electricity unethically and then can take necessary actions accordingly.

We first define a context with the set STATUS defining the two different statuses of the channels: sending and receiving, and two different status for the timestamp: true and false.

- Set: STATUS
- Constants: sending, receiving, true and false
- Axioms & invariants:
    - axm_1: Status_channel= sending, receiving
    - axm_2: Status_timestamp= true, false

Now we take 5 variables: |

- EED_signal
- DA_signal
- DA_timestamp
- Array_signal
- OHSM_signal (signal from one hop smart meters)

Invariants: inv_1: DA_signal=receiving if and only if DA_timestamp=true

Here the EED and DA are strongly synchronised but EED and other one hop smart meters (OHSM) are weakly synchronised. We will use the following pattern as shown in table 9.5, to instantiate the situation.

Figure 9.8 gives the series of events for this situation.

9.2 Conclusions

In this chapter, a new framework for configuration of components with compliance checking is proposed. This framework considers two main problems of CBSD: maintenance and compliance, and solves them by incorporating both configuration management and compliance management with CBSD. We have considered 2-level

9.2. Conclusions

Table 9.5: List of patterns for Phase 3

e	EED_signal
d	DA_signal
a	array_signal
ts	DA_timestamp
s	OHSM_signal
0	sending
1	receiving
t	true
f	false
ack	acknowledgement of excess electricity
s_rec	OHSM_signal_receives

```
ack
    when
        e = 0
    then
        s = 0
        d = 0
        ts = t
    end
ack
    when
        EED_signal = sending
    then
        OHSM_signal = sending
        DA_signal = sending
        DA_timestamp = true
    end
```

```
s_rec
    when
        ts = t
        a = 0
        d = 1
    then
        ts = f
        d = 0
        a = 1
        s = 1
    end
```

(a) Event 1: Acknowledgement of excess electricity

(b) Event 2: Excess electricity is sold to one of the OHSM.

Figure 9.8: List of Events in Phase 3

hierarchy between components, i.e., all the composite components are developed using primitive components. However, the level of hierarchy can easily increased in this model, so that we can consider a scenario where composite components are again assembled together to develop another composite component.

In chapter 7, requirements for configuration management for CBSD is discussed. Two main problems have been highlighted. One is due to version management, and another is due to the complex and nested relationship between the primitive and composite components. The model in this chapter is able to overcome these problems. In this model, the component management layer replaces each component with its latest version once it is accepted by the compliance layer, but the configuration management layer stores all the versions of a component to a database. Thus, the active system is always executed with current versions of each component, but the older versions are also stored in the database.

The component management layer is responsible for securing the compliance rules of the system. The algorithm for compliance checking further uses three sub algorithms to ensure three important aspects: entailment, consistency and minimality. The main concern in minimality checking is to identify the QoS parameters or soft goals which are relevant to the system and quantified each primitive component with respect to those soft goals. However, identifying system specific QoS variables and quantify them according to system specifications are altogether an independent topic for research and we would like to explore this topic as a future extension of this work. We have used Event-B to verify our framework. Event-B works as a complete modelling approach for systems like Smart Grid, as at every step of design, along with modelling, it verifies the consistencies between levels and also checks the correctness of the functionalities.

The advantage of Event-B is that it provides refinement at every stage of modelling. As a result we can modify the system according to the new requirements which has come along with the selected primitive component.

The configuration management layer uses an efficient algorithm to search all the related primitive and composite components for a particular primitive component. This helps the model to perform efficiently and provides an easily maintainable and compliant system.

An obvious question may arise in this situation: if we can achieve the goal of our algorithm using the semantic effect annotations in BPMN, then why a new algorithm is required at all? Identifying the effects of a change by semantic effect annotation in BPMN needs a certain amount of knowledge about both BPMN and propositional logic. Besides developing the BPMN model for a process and maintaining the semantic effect annotations is a complex task as changing any primitive component results in changing its immediate effect. This change in immediate effect needs to be propagated throughout the system so that the cumulative effects evaluated at different points within the system remain consistent with this change. Also, using BPMN requires maintenance of a graphical representation of the system. On the other hand, our algorithm is inherently simple as it does not require any graphical representations of the system or semantic effect annotations. A simple tabular data structure is sufficient for the execution of the algorithm. As a result, it is a less complex and more preferable solution compared to BPMN.

Although it is not a theoretical proof for correctness of the proposed algorithm, the validation using BPMN and Event-B indeed shows the effectiveness of the new algorithms. The proposed methodology builds the foundation for several meaningful extensions in future. We want to apply this model to the entire Smart Grid Architecture as a future work. For future scope we are trying to use Event-B method to model a better security system. We have modeled one non functional requirement which limited the access of excess electricity but we are trying to model an approach where we can stop unethical hacking of electricity.

CHAPTER 10

CONCLUSIONS & FUTURE WORKS

Though Smart Grid is an application domain, it grabs the attention of researchers due to its unique characteristics and high impact on society. The conventional electrical power grid that has been used over decades has met our needs in the past. However, as the society advances technologically so does the expectations from various infrastructures surrounding us. A smart grid is an intelligent electricity network that integrates the actions of all users connected to it and makes use of advanced information, control, and communication technologies to save energy, reduce cost and increase reliability and transparency.

Overall, the primary objective of this study is to provide security and autonomicity in Smart Grid. As we all know that Smart grid and especially AMI system enhances the efficiency, reliability, stability, security and economic facilities of traditional power grid systems. Advanced metering infrastructure (AMI) is arguably the most important and critical part of Smart Grid. AMI deals with the most sensitive information in the Grid and transmits them through the network. There already exist a good number of security solutions for AMI. However the percentage of security attacks is also increasing day by day and so does the innovative and intelligent ideas behind those attacks. Energy theft is always a serious concern for power industry. With traditional power grid, tapping, physical tampering of meters are the common sources to theft. Smart Grid and AMI can mitigate these attacks. However, with the recent advancement in the technology, the attackers also invent newer and sophisticated ideas to attack the grid. Thus our motive is to provide a secure communication in AMI, so that user information as well as utility properties cannot be harmed by intruders.

Integrating IPv6 with Smart Grid is quite natural, as only IPv6 could match the size of Smart Grid network. The large address space, auto configuration of addresses, QoS support technology helps Smart grid to construct a large network with a unique address specified for each and every device, efficient routing, end-to-end security. However, smart grid has very high security demand that needs to be considered before deploying IPv6 towards building Smart Grid. The proposed IPv6 addressing configuration will be useful for several Smart Grid applications. Our proposed methodology builds the foundation for several meaningful extensions in future. In continuation to the proposed work, it would be interesting to develop a new secure routing protocol for the last mile communication in Smart Grid.

Besides, accurate load forecasting model in Smart Grid works as a supporting tool to optimize demand scheduling. In this thesis we have tried to develop an accurate energy forecasting model that optimizes reliability and stability, while minimizing processing and computational load. In particular, we analyzed combinations of monthly user data and other predictor parameters to find some decision making information. This is used to find the coefficient for each parameter corresponding to different types of users to optimize the predicted demand.

As part of future work, we plan to develop an autonomic and dynamic forecasting tool based on our proposed approach that would use additive regression technique to generate the meta-model using previous 10 years' data. Existing models are mostly static, built using a fixed set of data, and are quite inaccurate in predicting electricity usage for future years. The proposed tool will automatically regenerate the forecasting model for every year using recent past data as sliding window of 10 years. As an example, for predicting monthly forecasting of 2016, the tool will build the forecasting model depending on the past trends during 2006-2015. However, for 2017, the model will rebuild automatically using the past data of 2007-2016. This would help us capture the recent trends of electricity usage of a region towards effective prediction of the near future electricity usage more accurately.

REFERENCES

[1] U.S Energy Information Administration, "International Energy Outlook 2017", September, 2017.

[2] A White Paper by United States Agency for International Development, USAID India, "The smart grid vision for India's power sector", March 2010.

[3] "Study of Security Attributes of Smart Grid—Current Cyber Security Issues", Department of Energy Office of Electricity Delivery and Energy Reliability, National SCADA Test Bed, April 2009.

[4] NIST Special Publication 1108R2, "NIST Framework and Roadmap for Smart Grid Interoperability Standards", Release 2.0, National Institute of Standards and Technology (NIST) Std., February 2012.

[5] S. Bera, S. Misra, J. J. P. C. Rodrigues, "CLoud Computing Applications for Smart Grid: A Survey", IEEE Transactions on Parallel and Distributed Systems, Vol. 26, No. 5, pp. 1477-1494, 2015.

[6] S. Bera, S. Misra, D. Chatterjee, "C2C: Community-Based Cooperative Energy Consumption in Smart Grid", IEEE Transactions in Smart Grid, Vol. 9, No. 5, pp. 4262-4269, 2018.

[7] A. Mondal, S. Misra, L. S. Patel, S. K. Pal, M. S. Obaidat, "DEMANDS: Distributed Energy Management Using Noncooperative Scheduling in Smart Grid", IEEE Systems Journal, Vol. 12, No. 3, pp. 2645-2653, 2018.

[8] R. Berthier, W. H. Sanders, "Specification-Based Intrusion Detection for Advanced Metering Infrastructures", IEEE 17th Pacific Rim Int'l Symp. on Dependable Computing, pp. 184-193, 2011.

[9] D. Mashima, A. A. Cárdenas, "Evaluating electricity theft detectors in smart grid networks", Research in Attacks, Intrusions, and Defenses (RAID), LNCS 7462, pp. 210–229, 2012.

References

[10] J. Nagi, K. S. Yap, S. K. Tiong, S. K. Ahmed, M. Mohamad, "Nontechnical loss detection for metered customers in power utility using support vector machines", IEEE Transactions on Power Delivery, vol. 25, no. 2, pp. 1162-1171, 2010.

[11] Md. A. Hamid, Md. S. Islam, and C. S. Hong, "Misbehavior Detection in Wireless Mesh Networks", International conference on Advanced Communication Technology, 2008, pp. 1167 – 1169.

[12] M. Alamaniotis, D. Bargiotas, L. H. Tsoukalas, "Towards smart energy systems: application of kernel machine regression for medium term electricity load forecasting", SpringerPlus-Engineering, Springer, vol. 5 no. 1, pp. 1-15, 2016.

[13] Y. Goude, R. Nedellec, N. Kong, "Local Short and Middle Term Electricity Load Forecasting With Semi-Parametric Additive Models", IEEE Transactions on Smart Grid, vol. 5, no. 1, pp. 440-446, 2014.

[14] S. J. Huang, K. R. Shih, "Short-term load forecasting via ARMA model identification including non-Gaussian process considerations", IEEE Trans. on Power System, vol. 18, no. 2, pp. 673–679, 2003.

[15] R. Jiang, R. Lu,Y. Wang,J. Luo,C. Shen,X. S. Shen, "Energy-Theft Detection Issues for Advanced Metering Infrastructure in Smart Grid", Tsinghua Science and Technology, vol. 19(2), pp. 105-120, 2014.

[16] D. Grochocki,J. H. Huh, R. Berthier, R. Bobba, W. H. Sanders, A. A. Cárdenas, J. G. Jetcheva, "AMI Threats, Intrusion Detection Requirements andDeployment Recommendations", Smart Grid Communications (SmartGridComm), IEEE, pp. 395-400, 2012.

[17] Amir Motamedi, Hamidreza Zareipour, William D. Rosehart, "Electricity Price and Demand Forecasting in Smart Grids", IEEE Transactions On Smart Grid, vol. 3, no. 2, pp. 664-674, June 2012.

[18] M. Kim, "A Survey on Guaranteeing Availability in Smart Grid Communications", Advanced Communication Technology (ICACT), pp. 314-317, 2012.

[19] A. Mayzaud, R. Badonnel, I. Chrisment, "A Distributed Monitoring Strategy for Detecting Version Number Attacks in RPL-Based Networks", IEEE Transactions on Network and Service Management, vol. 14, no. 2, pp. 272-286, June 2017.

[20] T. Zseby, "Is IPv6 Ready for the Smart Grid?", International Conference on Cyber Security, pp. 157-164, 2012.

References

[21] NIST Special Publication 1108R2, "NIST Framework and Roadmap for Smart Grid Interoperability Standards", Release 2.0, National Institute of Standards and Technology (NIST) Std., February 2012.

[22] NIST, "Guidelines for Smart Grid Cyber Security: Vol. 1, Smart Grid Cyber Security Strategy, Architecture, and High-Level Requirements, NISTIR 7628", 2010. [Online]. Available: http://csrc.nist.gov/publications/PubsNISTIRs.html

[23] S. M. Amin, B. F. Wollenberg, "Toward a smart grid: power delivery for the 21st century", IEEE Power and Energy Mag., vol. 3, no. 5, pp. 34-41, 2005.

[24] T. Baumeister, "Literature Review on Smart Grid Cyber Security", Tech Report, 2010.

[25] P. Parikh, M. Kanabar, and T. S. Sidhu, "Opportunities and Challenges of Wireless Communication Technologies for Smart Grid Applications", IEEE PES General Meeting, Minneapolis, USA, July, 2010.

[26] P. McDaniel, "Security and PrivacyChallenges in the Smart Grid", Security and Privacy, IEEE, Issue 3, pp. 75-77, 2009.

[27] H. K. Alfares, M. Nazeeruddin, "Electric load forecasting: literature survey and classification of methods", International Journal of Systems Science, vol. 33(1), pp. 3–34, 2002.

[28] L. Hernandez, C. Baladrón, J. M. Aguiar, B. Carro, A. J. Sanchez-Esguevillas, J. Lloret, and J. Massana, "A Survey on Electric Power Demand Forecasting: Future Trends in Smart Grids, Microgrids and Smart Buildings", IEEE Communications Surveys & Tutorials, Vol. 16, No. 3, pp. 1460-1495, Third Quarter 2014.

[29] J. Medina, N. Muller, and I. Roytelman, "Demand Response and Distribution Grid Operators: Opportunities and Challenges", IEEE Trans. Smart Grid, vol. 1, no. 2, pp. 193-198, Sept. 2010.

[30] Y. Yan, Y. Qian, H. Sharif and D. Tipper, "A Survey on Cyber Security for Smart Grid Communications", IEEE Communications Surveys & Tutorials, Vol. 14, No. 4, Fourth Quarter 2012.

[31] H. Farhangi, "The path of the smart grid", IEEE Power and Energy Mag., vol. 8, pp. 18-28, 2010.

[32] U.S. Energy Information Administration, "Monthly Energy Review", [Online]. available: https://www.eia.gov/totalenergy/data/monthly/

REFERENCES

[33] U.S Department of Commerce, Bureau of Economic Analysis, "Gross Domestic Product by State", [Online], Available: https://www.bea.gov/data/gdp/gdp-state.

[34] R. Jiang, R. Lu, Y. Wang, J. Luo, C. Shen, X. S. Shen, "Energy-Theft Detection Issues for Advanced Metering Infrastructure in Smart Grid". Tsinghua Science and Technology, vol. 19(2), pp. 105-120, 2014.

[35] D. Grochocki, J. H. Huh, R. Berthier, R. Bobba, W. H. Sanders, A. A. Cárdenas, J. G. Jetcheva, "AMI Threats, Intrusion Detection Requirements andDeployment Recommendations", Smart Grid Communications (SmartGridComm), IEEE , pp. 395-400, 2012.

[36] S. McLaughlin, D. Podkuiko, P. McDaniel, "Energy theft in the advanced metering infrastructure", 4th International Conference on Critical InformationInfrastructures Security, Springer, pp. 176-187 2010.

[37] J. Nagi, K. S. Yap, S. K. Tiong, S. K. Ahmed, M. Mohamad, "Nontechnical loss detection for metered customers in power utility using support vector machines", IEEE Transactions on Power Delivery, vol. 25, no. 2, pp. 1162-1171, 2010.

[38] D. Mashima, A. A. C´ardenas, "Evaluating electricity theft detectors in smart grid networks", Research in Attacks, Intrusions, and Defenses (RAID), LNCS 7462, pp. 210–229, 2012.

[39] S. Depuru, L. Wang, V. Devabhaktuni, "Support vector machine based data classification for detection of electricity theft", IEEE/PES Power Systems Conference and Exposition (PSCE), pp. 1-8, 2011.

[40] S. Depuru, L. Wang, V. Devabhaktuni, R. C. Green, "High performance computing for detection of electricity theft", International Journal of Electrical Power & Energy Systems, vol. 47, pp. 21-30, 2013.

[41] S. McLaughlin, B. Holbert, S. Zonouz, R. Berthier, "AMIDS: A multi-sensor energy theft detection framework for advanced metering infrastructures", IEEE Third International Conference on Smart Grid Communications (SmartGridComm), pp. 354-359, 2012.

[42] B. Khoo, Y. Cheng, "Using RFID for anti-theft in a chinese electrical supply company: A cost-benefit analysis", IEEE Wireless Telecommunications Symposium (WTS), pp. 1-6, 2011.

[43] Z. Xiao, Y. Xiao, D. H. C. Du, "Non-repudiation in neighborhood area networks for smart grid", IEEE Communications Magazine, vol. 51, no. 1, pp. 18-26, 2013.

[44] P. Jokar, N. Arianpoo, V. C. M. Leung, "Electricity theft detection in AMI using customers consumption patterns", IEEE Transactions in Smart Grid, vol. 7, no. 1, pp. 216–226, Jan. 2016.

[45] S. Amin, G. A. Schwartz, H. Tembine, "Incentives and security in electricity distribution networks", Decision and Game Theory for Security, Springer, pp. 264-280, 2012.

[46] A. A. C´ardenas, S. Amin, G. Schwartz, R. Dong, S. Sastry, "A game theory model for electricity theft detection and privacy-aware control in AMI systems", IEEE 50th Annual Allerton Conference on Communication, Control, and Computing (Allerton), pp. 1830-1837, 2012.

[47] Poly Sen, Nabendu Chaki, Rituparna Chaki, "HIDS: Honesty-Rate Based Collaborative Intrusion Detection System for Mobile Ad-Hoc Networks", Computer Information Systems and Industrial Management, pp.121-126, 2008.

[48] Novarun Deb, Nabendu Chaki, "TIDS: Trust-Based Intrusion Detection System for Wireless Ad-hoc Networks", Computer Information Systems and Industrial Management Lecture Notes in Computer Science Volume 7564, pp 80-91, 2012.

[49] Sung-Won Lee, Ji Yong Choi, Keun Woo Lim, Young-Bae Ko, Byeong-Hee Roh, "A Reliable and Hybrid Multipath Routing Protocol for Multi-Interface Tactical Ad Hoc Networks", The Military Communication Conference, pp. 1531–1536, 2010.

[50] S. Mueller, R. P. Tsang, D. Ghosal, "Multipath Routing in Mobile Ad Hoc Networks: Issues and Challenges", Calzarossa, M.C., Gelenbe, E. (eds.) MASCOTS 2003. LNCS vol. 2965, pp. 209–234, 2004.

[51] M. K. Marina and S. R. Das, "Ad hoc On-demand Multipath Distance Vector Routing", Computer Science Department, Stony Brook University, 2003.

[52] Y. Ganjali, A. Keshavarzian, "Load Balancing in Ad Hoc Networks: Single-path Routing vs. Multi-path Routing", IEEE International Advance Computing Conference, IACC, pp. 32–34, 2009.

[53] Ye Ming Lu, Vincent W. S. Wong, "An energy-efficient multipath routing protocol for wireless sensor networks", International Journal of Communication Systems, pp. 747-766, 2007.

References

[54] L. Xiong and L. Liu, "Building Trust in Decentralized Peer-to-Peer Electronic Communities", Proc. 5th Int'l Conf. Electronic Commerce Research (ICECR-5), 2002.

[55] Jie Zhang, Choong Kyo Jeong, Goo Yeon Lee, Hwa Jong Kim, "Cluster-based Multi-path Routing Algorithm for Multi-hop Wireless Network", International Journal of Future Generation Communication and Networking, 2009.

[56] J. Agrakhed, G. S. Biradar, V. D. Mytri, "Energy efficeient interference aware Multipath Routing protocol in WMSN", India Conference (INDICON), Annual IEEE , pp.1-4, 2011.

[57] Moufida Maimour, "Maximally Radio-Disjoint Multipath Routing for Wireless Multimedia Sensor Networks", 4th ACM workshop on Wireless multimedia networking and performance modeling, pp. 26-31, 2008.

[58] Maryam Dehnavi, Mohammad Reza Mazaheri, Behzad Homayounfar, Sayyed Majid Mazinani, "Energy Efficient and QoS Based Multi-path Hierarchical Routing Protocol in WSNs", International Symposium on Computer, Consumer and Control, pp. 414-418, 2012.

[59] Bashir Yahya, Jalel Ben-Othman, "REER: Robust and Energy Efficient Multipath Routing Protocol for Wireless Sensor Networks", Global Telecommunications Conference, GLOBECOM, IEEE , pp.1-7, 2007.

[60] Bashir Yahya, Jalel Ben-Othman, "RELAX: An Energy Efficient Multipath Routing Protocol for Wireless Sensor Networks", Proceedings of IEEE International Conference on Communications (ICC), pp. 1-6, 2010.

[61] Shirshu Varma, Uma Shanker Tiwary, Anshul Jain, Tarun Sharma, "Statistical Energy Efficient Multipath Routing Protocol", International Conference on Information Networking (ICOIN), pp. 1-5, 2008.

[62] Che-Jung Hsu, Huey-Ing Liu, Winston K.G. Seah, "Opportunistic routing – A review and the challenges ahead", Computer Networks, Volume 55, pp. 3592–3603, 2011.

[63] Wang Boa, Huang Chuanhea, Li Layuanb, Yang Wenzhonga, "Trust-based minimum cost opportunistic routing for Ad hoc networks", The Journal of Systems and Software, Vol 84, pp. 2107– 2122, 2011.

References

[64] V. Cagri Gungor and Frank C. Lambert, "A Survey on Communication Networks for Electric System Automation", Computer Networks, Vol. 50, pp. 877–897, Elsevier, 2006.

[65] Sung-Guk Yoon, Seowoo Jang, Yong-Hwa Kim, Saewoong Bahk, "Opportunistic Routing for Smart Grid With Power Line Communication Access Networks", IEEE Transactions on Smart Grid, vol. 5, no. 1, pp. 303-311, January 2014.

[66] Yuwen Qian, Cheng Zhang, Zhengwen Xu, Feng Shu, Linbin Dong, Jun Li, "A reliable opportunistic routing for smart grid with in-home power line communication networks", Information Sciences, Science China Press and Springer-Verlag Berlin Heidelberg, Vol. 59, pp. 1–13, December 2016.

[67] S. De, C. Qiao, H. Wu, "Meshed multipath routing with selective forwarding: an efficient strategy in wireless sensor networks", Computer Networks, pp.481-497, 2003.

[68] Siddiqui Muhammad Shoaib, Amin Syed Obaid, Kim Jin Ho, Hong Choong Seon, "MHRP: A Secure Multi-Path Hybrid Routing Protocol for Wireless Mesh Network", Military Communications Conference, MILCOM, IEEE , pp. 1-7, 2007.

[69] Zhiyuan Li, Ruchuan Wang, "A Multipath Routing Algorithm Based on Trafffic Prediction in Wireless Mesh Networks", Communications and Network, vol. 1, no. 2, pp. 82-90, 2009.

[70] Xiaoxia Huang, Yuguang Fang, "Multiconstrained QoS multipath routing in wireless sensor networks", Wireless Networks, Volume 14, pp. 465-478, 2008.

[71] Tan Ming-hao, Yu Ren-lai, Li Shu-jiang, Wang Xiang-dong, "Multipath routing protocol with load balancing in WSN considering interference", 6th IEEE Conference on Industrial Electronics and Applications (ICIEA), pp. 1062-1067,2011.

[72] Anfeng Liu, Zhongming Zheng, Chao Zhang, Zhigang Chen, Xuemin Shen, "Secure and Energy-Efficient Disjoint Multipath Routing for WSNs", IEEE Transactions on Vehicular Technology, Volume 7, pp. 3255-3265, 2012.

[73] S. M. Amin, B.F. Wollenberg, "Toward a smart grid: power delivery for the 21st century", IEEE Power and Energy Mag, Volume 3, No. 5, pp. 34-41, 2005.

[74] M. R. Asghar, D. Miorandi, "A Holistic View of Security and Privacy Issues in Smart Grids", SmartGridSec, Lecture Notes in Computer Science, Volume 7823, pp. 58-71, 2013.

REFERENCES

[75] J. Liu, Y. Xiao, S. Li, W. Liang, C. L. P. Chen, "Cyber Security and Privacy Issues in Smart Grids", IEEE Communications Surveys & Tutorials, Volume 14, No. 4, 2012.

[76] S. Axelsson, "Intrusion Detection Systems : A survey and taxonomy", Technical report 99-15, Department of Computer Engineering, Chalmers, March 2000.

[77] J. McHugh, "Intrusion and Intrusion Detection", International Journal of Information Security, Volume 1, pp. 14-35, August, 2001.

[78] N. Deb, M. Chakraborty, N. Chaki. "The Evolution of IDS Solutions in Wireless Ad-hoc Networks to Wireless Mesh Networks", International Journal of Networks Security & Applications (IJNSA), Vol. 3, Number 6, pp. 39-58, November 2011.

[79] Z. Zhang, F. Nait-Abdesselam, P. Ho, X. Lin, "RADAR: a ReputAtion-based Scheme for Detecting Anomalous Nodes in WiReless Mesh Networks", Proc. of Wireless Comm. and Networking Conf. (WCNC), 2008. pp. 2621-2626.

[80] H. Ye, M. Ektesabi, "RFIDS : Radio Frequency Indoor Intrusion Detection System", Proceedings of the World Congress on Engineering 2008, Vol I, July 2-4, pp. 401-404, 2008.

[81] A. Lakhina, M. Crovella, and C. Diot, "Diagnosing network-wide traffic anomalies", International Conference on Special Interest group of Data Commnunication, pp. 219-230, 2004.

[82] F. Hugelshofer, P. Smith, D. Hutchison, N. J.P. Race, "OpenLIDS: A Lightweight Intrusion Detection System for Wireless Mesh Networks", International Conference on Mobile Computing and Networking, September, pp. 309-320, Beijing, China, 2009.

[83] D. M. Shila, T. Anjali, "Defending Selective Forwarding Attacks in WMNs", Proc. of IEEE International Conference on Electro Information Technology, EIT, pp 96-101, 2008.

[84] J. Sen and K. Goswami, "An Algorithm for Detection of Selfish Nodes in Wireless Mesh Networks", Proceedings of the International Symposium on Intelligent Information Systems and Applications (IISA'09), pp. 571-576, October 2009.

[85] M. Gao, J. Tian, K. Li, H. Wu, "Community Intrusion Detection and Pre-warning System based on Wireless Mesh Networks", Proc. of IEEE Conference on Robotics, Automation and Mechatronics, pp. 1066 – 1070, 2008.

[86] D. Makaroff, P. Smith, N. J. P Race, D. Hutchison, "Intrusion Detection Systems for Wireless Mesh Networks", Proc. of the 5th IEEE International Conference on Mobile Ad Hoc and Sensor Systems, pp. 610 – 616, 2008.

[87] Z. Bankovic, D. Fraga, J. Manuel Moya, J. Carlos Vallejo, P. Malaga, A. Araujo, J. de Goyeneche, E. Romero, J. Blesa, and D.Villanueva, "Improving security in WMNs with reputation systems and self-organizing maps", Journal of Network and Computer Applications, 34(2), pp. 455-463, 2011.

[88] S. Tan, D. De, W. Z. Song, J. Yang, and S. K. Das, "Survey of security advances in smart grid: A data driven approach", IEEE Communications Surveys Tutorials, vol. 19, no. 1, pp. 397–422, 2017.

[89] M. Chakraborty, N. Chaki, "ETSeM: A Energy-Aware, Trust-Based, Selective Multi-path Routing Protocol", Computer Information Systems and Industrial Management, Lecture Notes in Computer Science, vol. 7564, pp. 351-360, 2012.

[90] D. E. Comer, "Computer Networks and Internets", Prentice Hall, pp. 476, 2008.

[91] S. McLaughlin, D. Podkuiko, and P. McDaniel, "Energy theft in the advanced metering infrastructure", 4th International Conference on Critical InformationInfrastructures Security, Springer, pp. 176-187, 2010.

[92] W. Stallings, "Cryptography and Network Security: Principles and Practice", 5th Edition, Prentice Hall Press Upper Saddle River, NJ, USA, 2010. ISBN:0136097049 9780136097044.

[93] ABB Inc., "Energy Efficiency in the Power Grid", ABB Inc., Fort Smith, 2007.

[94] R. Ruppe, S. Griswald, P. Walsh, R. Martin, "Near Term Digital Radio (NTDR) System", MILCOM '97, pp. 1282-1287, 1997.

[95] M. Chakraborty, N. Chaki, "An IPv6 based hierarchical address configuration scheme for smart grid", Applications and Innovations in Mobile Computing (AIMoC), Kolkata, pp. 109-116, (2015). doi: 10.1109/AIMOC.2015.7083838

[96] X. Fang, S. Misra, G. Xue, D. Yang, "Smart Grid - The New and Improved Power Grid: A Survey", IEEE Communications Surveys and Tutorials, vol. 14, no. 4, pp. 944-980, 2012.

[97] M. E. Khodayar, H. Wu, "Demand Forecasting in the Smart Grid Paradigm: Features and Challenges", The Electricity Journal, vol. 28, no. 6, pp. 51-62, 2015.

References

[98] D. Bassi and O. Olivare, "Medium Term Electric Load Forecasting Using TLFN Neural Networks", International Journal of Computers, Communications & Control, vol. 1, no. 2, pp. 23-32, 2006.

[99] H. S. Hippert, C. E. Pedreira, R. C. Souza, "Neural Networks for Shortterm Load Forecasting: a Review and Evaluation", IEEE Transactions on Power Systems, vol. 16, no. 1, pp. 44-55, 2001.

[100] H. T. Zhang, F. Y. Xu, L. Zhou, "Artificial Neural Network For Load Forecasting in Smart Grid", Proceedings of 9th International Conference on Machine Learning and Cybernetics, Qingdao, pp. 11-14, 2010.

[101] M. Q. Raza, A. Khosravi, "A review on artificial intelligence based load demand forecasting techniques for smart grid and buildings", Renewable & Sustainable Energy Reviews, Elsevier, vol. 50, pp. 1352–1372, 2015.

[102] T. Hong, M. Gui, M. E. Baran, H. L. Willis, "Modeling and Forecasting Hourly Electric Load by Multiple Linear Regression with Interactions", Proc. of IEEE Power and Energy Society Gen. Meeting, pp. 1-8, 2010.

[103] K. Song, Y. Baek, D. H. Hong, G. Jang, "Short-term Load Forecasting for the Holidays using Fuzzy Linear Regression Method", IEEE Transactions on Power Systems, vol. 20, no. 1, pp. 96-101, 2005.

[104] B. Bowerman, R. Oćonnell, A. Koehler, "Forecasting, Time Series and Regression: An Applied Approach", Thomson Brooks, California, 2005.

[105] N. A. Shikhah, F. Elkarmi, O. M. Aloquili, "Medium-Term Electric Load Forecasting Using Multivariable Linear and Non-Linear Regression", SGRE, Scientific Research, vol. 2, pp. 126-135, 2011.

[106] M. N. Mehr, F. F. Samavati, M. Jeihoonian, "Annual energy demand estimation of Iran industrial sector by Fuzzy regression and ARIMA", Eight International Conference on Fuzzy Systems and Knowledge Discovery, IEEE, vol. 1, pp. 593-597, 2011.

[107] Q. Huang, Y. Li, S. Liu, P. Liu, "Short term load forecasting based on wavelet decomposition and random forest", Workshop on Smart Internet of Things, Article No. 2, SmartIoT 2017.

[108] D. Zafer, L. C. Hunt, "Industrial electricity demand for Turkey: A structural time series analysis", Energy Economics, vol. 33, Issue 3, pp. 426-436, 2011.

[109] S. M. Ali, C. A. Mehmood, B. Khan, M. Jawad, et al., "Stochastic and Statistical Analysis of Utility Revenues and Weather Data Analysis for Consumer Demand Estimation in Smart Grids", PLoSONE, vol. 11, no. 6, 2016.

[110] T. Hong, M. Gui, M. E. Baran, H. L. Willis, "Modeling and Forecasting Hourly Electric Load by Multiple Linear Regression with Interactions",Power and Energy Society General Meeting, USA, pp. 1-8, 2010.

[111] W. Schellong, "Energy Demand Analysis and Forecast", Energy Management Systems P. Giridhar Kini, IntechOpen, DOI: 10.5772/21022. Available from: https://www.intechopen.com/books/energy-management-systems/energy-demand-analysis-and-forecast

[112] A. Molderink, V. Bakker, M. Bosman, J. Hurink, G. Smith,"A threestep methodology to improve domestic energy efficiency". In: Proceedings of IEEE PES conference on innovative smart grid technologies, pp 18, 2010.

[113] A. H. Mohsenian-Rad, V. W. Wong, J. Jateskevich, R. Schober, A. Leon-Garcia, "Autonomous demand-side management based on game-theoretic energy consumption scheduling for the future grid", IEEE Transaction of Smart Grids, vol. l, no. 3, pp. 3-20, 2010.

[114] J. Medina N. Muller I. Roytelman, "Demand response and distribution grid operations: opportunities and challenges", IEEE Transaction of Smart Grids, vol. 1, no. 2, pp. 193-198, 2010.

[115] L. Hernandez, C. Baladrón, J. M. Aguiar, B. Carro, A. J. Sanchez-Esguevillas, J. Lloret, J. Massana, "A Survey on Electric Power Demand Forecasting: Future Trends in Smart Grids, Microgrids and Smart Buildings", IEEE Communications Surveys and Tutorials, vol. 16, no. 3, pp. 1460-1495, 2014.

[116] A. Motamedi, H. Zareipour, W. D. Rosehart, "Electricity Price and Demand Forecasting in Smart Grids", IEEE Transactions on Smart Grid, vol. 3, no. 2, pp. 664-674, 2012.

[117] A. Molderink, V. Bakker, M. Bosman, J. Hurink, G. Smith, "A Three-step Methodology to Improve Domestic Energy Efficiency", Proceedings of IEEE PES Innovative Smart Grid Technologies, pp. 1 - 8, 2010.

[118] Wikipedia, "List of U.S. states by population density", https://en.wikipedia.org/wiki/List_of_U.S._states_by_population_density.

References

[119] Wikipedia, "List of states and union territories of India by population", https://en.wikipedia.org/wiki/List_of_states_and_union_territories_of _India_by_population.

[120] J. C. Lam, K. K. W. Wana, D. Liu, C.L. Tsang, "Multiple Regression Models for Energy Use in Air-conditioned Office Buildings in Different Climates", Energy Conversion and Management, SP Higher Education Press, vol. 51, pp. 2692-2697, 2010.

[121] L. J. Soares, M. C. Medeiros, "Modeling and forecasting Short-Term Electricity Load: A Comparison of Methods with an Application to Brazilian Data", Intl. Journal of Forecasting, vol. 24, pp. 630-644, 2008.

[122] I. H. Witten, E. Frank and M. A. Hal, "Data Mining: Practical Machine Learning Tools and Techniques", 3rd Ed., Morgan Kaufmann Publishers Inc, USA, 2011.

[123] Weka 3: Data Mining Software in Java, Class AdditiveRegression. [Online] Available: http://weka.sourceforge.net /doc.dev/weka/classifiers/meta/AdditiveRegression.html.

[124] Multiple Linear Regression-MLR, Investopedia [Online] Available:http://www.investopedia.com/ terms/m/mlr.asp.

[125] M5P, Opentox [Online] Available: http://www.opentox.org/dev /documentation/-components/m5p.

[126] W. Y. Loh, "Classification and Regression Trees", Wiley Interdisciplinary Reviews: Data Mining and Knowledge Discovery, vol. 1, no. 1, pp. 14-23, John Wiley & Sons, Inc, 2011.

[127] E. Ould-Ahmed-Vall, J. Woodlee, C. Yount, K.A. Doshi, "On the Comparison of Regression Algorithms for Computer Architecture Performance Analysis of Software Applications", Statistical and machine learning approaches applied to Architectures and compilation, Belgium, 2007.

[128] M. C. Baechler, T. L. Gilbride, P. C. Cole, M. G. Hefty, K. Ruiz. "Guide to Determining Climate Regions by County", vol 7.3, Pacific Northwest National Laboratory, Building America Program, U.S. Department of Energy, 2015.

[129] U.S. Energy Information Administration, "Industrial sector Energy Consumption", International Energy Outlook , pp. 113-126, 2016.

[130] U.S. Bureau of Labor, "Industry employment and output projections to 2024", December, 2015. [Online]Available:Statistics(BLS),https://www.bls.gov/

[131] U.S. Census Bureau, "State Population by Characteristics: 2010-2017", [Online]Available: https://www.census.gov/data/datasets/2017/demo/popest/state-detail.html

[132] National Centers for Environmental Information,NOAA,"Climate Data Online: Dataset Discovery"[Online]Available :https://www.ncdc.noaa.gov/cdo-web/datasets

[133] Weka 3:Data Mining Software in Java,Class Random Forest [Online]Available: http://weka.sourceforge.net/doc.dev/weka/classifiers/trees/RandomForest.html

[134] Weka 3.8.1 : Data Mining software in Java, [Online]Available :https://www.cs.waikato.ac.nz/ml/weka/

[135] S. Sackmann, M. Kahmer, M. Gilliot, L. Lowis, "A classification model for automating compliance", CEC/EEE. IEEE, pp. 79–86, 2008.

[136] G. Pour, "Component-Based Software Development Approach: New Opportunities and Challenges", Proceedings Technology of Object-Oriented Languages. TOOLS 26, pp. 375-383, 1998.

[137] I. Crnkovic, "Component-Based Software Engineering—New Challenges in Software Development", Journal of Computing and Information Technology. CIT 11. Vol. 3, pp. 151–161, 2003.

[138] J. Estublier, "Software Configuration Management: A Roadmap", International Conference on Software Engineering, The Future of Software Engineering, ACM Press, 2000.

[139] S. Sackmann, M. Kahmer, M. Gilliot, L. Lowis, "A classification model for automating compliance", CEC/EEE. IEEE, pp. 79–86, 2008.

[140] S. Herold, "Checking Architectural Compliance in Component-Based Systems", SAC '10: Proceedings of the 2010 ACM Symposium on Applied Computing. Pp. 2244–2251. ACM, New York, USA, 2010.

[141] The Institute of Electrical and Electronics Engineers, "Recommended Practice for Architectural Description of Software-Intensive Systems", ANSI/IEEE Std 1471-2000.

References

[142] N. Lohmann, "Compliance by design for artifact-centric business processes", 9th international conference on Business process management, pp. 99-115, 2011.

[143] C. Y. Cheng, C. C. Chuang, Ray. I. Chang, "Three-dimensional Location-based IPv6 Addressing for Wireless Sensor Networks in Smart Grid", 26th IEEE International Conference on Advanced Information Networking and Applications, pp. 824-831, 2012.

[144] C. Y. Cheng, C. C. Chuang, Ray. I. Chang, "Lightweight Spatial IP address Configuration for IPv6-based Wireless Sensor Networks in Smart Grid", SENSORS, IEEE, pp 1-4, 2012.

[145] X. Wang, S. Zhong, "A hierarchical scheme on achieving all-IP communication between WSN and IPv6 networks", International Journal of Electronics and Communications, vol. 67, pp. 414-425, 2013.

[146] X. N. Wang, H.Y. Qian, "An IPv6 address configuration scheme for wireless sensor networks", Computer Standards & Interfaces, Vol. 34, No. 3, pp. 334–341, 2012.

[147] R. Hinden, S. Deering, "RFC 4291-IP Version 6 Addressing Architecture", February, 2006.

[148] R. Hinden, S. Deering, E. Nordmark, "RFC 3587-IPv6 Global Unicast Address Format", August, 2003.

[149] T. Narten et al, "RFC 4861 for Neighbor Discovery protocol for IPv6", September, 2007.

[150] S. Groat, M. Dunlop, W. Urbanksi, R. Marchany, J. Tront, "Using an IPv6 Moving Target Defense to Protect the Smart Grid", Innovative Smart Grid Technologies (ISGT), IEEE PES, pp. 1-7, 2017.

[151] A. P. Castellani, G. Ministeri, M. Rotoloni, L. Vangelista, M. Zorzi, "Interoperable and globally interconnected Smart Grid using IPv6 and 6LoWPAN", 3rd IEEE International Workshop on SmArt COmmunications in NEtwork Technologies, pp. 6473-6478, 2012.

[152] Z. A. Baig, S. C. Adeniye, "A trust-based mechanism for protecting IPv6 networks against stateless address auto-configuration attacks", 17th IEEE International Conference on Networks. Singapore, pp. 171-176, 2011.

[153] R. Berthier, W. H. Sanders, H. Khurana, "Intrusion detection for advanced metering infrastructures: Requirements and architectural directions", First IEEE International Conference on Smart Grid Communications (SmartGridComm), pp. 350–355, 2010.

[154] P. Jokar, H. Nicanfar, V. Leung, "Specification-based intrusion detection for home area networks in smart grids", IEEE International Conference on Smart Grid Communications (SmartGridComm), pp. 208–213, 2011.

[155] R. Berthier, W. H. Sanders, "Specification-based intrusion detection for advanced metering infrastructures", IEEE 17th Pacific Rim International Symposium on Dependable Computing (PRDC), pp. 184–193, 2011.

[156] M. A. Saad, S. Ramadass, S. Manickam, "A Study on Detecting ICMPv6 Flooding Attack based on IDS", Australian Journal of Basic and Applied Sciences, Vol.7, pp. 175-181, 2013.

[157] S. Hogg, E. Vyncke, "IPv6 Security", 1st Edition, Cisco Press, Dec, 2008. ISBN: 978-1587055942.

[158] M. Hong, Z. Lu, Y. Fuqing, "A Component-Based Software Configuration model and its Supporting System", Journal of Computer Science and Technology. Vol.17, No.4, pp. 432-441, 2002.

[159] M. Mao, Y. Jiang, "A New Component-Based Configuration Management 3C Model and its Realization", ISISE, International Symposium on Information Science and Engineering, vol. 1, pp. 258-262, 2008.

[160] L. Ruan, Z. Yong, "A new configuration management model for software based on distributed components and layered architecture", Parallel and Distributed Computing, Applications and Technologies, pp. 665 – 669, 2003.

[161] M. Larsson, "Applying configuration management techniques to component-based systems", Licentiate Thesis Dissertation, Department of Information Technology Uppsala University, vol. 7, 2000.

[162] M. Larsson, I. Crnkovic, "Development experiences of a component-based system", 7th IEEE International Conference and Workshop on the Engineering of Computer Based Systems ECBS, 2000.

References

[163] M. Larsson, I. Crnkovic, "Component configuration management", ECOOP Conference, Workshop on ComponentOriented Programming Nice, France, June 2000.

[164] N. Lohmann, "Compliance by design for artifact-centric business processes"9th international conference on Business process management, pp. 99-115, 2011.

[165] R. I. Chang, C. C. Chuang, C. H. Chang, "A New Spatial IP Assignment Method for IP-based Wireless Sensor Networks", International Journal of Personal and Ubiquitous Computing, vol. 16, pp. 1–16, September 2011.

[166] S. Kaplantzis, S. A. Sekercioglu, "Security and Smart Metering", European Wireless 2012, pp. 18-20. Poznan, Poland, 2012.

[167] Amir Motamedi, Hamidreza Zareipour, William D. Rosehart, "Electricity Price and Demand Forecasting in Smart Grids", IEEE Transactions On Smart Grid, Vol. 3, No. 2, pp. 664-674, June 2012.

[168] "Object Management Group. Business Process Modeling Notation (BPMN) Version 1.0", OMG Final Adopted Specification. Object Management Group, 2006.

[169] N. Goel, R. K. Shyamasundar, "An executional framework for BPMN using Orc. APSCC", IEEE, pp. 29-36, 2011.

[170] K. Hinge, A. Ghose, G. Koliadis, G, "Process SEER: a tool for semantic effect annotation of business process models", Thirteenth IEEE International Enterprise Distributed Object Computing Conference (EDOC) Los Alamitos, USA, IEEE, pp. 54-63, 2009.

[171] G. Koliadis, A. Vranesevic, M. Bhuiyan, A. Krishna, A. Ghose, "Combining i* and BPMN for Business Process Model Lifecycle Management", BPM'06 Proceedings of the 2006 international conference on Business Process Management Workshops, pp. 416-427, 2006.

[172] R. Darimont, A. V. Lamsweerde, "Formal Refinement Patterns for Goal-Driven Requirements Elaboration", Proceedings 4th ACM Symposium on the Foundations of Software Engineering (FSE4), San Francisco, pp. 179-190, 1996.

[173] Jean-Raymond Abrial, "Modeling in Event-B: System and Software Engineering", Cambridge University Press, New York, NY, USA, 2010 ISBN:0521895561 9780521895569

[174] Jean-Raymond Abrial, Michael Butler, Stefan Hallerstede, Thai Son Hoang, Farhad Mehta, Laurent Voisin, "Rodin: an open toolset for modelling and reasoning in Event-B", International Journal on Software Tools for Technology Transfer (STTT) - Special Section on VSTTE 2008, Springer-Verlag Berlin, Heidelberg, Vol. 12, Issue. 6, pp. 447-466, 2010.

[175] S.K.A. Zaidi, H. Mansoor, S.R. Ashraf, and A. Hassan, "Design and implementation of low cost electronic prepaid energy meter," Proc. IEEE International Multitopic Conference, Karachi, Pakistan, Dec. 2008, pp. 548–552.

[176] S. Lee and M. Gerla, "Split Multipath Routing with Maximally Disjoint Paths in Ad Hoc Networks," Proceedings of IEEE International Conference on Communications, Vol. 10, pp. 3201-3205, 2001.

[177] M. K. Marina and S. R. Das, "On-demand Multi-path Distance Vector Routing in Ad Hoc Networks," Proceedings of the IEEE International Conference on Network Protocols, pp. 14 – 23, Nov. 2001.

[178] L. Bononi and M. D. Felice, "Performance Analysis of Cross-layered Multi-path Routing and MAC Layer Solutions for Multi-hop Ad Hoc Networks," Proceedings of the ACM International Workshop on Mobility Management and Wireless Access, pp. 190 – 197, 2006.

[179] A. Acharya, A. Misra and S. Bansal, "A Label-Switching Packet Forwarding Architecture for Multihop Wireless LANs," Proceedings of the 5th ACM International Workshop on Wireless Mobile Multimedia, September 2002.

www.ingramcontent.com/pod-product-compliance
Lightning Source LLC
LaVergne TN
LVHW011935070526
838202LV00054B/4661